RISK

RISK

A USER'S GUIDE

GENERAL STANLEY A. McCHRYSTAL,
US ARMY, RETIRED

& ANNA BUTRICO

BUSINESS

PENGUIN BUSINESS

UK | USA | Canada | Ireland | Australia
India | New Zealand | South Africa

Penguin Business is part of the Penguin Random House group of companies
whose addresses can be found at global.penguinrandomhouse.com.

First published in the United States of America by Portfolio / Penguin 2021
First published in Great Britain by Penguin Business 2021
001

Printed and bound in Great Britain by Clays Ltd, Elcograf S.p.A.

The authorized representative in the EEA is Penguin Random House Ireland,
Morrison Chambers, 32 Nassau Street, Dublin D02 YH68

A CIP catalogue record for this book is available from the British Library

HARDBACK ISBN: 978–0–241–48192–9
TRADE PAPERBACK ISBN: 978–0–241–52935–5

Follow us on LinkedIn: https://www.linkedin.com/company/penguin-connect/

www.greenpenguin.co.uk

To the health-care and other essential workers who,
when faced with risk that is often difficult to effectively assess—
and impossible to completely mitigate—respond with
quiet courage, and too often sacrifice themselves for others.

———————————————

Contents

| *Part Three* |

STRENGTHENING THE SYSTEM

Crimson Contagion

We are too much accustomed to attribute to a single cause
that which is the product of several, and the majority
of our controversies come from that.

—MARCUS AURELIUS,
PHILOSOPHER AND EMPEROR
OF ROME

You may remember how it started.

A Chicago tourist returned from China carrying a deadly respiratory virus. The fifty-two-year-old traveler was the first confirmed American carrier of a novel influenza virus. The virus spread quickly through human-to-human contact, and within days, hospitals across the country were overrun with patients experiencing fevers, chills, low energy, and unrelenting coughs. America's medical supply chain failed, and critical resources, like protective gear and essential medical equipment, fell in short supply.

In mere weeks, the situation went from bad to worse. Medical professionals—the critical front line of the response to the virus—quickly became patients themselves, further straining systems that buckled under the weight of a pandemic-inflicted population.

An ill-defined leadership structure, combined with mixed communications from Washington, thwarted a competent response to the outbreak. Within months of the initial case emerging in Chicago, the virus was on track to infect 110 million Americans and kill 586,000, a mortality rate roughly five times greater than that of the common seasonal flu. It constituted a national calamity of the first order.

You may *think* you recall these events—but they didn't actually happen.

In fact, the outbreak starting in Chicago was the scenario for a series of exercises called Crimson Contagion that the Department of Health and Human Services (HHS) convened in 2019 to test the United States' capacity to respond to a severe pandemic. Its results were as alarming as they were conclusive: our nation was woefully underprepared.

Crimson Contagion was a wake-up call—but the nation slept through the alarm. Although key members of the administration were aware of what the exercises revealed—issues that ranged from severe equipment shortages to uncoordinated federal and state responses—the White House stood by its 2018 decision to dismantle the National Security Council directorate that was responsible for pandemic preparedness. And there is scant evidence that Crimson Contagion's findings—specifically recommendations about school closures and fast, widespread testing—led to changes in policy.

Tragically, in a matter of just a few short months, the systemic weaknesses that were identified by the exercise were proved all too real: the foreboding crimson bubbling back to the surface with a virus of a different name—COVID-19.

■

COVID-19 is a contagious respiratory and vascular disease caused by severe acute respiratory syndrome coronavirus 2 (SARS-CoV-2).

Put simply, the virus is a thief that breaks into bodies and corrupts cells in human airways. Once in position, the pathogen passes harmful RNA into healthy cells, which then produce proteins that, like accomplices, aid in creating copies of the virus. The virus travels from host to host in fluid droplets originating in airways that are spread through coughing, or even breathing—making transmission possible without direct human contact.

COVID-19's collision with the world began modestly in late December 2019, when doctors identified cases of pneumonia of unknown origin in Wuhan, China—tracing these cases back to one location: the Huanan Seafood Wholesale Market.

Initial responses were contradictory. The Wuhan Municipal Health Commission released an "urgent notice" to doctors about this mysterious new illness, but health professionals who publicly posted about the pneumonia were reprimanded for "spreading rumours," and—most critically—Chinese officials did not immediately report their concerns to the World Health Organization (WHO).

Still, online murmurs of these concerns grew louder, eventually springing up on the "US-based open-source" Program for Monitoring Emerging Diseases (ProMED) platform, created to share information about outbreaks with the public. On New Year's Eve 2019, the WHO confirmed twenty-seven cases in China's Hubei Province, and eleven days later, the first COVID-19 death. Attempting reassurance, authorities stressed there had been no new cases since January 3, no proof of the virus spreading person-to-person, and no infections among medical professionals.

Then on January 13 the virus sprang up in Thailand—the first case outside China. By the following week cases had spread to Japan and South Korea, and Chinese officials reversed their January 11 announcement—confirming that the virus *had* infected health-care workers and can be spread person-to-person. The first American case was confirmed on January 21—a small red dot of infection on the global map.

Two days later, Chinese authorities suspended transportation out of the city of Wuhan, at that time assessed to be the virus's point of origin. But the gesture was too late, the equivalent of using a garden hose to douse a fire that had already engulfed the house, with its flames now racing to the buildings down the street. The red dots that started in Wuhan were spreading rapidly. By the beginning of February, COVID-19's global death toll had climbed to at least 360. The pathogen was now statistically more lethal and spreading faster than any pandemic in living memory—the infected air droplets dispersing and sickening citizens around the globe.

The WHO moved cautiously, declaring a Public Health Emergency of International Concern (PHEIC)—a balancing act attempting to raise a red flag without inducing global panic. But by late February the menace was starkly evident when an American with no travel history to an outbreak area and no known contact with anyone infected was diagnosed with COVID-19. The implication was huge. With no way of re-creating the pattern of transmission, scientists realized that the extent of the virus's presence in America remained largely unknown.

Over the next two weeks, cases in Italy skyrocketed, and death tolls steeply rose in Iran, Spain, the United Kingdom, and elsewhere—causing nations to start to declare national stay-at-home orders. On March 11, the WHO—no longer trying to avoid raising unnecessary alarm—declared a pandemic. The balancing act was over—a war that had begun three months before was finally declared.

The world haltingly girded for combat, but the enemy had already gained crucial ground, and just over a week later, reported global infections passed two hundred thousand.

To be sure, COVID-19 is highly infectious and too often lethal, but it is not unconquerable. And, as a variant of SARS, it is not particularly novel. Human history has borne witness to countless pandemics: the deadly 1918 Spanish flu and, more recently, the public health crises of SARS, H1N1 (aka, the "swine flu"), Ebola, and the Zika epidemic.

In earlier eras of limited medical knowledge, the effectiveness of the public health response to pandemics had been uneven. In 2020, however, armed with greater medical understanding and expertise, and a vastly more robust medical infrastructure—hospitals, intensive care units, testing and research laboratories, etc.—we were not defenseless.

But we appeared to be.

From the outset, political dynamics hampered rapid sharing of data on the pathogen's spread and delayed containment measures. A lack of a clear narrative only made matters worse: the WHO's tentative declarations on the severity of the outbreak initially delayed full mobilization against the virus.

Weaknesses at the helm made things worse. In crisis, leadership is the unifying force that inspires and coordinates the efforts of many. In a

*The biggest pandemic to hit the United States before
COVID-19 had been the Spanish flu of 1918.*

moment demanding honesty, clear direction, and decisiveness, too many leaders fell short. Some decision-makers, like those in Taiwan, New Zealand, and South Korea, moved swiftly. But their success contrasted painfully with the haphazard method of leaders in larger countries like the United States and Brazil, where denial and minimization of the danger resulted in uneven responses that were too late and too modest to halt COVID-19's march.

Lacking a coherent defense, the line crumbled, and the pathogen rushed in.

■

Why was there such unmitigated failure in the face of an all-too-familiar threat?

Soldiers and athletes know from experience that the most dangerous opponent is one who lost the last contest but has the humility to learn why—and the discipline to correct their weaknesses.

In retrospect, Crimson Contagion was a diagnosis whose illness went untreated. The simulation accurately predicted our unpreparedness, and the subsequent outbreak of COVID-19 revealed failures across a range of factors that were ultimately in our control—factors we must learn to understand and influence if we are to effectively manage risk.

It took a mere three months from Crimson Contagion's findings in October 2019 for the exercise's warnings to become a reality—ventilators whisked to intensive care unit bedsides as the distance between Americans grew by six feet.

As the Roman emperor and philosopher Marcus Aurelius reminded us, we are too often tempted to attribute our failure to the magnitude of a single outside threat. But as we have seen, COVID-19's most significant strength lay in our own weakness.

We may not be able to see the future, but we can improve our resistance and build a strong defense against what we know—and what we don't.

TIMELINE OF COVID-19

DECEMBER 30, 2019: The Wuhan Municipal Health Commission warns of pneumonia of unknown cause.

DECEMBER 31, 2019: The outbreak is posted to ProMED platform.

JANUARY 1, 2020: The WHO requests verification of virus.

JANUARY 11, 2020: China announces its first virus death.

JANUARY 13, 2020: The WHO identifies the first case outside of China in Thailand (the infected woman had just left the Wuhan region).

JANUARY 20–21, 2020: Japan, South Korea, and Thailand report infections. On January 21, the United States confirms its first case.

JANUARY 23, 2020: The virus has infected more than 570 and has killed at least 17 in China. Chinese authorities suspend transportation out of the city of Wuhan.

FEBRUARY 2, 2020: COVID-19's global death toll reaches at least 360 and the WHO confirms the first death outside of China in the Philippines.

FEBRUARY 26, 2020: An American with no travel history to an outbreak area or known contact with anyone infected is diagnosed with COVID-19.

FEBRUARY 29, 2020: The United States reports its first COVID-19 death (at least two others had died from it earlier, but it hadn't been known or reported as such at the time).

MARCH 11, 2020: The WHO declares COVID-19 a "pandemic." Thirty-eight Americans have died, and the country has 1,267 cases.

DECEMBER 11, 2020: As a result of Operation Warp Speed, two vaccines are approved by the FDA for emergency use authorization: the Pfizer-BioNTech COVID-19 vaccine is granted emergency use authorization on December 11 and the Moderna COVID-19 vaccine is authorized a week later, on December 18. The FDA grants the Johnson & Johnson vaccine emergency use authorization on February 27, 2021.

DECEMBER 31, 2020: Though officials intended to vaccinate 20 million people by the year's end, only 2.8 million have received their first dose by December 31.

FEBRUARY 22, 2021: Five hundred thousand Americans have died from COVID-19.

A Question of Risk

They couldn't hit an elephant at that distance.

> —MAJOR GENERAL JOHN SEDGWICK,
> IMMEDIATELY BEFORE BEING SHOT
> AND KILLED AT SPOTSYLVANIA
> COURT HOUSE, MAY 9, 1864

WHY READ A BOOK ON RISK?

Why spend time trying to dodge or defeat things over which you have no control—hurricanes, nuclear war, or, God forbid, a pandemic?

Because we have far more control than we think we do. That means we have more responsibility than we often accept. Upon examination, we may discover just how much of the risk we face depends on us—and how much control we can exert in the face of the unknown.

A few years back, aided by Dr. Kristina Talbert-Slagle, a brilliant Yale immunologist, I studied the human immune system to compare it to the complexity of counterinsurgency operations. Our body's natural defenses are a lifesaving marvel that we often take for granted. On a daily basis, it is able to reconnoiter, identify, defeat a dizzying array of threats, and then remember those threats to more easily combat them in the future. But when the body's defenses are unprepared or weakened, such as when it is impacted by acquired immunodeficiency syndrome (AIDS), we become susceptible to viruses, diseases, and other maladies we would normally brush aside with ease.

I was struck by the fact that while there's little we can do to avoid or eliminate many of the threats we encounter in daily life, our ability to effectively defend against external risks is something we *can* control.

Although most of us are unaware of it, we all possess a Risk Immune System. If we can keep it healthy by adjusting and controlling for the factors that affect it, just like our immune system does for our bodies, then we can handle risk in the most effective way.

The outcome depends largely on us.

WHAT WILL ANOTHER BOOK ON RISK TEACH ME?

We've heard the warnings about global warming, poor diet, lack of exercise, fake news, the dangers of this or that political dogma. A ceaseless drumbeat of cautionary messages creating a cacophony that deadens our senses and stifles action. Too many boys crying wolf too often.

Still, we understand that risk is real and ever present. Small and large, obvious and invisible, it shapes our behavior and impacts our lives. So we buy insurance, install home security systems, and take the obvious precautions. Yet despite our best efforts, risk retains an ominous, amorphous quality—like the sounds and shadows in a darkened forest. We do the best we can to prepare for the possibility that things will not go as planned—and yet we still worry.

We *should* worry. The precarious nature of our jobs in a changing economy, violent crime in our neighborhoods, and countless other realities threaten our health and livelihoods. Whole industries and media outlets focus on different categories of risk, offering explanations and solutions. Countless books exist to educate us on specific threats—from financial turmoil to global warming to geopolitical strife—and they can be of great value.

But this book won't attempt to do that. There is an even more important message here. The message is that while we *should* worry, we must also *act*.

Too often and to great cost, individuals and organizations fail to mitigate risk because they focus on the probability of something happening—

instead of what they can do about it. We will show that, in reality, *the greatest risk to us—is us*. And yet, conversely, we can also be our own greatest asset in overcoming whatever life throws our way.

Although we cannot predict the future and lack control over a vast number of things in life, we *do* have dominion over ten key dimensions that we can adjust at any given time to take control over our response: communication, narrative, structure, technology, diversity, bias, action, timing, adaptability, and leadership.

By closely monitoring these controls, we can maintain what I call a healthy Risk Immune System that allows us to effectively anticipate, identify, analyze, and act upon the always present possibility that things will *not* go as planned.

Through stories—some personal, some historic, some a bit of both— these pages will explore how these factors impact our ability to assess and respond to the countless things that can cause us harm or failure. Rather than fixate on external risks, we will look inward to examine the factors that are so ubiquitous that we cease to see them, and so stubbornly enduring that we too often accept them as constants, rather than as variables we can affect.

But we *can* affect them, and my hope is that this book will shape a new understanding of your relationship to risk and how you respond to it. It is based upon the fundamental concept of the Risk Immune System. Like our body's natural immune system, it functions to:

Detect threats.

Assess the risk they represent, based on our own vulnerabilities.

Respond to avoid or mitigate any negative effects of the risk.

Learn so that we are well prepared if the risk reappears.

This is not a book about different types of risks. Nor is it a catalog of famous mistakes. It offers no pat solutions or "foolproof" checklists. Rather, it explores the factors by which we can strengthen our ability to respond to risk, and how we can turn the dials up and down to make our responses more effective.

Make no mistake, this isn't a secret formula for success. It is more an exercise in self-reflection and disciplined thinking, a unique approach to keeping *risk fit* and creating resilience throughout an organization.

Through historical and current vignettes, I will explore these factors to reveal why risks are so often overlooked or ignored, why organizational structures and processes designed to cope with risk frequently increase it exponentially—and, most crucially, *what we can do about it.*

WHY WRITE A BOOK ON RISK?

You would think that having lived a life associated with the deadly risks of combat, I'd either have mastered the subject or be sick and tired of it. Neither is the case. I've long pondered why some leaders and units dealt with risk so differently than others. I noticed over and over again that the same threat would impact seemingly identical organizations in entirely different ways. One unit swept away the enemy with apparent ease while another suffered casualties and frustration. Why was that? Why did similar risks result in such divergent outcomes? I have thought a lot about these kinds of questions.

I have also been struck by the realization that dealing with risk is often more mundane and counterintuitive than one might initially think. For example, in a well-intentioned but misplaced effort to limit the risks to our troops, the Pentagon prescribed that every soldier leaving a secure base in both Afghanistan and Iraq wear body armor, and required each casualty report to include a detailed accounting of every piece worn. The overall intent was to ensure that American service members were as "bulletproof" as possible—an admirable goal to be sure.

But unfortunately wearing protective gear simply wasn't always realistic. Many activities, including climbing Afghanistan's towering mountains, were literally impossible in the heavy armor, and the perception was that the decision-makers above, clueless to the realities on the ground, were covering themselves to evade accountability by ordering maximum protection. To accomplish their missions, soldiers would now have to assume both the normal risks of combat and the added risk of disobedience.

Too often our efforts to manage risk create further risks. Whether in combat or in day-to-day life, we encounter situations that call for us to assume a reasonable amount of risk to achieve our goals, and if we try to make ourselves "bulletproof," we may ultimately collapse under the weight of our gear.

So it is on the battlefield, in the office, and at home. Developing the ability and habit of mind to effectively assess and respond to the range of risks that constantly emerge is an essential survival skill. This book will provide the insights for individuals and organizations to do just that.

THE JOURNEY AHEAD

Our journey will be conducted in three parts along a route that examines how we think about and respond to risk—and how we can do it better.

In **Part 1** we begin at Pearl Harbor on the seventh of December 1941, but soon move to the present day to look at how we have traditionally thought about risk, and propose a new paradigm built around the concept of maintaining a healthy Risk Immune System.

With the foundation set, **Part 2** studies each of the ten Risk Control Factors by which we can maintain this healthy system. With examples drawn from history, from the business world, and from my personal experience on and off the battlefield, we will explore the role of communication, narrative, structure, technology, diversity, bias, action, timing, adaptability, and leadership in identifying, analyzing, and ultimately controlling risk.

We'll start by looking at how the failure of communication casts a shadow over the tragedy of 9/11, and discover, from foxholes in Korea to Google's San Francisco headquarters, how alignment in narrative and structure can be a fundamental strength—or a fatal condition.

We will witness how inertia doomed the video giant Blockbuster, and how bias led America into the cauldron of Iraq. With Dr. Martin Luther King Jr., we'll write a letter from Birmingham's jail, and with John F. Kennedy, we will avert a nuclear war—in both cases embracing a bias for action that values diverse perspectives. In the pit with a Ferrari Formula 1 team, we'll learn how timing is not all about speed, and alongside gangly

Dick Fosbury, we'll stun the world with a new approach to the high jump—seeing firsthand how an ability to adapt is impotent without a willingness to do so.

Finally, marching with a British general into the American wilderness and alongside Franklin D. Roosevelt at the outset of the New Deal, we'll see how leadership is the essential enabler—the hand on the dials that orchestrates a successful response to risk.

After exploring all the factors by which we can exert control, **Part 3** offers proven tools and practical exercises that can first assess, then build and strengthen our Risk Immune Systems. We'll start by examining the story of how the city of Boston battled COVID-19, exploring how the mayor and his team leveraged the Risk Control Factors on a daily basis to impressively calibrate their response to the multifaceted crisis. We will then then outline how organizations themselves can diagnose and improve the health of their Risk Immune Systems.

Finally, by looking at common problems our organizations experience, I'll provide a range of concrete steps that leaders can take with their teams. Detailed descriptions for solutions as diverse as Assumptions Checks, Red Team exercises, and After-Action Reviews offer prescriptive road maps to address common problems.

By the end, you'll be equipped with the tools you need to strengthen both yourself and your organization. You will have a new understanding of your relationship with risk and how to work with the factors within your control to successfully **Detect**, **Assess**, and **Respond** to hazards—no matter what the risk may be.

Part One

ON RISK

RISKY BUSINESS

In May 2006, during a daylight raid against a target in Yusufi-yah, Iraq, one of two AH-6M Little Bird helicopters was shot down and the pilots killed. The small aircraft, modified by the Night Stalkers of the 160th Special Operations Aviation Regiment to serve as a gunship for counterterrorist operations, lacked the protection of larger attack helicopters like the AH-64 Apache, but it was an extraordinarily agile, lethal weapon when flown by the right pilots.

The AH-6M Little Birds were flown that day by such men, specially selected professionals who were seasoned by the relentless combat in which our Special Operations Task Force was engaged. And the operation was successful—another hammer blow against al-Qaeda in Iraq. But with the downing of our helicopter, and the loss of two brave pilots, the question necessarily arose: Was this operation—was any operation—worth the risks involved?

The question became even more poignant when the father of one of the downed pilots asked why his son was dead. But the question wasn't merely the pained expression of a grieving parent. This father had been an Army aviator in Vietnam himself—a distinguished pilot intimately familiar with the mission, tactics, and culture of our force. He didn't ask why his son was fighting in Iraq. Instead his question was very specific: Why were we conducting a daylight operation when the effectiveness and survivability of the AH-6M Little Bird was based on leveraging the advantage of darkness?

It was a fair question, although our answer was likely less than satisfying.

The grim reality was that although our forces had been designed and equipped to conduct "surgical" operations leveraging surprise, technology-driven superiority during darkness, and the proficiency of highly skilled professionals, the struggle against al-Qaeda in Iraq was a far different fight. Often forced into head-to-head combat during daylight—because that was when the enemy was operating—we forfeited many of our normal advantages and relied on the skill, raw courage, and commitment of our force. The fallen pilot's father understood.

At that point, I had been three years in the fight and knew that the unsurprising effect over time had been to harden my comrades and me to what we did to the enemy—and what they did to us. To be clear, I hadn't become bloodthirsty or uncompassionate, but slowly, subtly, the pressure to finish the fight by destroying al-Qaeda in Iraq had taken its toll on all of us. As the *risks rose, like General Ulysses Grant did at his relentless siege of Confederate Petersburg, Virginia, nearly 150 years earlier, we steeled ourselves to the cost and pressed on.*

Even now, years later, it is difficult to say whether or not we were right. I feel like we were—but I also recognize that I'm a prisoner of my personal perspective. More broadly, however, the question of risk arises. How did I think about risk? How did I rank the risks of losing the fight versus losing comrades? Was the risk of losing our humanity a factor in my decision-making? Most crucially, how do we make ourselves, and our organizations, better able to respond effectively to risk?

CHAPTER ONE

What If?

*The art of war teaches us to rely not on the likelihood of the
enemy's not coming, but on our own readiness to receive him;
not on the chance of his not attacking, but rather on the
fact that we have made our position unassailable.*

—SUN TZU, CHINESE PHILOSOPHER
AND MILITARY STRATEGIST

*To study risk is to reconsider what we think
we know about being prepared.*

THE COMMANDER

It was the summer of 1965. I was ten years old, and in the weeks before my
father deployed to Vietnam for another tour of combat, my parents took
my five siblings and me to Lookout Mountain, Tennessee, where my
mother had been raised and family abounded. My soldier father was my
hero, but on a warm evening at my aunt Margaret's lovely mountain
home, she showed me a black-and-white photograph of a young-looking
naval officer and told me a fascinating story about another member of my
family. For a ten-year-old history buff, the story was a seductive mystery.

The officer was Commander Thomas Calloway Latimore, a 1914
graduate of the United States Naval Academy at Annapolis. After a twenty-
seven-year career of shipboard and shore assignments, including a tour in
military intelligence and a brief stint as the governor of American Samoa,
Latimore was given command of the USS *Dobbin*, a destroyer tender
stationed at Pearl Harbor, in April 1941. The USS *Dobbin* supported the
US Pacific Fleet that had been forward positioned from the West Coast to

My relative Thomas Latimore had once commanded the USS Dobbin,
a destroyer tender in the Pearl Harbor waters on December 7, 1941.

Hawaii by President Franklin D. Roosevelt to counter increasingly aggressive Japanese moves in the region.

By all accounts, Latimore was a quiet man and an avid hiker who liked to walk the hills overlooking the sprawling Hawaiian naval base. Once, he injured his arm while hiking, telling crew members that he had fallen. The injury required a cast, but after a time he appeared to fully recover.

In July 1941, Latimore went out again. Clad in a hat, a khaki uniform, and comfortable shoes, and carrying a walking stick, the commander left the trailhead alone, hiking into the Aiea Range above the base—and he disappeared forever. Late that day, his crew, concerned about his well-being, unsuccessfully combed the hills before a wider effort involving local authorities joined the search, all with the same result. No sign or any clue of what had happened to Commander Latimore was ever found.

Like most stories, it got a bit better in the telling. I remember it described as having happened only days before the Japanese attack, so it was assumed that Latimore had unexpectedly run into Japanese agents collecting intelligence on the US fleet and they had kidnapped or killed him. No evidence supports that hypothesis, but it's too enticing to ignore.

A less romantic but far more likely risk came from the danger inherent in a fifty-one-year-old sailor hiking alone. The terrain above Pearl Harbor is not obviously treacherous, but Latimore had already been injured earlier doing the same thing. Risks are not always obvious, nor are they often

NAVY INQUIRY INTO OFFICER'S DISAPPEARANCE IN HAWAII

WASHINGTON, July 26 (AP).— The Navy ordered an official investigation today into the disappearance of Commander Thomas C. Latimore, missing in Hawaii for more than a week. The Navy said search had been abandoned, although Honolulu police were continuing an investigation.

Commander Latimore, whose home was Chattanooga, Tenn., disappeared July 18 on a hike into the hills on Oahu Island.

My relative's disappearance still remains a mystery—nearly sixty years later.

legend-worthy. We may never know the truth of what happened, but in any event, Commander Thomas Calloway Latimore had vanished—his family and nation were left to wonder how things might have been different. And less than five months later, his disappearance became forever associated with the Japanese attack on Pearl Harbor. Some pondered whether it could have been part of a larger failure to effectively assess and respond to potential risks.

Though I was just ten years old that summer in 1965, I was already very familiar with the story of Japan's surprise attack on Pearl Harbor. Just before 8:00 A.M. on Sunday morning, December 7, 1941, six Imperial Navy carriers infiltrated the base along a northern route to a position 230 miles from Oahu before launching 353 bomber, fighter, and torpedo aircraft in two waves against a series of US naval targets on the most developed of Hawaii's islands.

By midmorning the United States counted 8 battleships severely damaged or destroyed, 11 other vessels bombed and strafed, 328 aircraft damaged or destroyed—and 2,403 souls killed with more than 1,100 wounded. For days oil fires burned in the harbor and desperate taps could be heard from sailors caught in the bowels of capsized ships.

The effect was devastating. But should the attack have been a surprise?

Conflict between Japan and the United States had long been brewing. With the 1898 US annexation of Hawaii and occupation of the Philippines following the defeat of Spain, America became a true Pacific power, putting Japanese and US objectives increasingly at odds. Logically, the United States began to fortify its possessions in the region, and naval officers at Newport's Naval War College conducted regular war games to refine strategies for conflict with Japan.

After 1931, the friction between the two nations rose. Japan's increasingly militaristic government, its aggressive expansion in Manchuria and then China proper, and its symbolic alliance with Germany and Italy convinced American diplomats and the military that war was not only likely but inevitable.

In the months before December 7, American pushback targeted Japan's dependence on foreign resources to fuel its increasingly industrialized economy. The United States imposed embargoes on oil and scrap metal shipments, leaving the proud Japanese to face the prospect of humiliating retreat—or war. If unable to trade for these goods, surely Japan would take them by force. It would only be a question of when and how.

In July 1941, Japanese leaders began a series of meetings to set a strategic course. The game of chess became more complex when Nazi Germany, Japan's nominal Axis ally, invaded the Soviet Union and requested that Japan join the attack on Stalin's enormous communist state. The Japanese deferred but committed themselves to securing a political and economic order for Asia that would extend far beyond their home islands and subordinate hundreds of millions to Japanese rule.

The outcome of the meetings did not remain secret for long. US intelligence had broken the Japanese code used for diplomatic messages, and within weeks had intercepted a coded message from the Japanese Foreign Ministry to its embassies overseas, communicating to the Imperial Conference that their nation would not hesitate to use force to secure its strategic objectives.

These messages also included instructions for Japanese diplomats to report on American military facilities like Pearl Harbor, thereby giving the United States advance notice of potential targets. Simultaneously, the US military, government sources, allied countries, and the press continued to collect information about Japan's designs.

THE GREATEST RISK IS US

Unless we believe the story of Japanese spies, Tom Latimore likely died from a mistake he made while hiking—a stumble, a misplaced step, perhaps dehydration. On an island devoid of likely predators, and crossing inanimate terrain, the likely determining variable, and responsible party, is Latimore himself.

The Japanese attack on December 7, while far more famous, shares DNA of sorts with my lost relative. Although Pearl Harbor has long been used as a synonym for treachery, the risks—of war with Japan, of a Japanese first strike, even of an attack on America's Pacific Fleet's primary base (although considered less likely than other targets such as the Philippines)—were well known. Indeed, responsibility for much of Japan's success lay with the failure of American leaders to effectively assess and respond to the risk.

Why didn't the United States have the ability to better estimate Japanese strategic plans? Why was the attack on Pearl Harbor such a devastating surprise?

It is a familiar pattern. Fixated on external factors, individuals and organizations fail to tend to their Risk Immune System and become vulnerable even to perceivable risks.

Time and again we see that *the greatest risk to us as individuals, and to our organizations, is us*.

Like Latimore, whose personal miscalculation likely cost him his life, his nation ultimately posed the greatest danger to itself by failing to respond to a well-understood threat. Both Latimore and American officials had at their disposal the dials needed to control their own response to risk, and both failed to calibrate them. This is not uncommon. Unable or unwilling to calibrate for important factors like communication, structure, and bias, we remain vulnerable to threats.

That is why it is so important to change our approach from one that is focused on external factors to one that looks inward at the factors that determine our own response.

But before we go further, it is essential that we first consider the very concept of risk—it is less clear-cut than we pretend.

Threats—people or things that could potentially do us harm—are omnipresent. But it is our ability to prevent, avoid, or mitigate a threat that determines to what extent it constitutes a risk. For example, if I am in an armored vehicle, an individual with a handgun isn't a risk to me. But if I am unarmed on a crowded street, that armed person could constitute a tremendous risk.

In the unrealistically perfect world where no threats exist, the strength of my ability to deal with threats is irrelevant—I'm not at risk. Conversely, and equally unrealistically, in a threat-filled environment where my ability to deal with threats is absolute, I have no risk to worry about. To sum it up:

> *If there are no threats—our vulnerabilities don't matter.*
> and
> *If we have no vulnerabilities—threats don't matter.*

For the mathematically inclined, it would be depicted as an equation:

$$\textbf{Threat} \times \textbf{Vulnerability} = \textbf{Risk}$$

Which means that if the value of either Threat or Vulnerability is zero, there is no Risk (Anything $\times$ 0 = 0).

But I've never experienced either situation, and it's likely you haven't either—we live somewhere in the middle. We try to minimize the threats we are exposed to, but knowing that our efforts will be imperfect at best, we rely on our Risk Immune System to help **Detect** the risk, **Assess** it, and **Respond** to it appropriately.

Wait a minute. I've just drawn an analogy to our human immune system, a confusing approach if most of us have, at best, a hazy understanding of what it actually does—and how. Well, here it is in terms even an infantry soldier can understand.

The miracle of the immune system lies in its ability to rapidly and accurately identify friend (good cell), from foe (potentially harmful pathogen), mount an effective response to defend the body, and then remember what it learned, maintaining the ability to respond even more effectively should the threatening pathogen reappear.

Immunologists view our immune systems as bounded by the outside (skin) of our bodies. As individuals, most of us make reasonable efforts to augment and extend our natural defenses by avoiding or mitigating threats through good hygiene, diet, and exercise. Still, our immune systems do the lion's share in defending our health.

Organizations have, in fact, a very similar capability.

The analogy isn't perfect (few are), but what we call the Risk Immune System performs a similar function to identify, assess, and combat threats to our well-being. And it provides a helpful construct through which to understand how we can strengthen our ability to survive and prosper in a world of constant risk.

As we mentioned earlier, to be effective, Risk Immune Systems must perform four functions: **Detect—Assess—Respond—Learn.** In today's environment, driven by increasing speed and complexity, adeptly fielding a wider range of fast-moving threats is more challenging than ever. But while the threats we face are daunting, our condition need not be fatal. To be sure, there are external threats that constitute challenges individuals and organizations cannot dodge, but the capacity to respond effectively is typically within reach. With thoughtful attention to the health and effectiveness of our Risk Immune System—by paying particular attention to what we *can* control—we reshape our ability to deal with risk; hence this book.

I have identified ten dimensions of control present in every organization, typically at varying levels of effectiveness, that can be monitored and adjusted to maintain a healthy Risk Immune System.

COMMUNICATION: *How we exchange information with others*
NARRATIVE: *How we tell others about who we are and what we do*
STRUCTURE: *How we design our organizations and processes*
TECHNOLOGY: *How we apply machinery, equipment, resources, and know-how*
DIVERSITY: *How we leverage a range of perspectives and abilities*
BIAS: *How the assumptions we have about the world influence us*

ACTION: *How we overcome inertia or resistance to drive our response*
TIMING: *How when we act affects the effectiveness of our response*
ADAPTABILITY: *How we respond to changing risks and environments*
LEADERSHIP: *How we direct and inspire the overall Risk Immune System*

These Risk Control Factors are not a set of strengths to celebrate, nor are they vulnerabilities to be mitigated. Instead, think of the factors as a set of dials that we can adjust or calibrate to improve the operation of the Risk Immune System. Each factor needs to be healthy and functioning (and strengthened, if necessary) and then adjusted, or dialed, to achieve the appropriate response to each situation.

Complete malfunctioning of any Risk Control Factor can be problematic. It's more important, however, to consider each factor as part of an interconnected system, one that can be set and adjusted as appropriate. As we'll see throughout the book, in some instances one or more of the Risk Control Factors assume dominant importance (in how well or how poorly they function)—but by and large, the factors are interdimensional. Most outcomes are determined by a broad combination of the factors.

This can prove frustrating. We crave a "one big thing" answer to any success or failure. But most often the "one big thing" is our appreciation for the complexity of the system, and our ability to keep it healthy and properly functioning. We can blame outside threats all we want, but there is much we can do to prepare for them—often far more than we care to admit.

Though in practice we employ Risk Control Factors in combination, for the purpose of this book, they are organized by chapter. The stories used to illustrate each factor are meant to demonstrate some particular quality or emphasize its priority in decision-making, but careful readers will notice multiple Risk Control Factors at play. For example, an anecdote about communication may also speak to structure and technology. The system is interdimensional by design. So keep in mind that the factors making up the Risk Immune System are interrelated parts of a whole, connected by communication and overseen by the tenth factor, leadership.

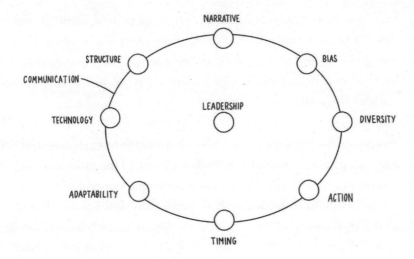

Another way to think of the Risk Immune System is like a series of interconnected dials, or gears, where the movement of one affects the shifting of all. Leadership is the wrench that orchestrates everything.

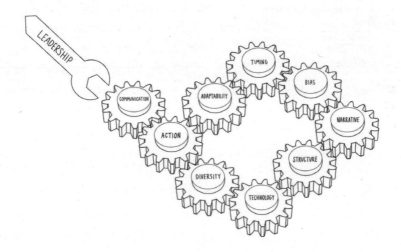

If several factors, or gears, fail, then the whole Risk Immune System breaks down.

The cost of failure in our body's immune system is well known—we become vulnerable to maladies we might normally ignore. In a sense, our

Risk Immune System works the same way: a weakened ability to detect and respond to risks carries a punishing cost. The chapters in Part 2 explain each Risk Control Factor in detail and call out some common symptoms of failures for each, and the final part of this book provides some proven solutions.

Beginning in late 2019, the COVID-19 pandemic offered a stunningly clear demonstration of the importance of the effectiveness of these factors in maintaining a healthy Risk Immune System. Faced with a virus that represented a fairly consistent threat across the globe, the relative success and failure of individual nations in dealing with it has spanned a wide spectrum. Even allowing for differing governance, wealth, and health-care systems, the gaps between the most and least effective nations—measured in lives—is noteworthy.

What countries did before, and during, the pandemic determined the outcome they ultimately experienced. The lesson is clear. We are, most often, the architects of our fate.

THE BOTTOM LINE

We can't control the emergence of threats—but we can make our organizations less vulnerable.

CHAPTER TWO

Damocles and Me

I wish to have no connection with any ship that does
not sail fast; for I intend to go in harm's way.

—CAPTAIN JOHN PAUL JONES,
"FATHER OF THE US NAVY"

In reality, risk is neither mathematical nor
finite. Its impact depends to a great extent on
how we perceive, process, and respond.

THE BLADE ABOVE

The heavy sword hung from the palace ceiling by a single horsehair, its sharpened blade pointed downward as if an invisible hand executing a lethal thrust from above had been suddenly stopped. Directly below, in sharp contrast to the image of imminent violence, a man sat on a regal bed of gold, surrounded by delicacies of food and drink while servants attended to his desires.

The sword belonged to Dionysius II, the king of Syracuse, and it loomed over Damocles, a subject of the monarch who was receiving an unsubtle lesson in the perils of power, simultaneously enjoying its benefits while being made acutely aware of its mortal dangers.

I remember the story from my youth. The aging volume my mother gave me showed Damocles staring upward at the sword, his entire body tensed in apprehension, the onlookers exhibiting both horror at his predicament and relief in not sharing it. I don't remember giving much thought to the likelihood that the tiny strand of horsehair would give way, letting the sword plunge into Damocles, or whether the weight of the

Though thrilled to be seated on the throne, Damocles
is terrified by the sword hanging by a horsehair.
(PAINTING: RICHARD WESTALL, *The Sword of Damocles*)

sword, height of fall, and sharpness of the blade combined would inflict a serious wound. Even then I understood the probabilities of those factors were beside the point. The lesson was that frequently individuals, and most particularly leaders, operate in an environment of constant risk. The sword may not be so evident, but it is there. We must learn to live with risk, and even better, do something about it.

THINKING ABOUT RISK

It's worth stating the obvious here at the start that this book isn't an academic exploration of risk. Theory is one thing. How we actually perceive and act upon risk is another thing entirely. For our purposes, we intend to approach the subject from a practical perspective, focused not on odds— but on readiness to respond.

Although many brilliant minds have studied risk in detail, their theories and prescriptions rarely determine how each of us actually approaches the ever-present challenge of risk. At least that hasn't been the case for me or any of the organizations I've been a part of. So while understanding the more theoretical aspects of risk can be valuable, knowing how each of us—and our teams and organizations—actually *perceives* risk is essential.

This is easier said than done. There's something highly subjective about how we consider risk, both individually and collectively. At the most basic level, I have always viewed risk as the probability of something unwanted happening (e.g., Damocles's horsehair breaking), and the potential consequences if it did. At the most basic level, the combination of those factors constituted my estimation of the risk involved.

Regardless, in the long run, what *might* happen holds less interest to me—and certainly less practical importance—than what I intend to do about it.

In some cases, as with life insurance or seat belts, I dutifully take steps to mitigate the impact of a negative event. In other cases, like when I'm driving or managing my finances, I try to maintain the agility to react to changing conditions and emerging threats. And in some instances, I irrationally deny the existence of the risk or hope that probability will work out in my favor, like those who ride motorcycles without helmets or smoke two packs a day. Sometimes I'll study situations extensively, but on the vast majority of risks I encounter (even some big ones), I rarely do the due diligence to determine mathematically what the best move is. I'm guessing I'm about average on all these.

By way of example, in December 2019, I arranged for a long-needed spine surgery. To give myself the best probability of having a good outcome, I contacted a friend of mine at a prominent hospital to seek his advice. He recommended a highly experienced surgeon. During the consultation, the surgeon dutifully outlined for me the potential risks associated with all major operations as well as those specific to the spine. I listened intently, but in every case where bad outcomes or complications were accurately described as being rare, I assumed I would naturally fall into the far larger population that suffered no difficulties.

The surgery was almost twelve hours long, complicated by scar tissue from two earlier back operations, but seemingly successful, and soon I began my recovery. But four weeks into that process complications arose. Two more operations followed and then almost a month flat on my back in hospital beds. Months later the problem seems to have been fixed, but it gave me a new appreciation for how I perceive and act upon risk.

Could I have done anything differently? The surgery was necessary, and I sought out the most qualified doctor I could find to perform it. But I admit that, during the period of complications, his assurances that I was the first person to suffer this problem in more than four thousand such surgeries gave me no comfort. Risk is theoretical, psychological, emotional—an unreal bolt of lightning that always hits someone else. Until it doesn't.

The point I want to make here is that while we need to do our due diligence and make well-informed choices, we can't live life inside a spreadsheet trying to tabulate the countless risks that we encounter every day. Even if we *were* to determine mathematically what the best move is, we can't ever account for all factors, and in a fast-moving, complex environment, such an approach would likely *increase* risk by giving an illusion of completeness impossible to attain. However, developing a thoughtful appreciation of the threats we face, our vulnerabilities, and the resulting risks can be hugely beneficial.

In the end, the real question is not one of odds but attitude: How should we *think* about risk, and, even more important, how should we react to it?

LEARNING ABOUT RISK

The study and calculation of risk is a respected science that has accelerated dramatically in depth, breadth, and utility in the last two centuries. Useful concepts outlined in decision theory, dual-process theory, game theory, and expected utility theory—and a host of other research-based conclusions—are available to educate and improve how we understand and deal with risk. Our ability to appreciate and leverage technology to calculate probabilities is also vastly increased over that of our ancestors. As a result, we have established rules, tools, and jobs (e.g., chief risk officer) to reflect our increasing mastery over the vagaries of risk.

But that's not what this book is about. It offers a new way to understand and manage risk: a system that acknowledges and improves upon mere instinct by shining a light beyond the approaching threat to illuminate the *capabilities* that we can apply to its resolution.

This approach is born out of my experience that we rarely knowingly leverage academic study or theory in dealing with risk in real life. I have sat through countless briefings that tabled extensive, sometimes impressive, data-driven conclusions, but more often than not saw decisions made more informally and more intuitively than strict science would ever have approved. Even calculated comparisons of relative risks depicted with seeming numerical precision, were, when dug into, actually based on subjective assessments by all-too-human operators. We interpreted or adjusted the data until it fit comfortably with our intuition.

That's not necessarily a wrongheaded approach. As researchers John Kay and Mervyn King argue in their book *Radical Uncertainty: Decision-Making Beyond the Numbers*, the inherent uncertainty that underlies most situations, and challenges decision-making, means that even massive amounts of information can rarely eliminate the element of chance. It's both that simple and that complex. We can't eliminate risk, but as this book will show, we can develop and maintain our resiliency.

In practice, most of us learn about risk through experience. Raised in the late 1950s and 1960s as one of six children, I rode countless miles on my bicycle but never owned a helmet. I was crammed uncomfortably for hours in the family station wagon, but never wore a seat belt. I don't think my two little brothers (six and ten years my junior) ever sat in a car seat, and like other kids in the neighborhood, we were "free-rangers" who disappeared in the morning and reappeared dirty and hungry that evening. We wouldn't have considered ourselves as risk-takers or our parents as irresponsible—I suspect we were just largely oblivious.

Risks were considered differently then. I distinctly remember when the front yard of my third-grade schoolmate's home was dug up for the construction of a bomb shelter, and green fifty-five-gallon drums of civil defense supplies lined the halls of Stonewall Jackson Elementary School's basement in Arlington, Virginia. But what appeared to be thoughtful mitigation of an unthinkable risk was a futile gesture given that our proximity to Washington, DC, and the Pentagon made surviving a serious Soviet nuclear strike, even in my schoolmate's shelter, an unlikely possibility.

As I got older, I found myself, probably like most people, unconsciously calculating risk using a simple model that balanced the probability of an event or outcome and the consequences if it did happen. If I climbed on the roof of our home, I simply had to judge how likely it was I would fall, and if I did, how badly it would hurt. If both the probability of falling was low and the consequences limited—there wasn't much risk. If either the probability or the potential cost was high, it was cause to reconsider. As shown in Figure 1, the concept isn't complicated.

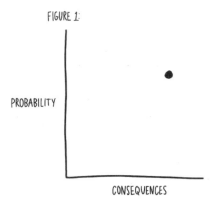

FIGURE 1:

PROBABILITY

CONSEQUENCES

I chose a soldier's life for many reasons, one of which was the desire to perceive myself as a courageous risk-taker. I liked the idea of taking risks that others would not. Like other comrades I would eventually serve alongside, I pursued becoming a paratrooper, a Ranger, and a Green Beret (Special Forces officer), and I joined elite units partly for the cachet of appearing to disdain risks others shrank from.

However, although I hoped to define myself as a risk-taking warrior, it's important to understand that overall, to the very marrow of its bones, the United States military is an intensely risk-averse entity. That doesn't refer to the physical courage of the women and men in uniform, or even to the audacity of many of the operations they conduct, but instead to the bedrock belief that, charged with the defense of the nation, our armed forces can simply not afford to fail. In this regard, in matters of importance, most military leaders prefer belt and suspenders, and a backup set of each.

For observers, and often for lawmakers, this can be frustrating—a military that always wants more. Accepting a force structure of units, ships, tanks, aircraft, and other elements of military power that produces less than an overwhelming probability of victory is incredibly difficult for military leaders. Despite the romanticism of last stands by small bands of heroes, given the option, soldiers never want to fight outnumbered or outgunned.

On a more personal level, military leaders, like all people in a position of accountability, instinctively seek to avoid failure. History often classifies generals and admirals into two categories: winners and losers. While the reality is less binary, no military leader wants the personal or public burden of responsibility for defeat. Many commanders, frightened by the prospect of making a costly mistake, find themselves frozen in fear and fall to those who act decisively in the face of risks. Fortune, it is said, favors the bold.

Added to this is the sense of responsibility leaders feel for the men and women they lead. For most, even superficially hard-bitten warriors, there is a deeply emotional, almost visceral, obligation to do everything in their power to protect the lives of those entrusted to them. Even operations sure to result in painful losses, like bloody assaults on Pacific islands or Omaha Beach, are considered against the imperatives of the broader effort. Risks are rarely ignored—they are the source of angst and stress in compassionate leaders.

Combat aside, I found that military leaders in a peacetime environment struggle with everyday risks—and with teaching and learning from risk—much as their counterparts in the civilian sector do; and this struggle can produce some predictable, albeit interesting, behaviors.

Although after-action reports from veterans of World War II combat emphasized the importance of live-fire training in preparation for combat, training with lethal ammunition carries some obvious risks. While static positions with constant oversight by noncommissioned officers, or sergeants, minimize the likelihood that soldiers will mistakenly shoot themselves or others, they hardly approximate actual battle. Maneuvers with live ammunition, particularly in darkness, when the US Army hopes to fight in order to leverage its technological strength in night-vision equipment, are infinitely more difficult to control. Ultimately, commanders must weigh the reality and value of training with risk.

In my career, I saw a wide range of reactions to this challenge. In the best units, commanders worked tirelessly to balance realism and controls to achieve the most effective training possible. Special Operations Forces with more mature operators were able to go furthest to create the most realistic scenarios, but even some conventional forces produced impressively valuable training experiences for their soldiers. Accidents, even tragically lethal ones, periodically occurred, but when they did, the organizations received training on how to prevent recurrence and balanced the risks with the value the training provided.

But it was never easy or straightforward. Often success depended upon the commanders, and the tension involved was significant. If their units were realistically prepared for combat, commanders were well regarded by the chain of command, but the scrutiny that followed a training accident often acted as a more powerful disincentive to avoid risk. For too many it was safer to pull back on the realism in their training to reduce the risk of accident. And organizationally it was hard to pressure them to do more—leaders who pushed to approximate combat conditions could be seen to be accepting responsibility for the risks involved. Career-wise, fielding a battle-ready unit was good, but the reality was that responsibility for a lethal training accident could be a career killer.

The predicament was clear: "Do I incur the risk of harming my career to prepare my soldiers for the rigors of combat—or pull my punches?" There was always a siren call to rationalize taking the less risky course.

LIVING WITH RISK

There is a common misperception that soldiers transitioning from peacetime to combat undergo a metamorphosis—laggards become lions and the risks of combat bring out the best in even the worst in uniform.

Periodically that does happen, and certainly the danger of battle focuses the attention of most soldiers. But my experience was that while combat seasons and matures everyone involved, an individual's relationship with risk remains largely constant. Those who are comfortable with assessing and responding to risks in peacetime are the same under fire. For those whom the uncertainty of amorphous negative possibilities breeds caution, and even timidity, combat reflects an uncomfortable extension of those tendencies.

And this phenomenon isn't just limited to combat—it also occurs at the organizational level. The low casualty rate and rapid victory of Operation Desert Storm, America's rout of Saddam Hussein's army in 1991, was a wonderful contrast to the slow agony of Vietnam and seemed to reset expectations. Future war, we hoped, would be brief and less costly. Then, in October 1993, a brutal but highly reported gunfight in Somalia's smoldering capital of Mogadishu resulted in the death of eighteen American servicemen, followed quickly by our withdrawal from the troubled country. Overnight it became dogma that Americans were superb at technology-enabled wars from afar but were unable to withstand casualties, particularly in confused, difficult fights.

Ghosts of Somalia traveled with US forces reluctantly deployed in 1995 into the war-shattered Balkans. There, working under the concept of a peacekeeping mandate, force protection became the highest priority. While it's difficult to criticize the inclination to do everything possible to protect soldiers from harm, America and its military began to create a perception (inside and outside the force) that any casualties would reduce the resolve necessary for armed conflict. When foes believe that the United States is more determined to limit its costs in blood than to ultimately prevail, they will adjust their strategies accordingly.

In this vein, North Vietnam prevailed largely because it was able to convince the United States that there was no level of loss that would deter it from its objective. Faced with the unacceptable options of either devastating North Vietnam, probably with nuclear weapons, or fighting indefinitely, the United States threw in the towel.

Both al-Qaeda across the globe and the Taliban in Afghanistan have gone to school on the American experience. Each seeks to communicate

Soldiers were at constant physical risk in Afghanistan. Here, an Afghan National Army soldier and US forces carry a wounded American.
(AP PHOTO/RAFIQ MAQBOOL)

that the risks of continuing to actively oppose them on battlefields in the region aren't worth the sacrifice. Particularly in a democracy, absent a clear existential threat, it is difficult to sustain a compelling case for incurring casualties in support of physically and psychologically distant foreign policy objectives.

COMMUNICATING RISK

In the fall of 2008, not long after I'd relinquished command of a Special Operations Task Force, the new commanding general proposed a cross-border operation into Pakistan to strike Taliban who were using border areas for safe haven. I had assumed the position of director of the Joint Staff in the Pentagon and monitored the plan as it was briefed to the required decision-makers in Washington, DC, and ultimately approved. As I remember, the plan was characterized as "high risk," but it was well within the capability of the force assigned to conduct it. Except for the fact that the target's location was in Pakistan, which carried significant political sensitivities, the mission was not unlike countless others the command was conducting nightly in Iraq and Afghanistan.

As it unfolded, the mission lost its surgical quality and became a very visible gunfight in which a number of Taliban were killed, and the public violation of sovereignty aroused the ire of the Pakistanis. In the immediate aftermath I received several calls to my Pentagon office asking me, in effect, "How could this happen? Why did our forces screw it up?"

In reality, they hadn't. Nothing goes perfectly in combat, and every operation carries risks that the enemy will exceed expectations, that extraneous factors will intervene, and in this case that it had simply become less clandestine than hoped. I remember asking one agitated caller, "I listened to the briefing describe the operation as 'high risk'—what about that didn't you understand?"

I realized later that, under the circumstances, maybe my question was unfair. Although in the lexicon of military special operators "high risk" communicated the clear possibility that things wouldn't go as planned— and might well go badly wrong—someone from another background lacked that context. Terms like "high" and "strong" had a hollow quality, devoid of effective meaning to the uninitiated. Watching a series of "high risk" operations executed successfully by Special Operations Forces likely deadened their appreciation that over time the probability of failure will prove true. Even operations with a 90 percent chance of success will fail 10 percent of the time.

In today's environment it's always a struggle to communicate risk. Understatement is ignored and exaggeration is discounted. Sources are viewed with suspicion, and even well-intentioned advocates deliberately amp up the message of impending risks in order to be heard over the cacophony of competing alarms. The result is that it is difficult to separate the signal of real risks from the noise that bombards us.

Twenty-eight years before the raid into Pakistan, another operation was conducted that shaped much of the remainder of my career—and I wasn't even part of it. It was the spring of 1980 and I was a young Special Forces lieutenant working in Thailand. Five months earlier, in November 1979, Iranian students had seized the US embassy in Tehran and were now still holding fifty-three American hostages.

On April 11, 1980, after several months of frustrating attempts to negotiate their release, President Jimmy Carter received a briefing on a rescue plan devised to be executed by American Special Operations Forces. But communicating the risks associated with such an operation is never easy.

Air Force General David Jones, the chairman of the Joint Chiefs of Staff, as well as key leaders of what came to be called Operation Eagle Claw, briefed the mission to the president. Major General James Vaught would serve as the overall mission commander, and Colonel Charlie Beckwith would lead the embassy assault. Vaught, a veteran of combat in Korea and Vietnam, was an imposing figure, and Beckwith, the boomingly confident founder of America's nascent counterterrorist force, was instinctively passionate in his advocacy.

In the session, President Carter asked Vaught for his assessment of the probability of success, or degree of risk, and the estimated number of casualties. Vaught, after orchestrating almost five months of intensive planning and rehearsals, expressed confidence that the mission had an 85 percent probability of success. He highlighted risks associated with the time spent on the objective, entering the embassy compound, but said the force had prepared for even the most difficult circumstances—the hostages secured by a truly active guard force. He told the president that he expected a limited number of casualties among the operators and hostages, but that some were likely.

Colonel Charlie Beckwith and Major General James Vaught were key commanders of Operation Eagle Claw.

When asked, Jones and Beckwith indicated that they agreed. President Carter approved the mission as briefed. The operation would be conducted less than two weeks later, on April 24, 1980. It was an audacious effort by some of the best a nation had to offer—but it ended in humiliating failure.

The challenges of the mission resulted in a plan that was necessarily complicated and undeniably high risk. Constructed after weeks of intensive analysis of options, it included a series of steps, or phases, conducted in sequence to infiltrate and position the force for the rescue, then to extract the hostages and everyone involved from Iran. Launching from an aircraft carrier in the Arabian Gulf and from other bases in the region, the raiders would simultaneously infiltrate Iran by fixed- and rotary-wing aircraft to conduct a hostage rescue raid on the American embassy in downtown Tehran before exfiltrating the captives and operators.

Infiltration involved flying nighttime routes to avoid Iranian radar, transloading commandos from cargo aircraft to helicopters in darkness on a deserted piece of desert named Desert One, then positioning the raid force outside of Tehran. The following night the raiders would strike the embassy compound (and one other location in downtown Tehran) and hopefully secure the hostages. So far, so good.

But they then had to get out of Iran. After the raid, which was expected to involve some level of firefight, exfiltration included securing Tehran's soccer stadium as a helicopter pickup zone and seizure of another airfield for cargo aircraft to extract the force. Because of the sequential nature of the mission, each step depended on the successful completion of all the steps preceding it (e.g., no assault of the embassy could be conducted if the raid force had not infiltrated successfully).

Each of these tasks was difficult, but theoretically within the capability of the elite force assembled for the mission. Training and rehearsals had been rigorously conducted, but experience has shown that even with practice, it is impossible to perfectly predict the weather and other conditions under which the operation tasks would have to be performed, and thus impossible to accurately assess their statistical probability of success. But for the purposes of this mission, let's say that each of Eagle Claw's tasks (or phases) had a roughly 90 percent chance of working as planned.

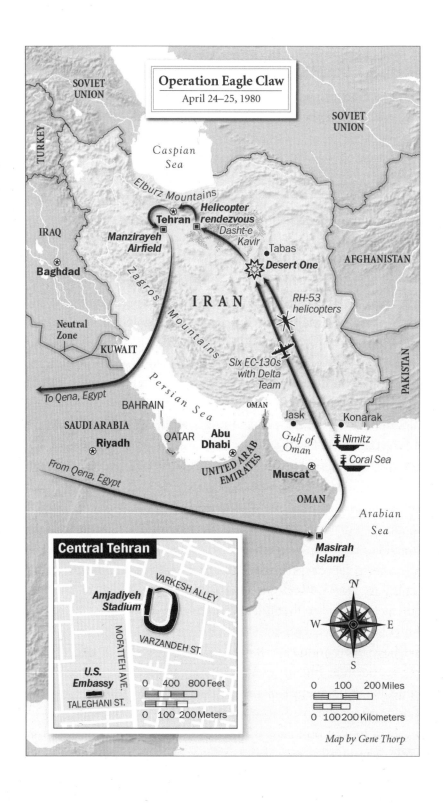

Operation Eagle Claw
April 24–25, 1980

SOVIET UNION

SOVIET UNION

TURKEY

Caspian Sea

Elburz Mountains

Tehran
Helicopter rendezvous
Dasht-e Kavir

Manzirayeh Airfield

IRAQ

Tabas

Baghdad

AFGHANISTAN

Desert One

I R A N

RH-53 helicopters

Neutral Zone

Zagros Mountains

KUWAIT

Six EC-130s with Delta Team

PAKISTAN

To Qena, Egypt

Persian Sea

BAHRAIN

OMAN

Jask

Konark

SAUDI ARABIA

QATAR

Abu Dhabi

Gulf of Oman

Riyadh

Nimitz

From Qena, Egypt

UNITED ARAB EMIRATES

Muscat

Coral Sea

OMAN

Arabian Sea

Masirah Island

Central Tehran

VARKESH ALLEY

Amjadiyeh Stadium

MOFATTEH AVE.

VARZANDEH ST.

U.S. Embassy

0   400   800 Feet

TALEGHANI ST.

0   100   200 Meters

N

W   E

S

0   100   200 Miles

0 100 200 Kilometers

Map by Gene Thorp

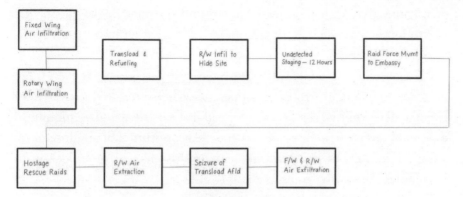

The fixed wing (F/W) and rotary wing (R/W) aircraft would depart from their aircraft carriers and bases throughout the Middle East. They'd meet to transload and refuel at a landing strip known as Desert One. From there, the rotary-wing aircraft would infiltrate to the hide site, where they'd wait (undetected) during daylight hours before the raid force then moved by truck to the embassy. Then they would extract the hostages using the rotary-wing aircraft and transload them onto an airfield, where the cargo aircraft would remove the hostages and return them safely to the United States.

So, the likelihood Operation Eagle Claw would rescue our hostages was 90 percent—right?

No, not even close. It is crucial to remember that because every step in the operation was essential to the whole, every step must succeed. And even if the realistic probability of the force's completing each step was 90 percent (or .9), the overall probability Eagle Claw would succeed was not 90 percent. In actuality it was:

$$.9 \times .9 \times .9 \times .9 \times .9 \times .9 \times .9 \times .9 \times .9 \times .9 = .348$$

Imagine President Carter's dilemma if the briefing had described the operation as having a less than 35 percent probability of success?

Obviously, this exercise itself is flawed. The probabilities assigned would have been arbitrary at best—although the low probability would have been jarring. But in my experience, when faced with a relatively complicated mathematical evaluation or the earnest faces of experienced operators saying they can accomplish the mission—I think most of us would lean toward optimism. After all, we have every reason to *want* it to work. A numerical equation pales in comparison to the confidence of veterans like Major General Vaught and Colonel Beckwith. In that environment, risks seem to shrink, and we are sorely tempted to believe — as Jimmy Carter did.

The case of Eagle Claw, like most difficult decisions, was even more complex than might be readily apparent. When President Carter went into the decision-making process, he had just experienced five months of diplomatic impasse and was under the clear pressure that a failure to resolve the hostage crisis would likely doom his chances of reelection in November. Naturally his assessment of risks to the mission was going to account for likely political costs of inaction.

The military leaders had developed their complicated plan over several months, and after extensive consideration, felt they had crafted not the best plan, but the *only plan* that would work. They had assessed the two biggest risks as the helicopters completing the mission, and the emergence of an Iranian mob gathering around the embassy before evacuation of the hostages and raid force could be completed. Both risks had been mitigated, as much as possible, by utilizing two helicopters above the six needed, and by implementing crowd-control measures in the vicinity of the embassy compound.

There was another pressure—that of lengthening daylight. As the weeks passed from the long nights of winter into spring, the reduced periods of darkness would soon make the operation impossible until the fall, which was months away. There was an overriding feeling that if the operation was to go, now was the time.

From the cheap seats, it is easy to find fault with the plan crafted and the decisions made—until you've been in the position of the people involved. Then it looks and feels different.

In the aftermath of Operation Eagle Claw, with destroyed and abandoned American equipment sitting like a monument to failure in the Iranian desert, leaders in the White House and Pentagon went to work on creating a permanent force capable of successfully completing such missions. I would serve in and ultimately command that force, finding myself repeatedly in the position of assessing and communicating risks that were difficult for both the uninitiated and even the experienced to fully understand.

ASSESSING RISK

Even when I was out of uniform, risk followed me. For two years I had the opportunity to sit on the board of directors of Deutsche Bank USA, the American division of the German bank. It was a fascinating experience as I watched truly dedicated professionals wrestle to repair organizational and reputational damage caused by a combination of factors that were further complicated by a large measure of internal dysfunction. Much of the work revolved around risk.

Risk assessments are more formalized in banking than in almost any other part of the commercial sector. The Great Depression, dot-com crash, and Great Recession were all followed by periods of increased scrutiny that attempted to identify and analyze the roots of the problems. In the wake of the 2008 financial crisis, risks were identified in the emergence and popularization of financial tools like CDOs—collateralized debt obligations—as well as other less publicized activities and products. Taken as a whole, these risks created an existential threat for global financial institutions that traditionally had portrayed themselves as being rock-solid.

As a result, governments sought to restore the soundness of the financial sector by increasing oversight and demanding discipline from banks in maintaining liquidity and limiting exposure to risky loans or investments. To some degree it has worked, but a fundamental tension remained: riskier investments typically bring higher returns, and money sitting in the bank to provide liquidity doesn't yield a profit. Bankers compete and are usually personally compensated for the revenue they generate for their financial institutions, and a conservative, low-risk approach brings lower returns. Therefore, governments at every level, led by the US Federal Reserve, now demand detailed risk assessments to ensure that the banks remain safely out of harm's way.

This has produced some elegantly complex computerized models that incorporate a variety of factors or variables (interest rates, gross national products, etc.) that all impact a bank's financial health. No doubt these models have value, but my eyes glazed over every time we reviewed them. They did provide a good way to calculate metrics like levels of liquidity the bank should maintain, but the far more fundamental risks to Deutsche Bank lay, as everyone who worked there understood, in factors like reputational damage, the ability to retain key talent, and the underlying culture of how the organization operated.

My point is that sometimes models or other dashboard-like systems tell us all is well even when we can look out the window and see a monstrous meteor headed directly toward us.

CONCLUSIONS

There is a humorous story, probably apocryphal, passed among special operators about an incident that took place during the very real chaotic withdrawal from Desert One, the transload location for Operation Eagle Claw. In the dust-filled darkness of the remote desert landing location, the mission had been aborted due to a shortage of operational helicopters, and the raiders reloaded cargo aircraft for the long exfiltration. Mattresses had been spread across the floors of the aircraft and some of the disappointed commandos lay down and fell asleep.

The exfiltration did not go well. The RH-53 helicopters that had just endured a nail-biting flight into Iran through unexpected sandstorms now had to refuel off EC-130 cargo planes for the flight back, a procedure that brought whirling rotors, propellers, and hulking airframes in close proximity in darkness. A mistake occurred and an EC-130 and RH-53 collided. The resulting fire ultimately killed eight Americans and destroyed both aircraft—an ignominious end to an already failed mission.

The story goes that there was time for the commandos in the cargo compartment of the EC-130 to flee the aircraft. One veteran operator, awoken suddenly from a sound sleep, leapt to his feet, moved to the door, and thinking the aircraft was already in flight and at high altitude, dove out and assumed a free-fall parachute posture—which he maintained until his body hit the ground with a thud—eight or so feet later. As always, even in tragedy, the operators found this reaction hilarious, and later, to further poke fun at the operator, asked why he threw himself out when he had no parachute. The veteran replied, "You have to solve one problem at a time."

Risk is like that. It comes at you from out of the blue, from every angle, when least convenient. There is a cost both to becoming overly focused on risk and to ignoring it. And the sweet spot between the two extremes moves with the circumstances around you.

Dealing with risk is part art, part science, and always depends heavily on the personality of an individual or the culture of an organization. There's no perfect formulaic approach to assessing risk nor an effective checklist to avoid or mitigate it. And there will be special dangers waiting for those who blindly follow the technology solution. The emergence of data-fueled artificial intelligence will help identify potential risks with greater clarity, but probabilities will always be impacted by too many variables to let us master risk by taking a purely mathematical approach.

But there's much we can do. An essential first step is to accept the reality that the greatest risk lies inside you and your organization. Focusing on myriad external flaming arrows directed at you is less valuable than focusing on your strengths and vulnerabilities. The consequences of an external threat must always be calculated in the context of your life or your organization.

To this end, understanding how you perceive risks is fundamental. It begins with opening your senses and suppressing the biases that cause you to ignore or discount many risks. History offers countless examples of how Western nations' hubris about the inferiority of other races and cultures resulted in painful setbacks and humiliating defeats. At the outset of World War II, Japanese pilots were thought to be less capable in aerial combat because of poor eyesight. Humbling reality disproved that racist misconception.

Planning for specific risks is important, but only goes so far. John Paul Jones, whose quotation opened this chapter, sought a fast ship because he anticipated the risks of naval combat, and indeed, in many cases, we can plan for the most likely risks that will arise to challenge us. But although every special operation I was ever involved with included detailed contingency plans, rarely did we execute any of those contingencies as planned—the risks that arose were always a bit different from what we'd expected. Still, there was tremendous value in assessing and planning for those contingencies because they gave us a better understanding of our ability to respond and the need to remain agile enough to do it.

In the end, we don't know what a baseball pitcher's next throw will bring. We must be well practiced in hitting, in a stance that allows us to watch him release the ball, decide whether we should swing, watch, or duck—and then act.

And it's useful to remember that baseball's iconic Ted Williams, who set an unmatched standard when he batted .406 in 1941—failed 60 percent of the time he strode to the plate. Just as Williams, a doggedly hard worker, did everything in his power to improve his swing, it's up to us to do all it takes to develop a strong Risk Immune System.

THE BOTTOM LINE

While risk is often portrayed mathematically, our response to risk is more often instinctive. Understanding the factors that drive how we think about and act upon risk is critical.

Part Two

RISK CONTROL FACTORS

A COMBINATION OF SHORTCOMINGS

Candidly, I think we all took it for granted—and we shouldn't have. All we had to do as the enemy approached was to shut the gate, and yet it remained wide open.

In January 1984, my battalion, part of General H. Norman Schwarzkopf's 24th Infantry Division, was on a rotation to the US Army's technology-enabled training center in the Mojave Desert. I was commanding a mechanized rifle company, 120 or so soldiers mounted for combat in M113 armored personnel carriers.

The training was harsh but exhilarating. Nowhere else could our maneuvers approach the realism of this experience. It was an opportunity to test our tactics, our unit, and ourselves against a brutally objective yardstick of effectiveness. Like all units, we were put through a series of missions in an area designed to approximate a Middle Eastern battlefield against a well-equipped and proficient enemy labeled "Krasnovians," who mimicked the Soviets in every regard.

Partway through the rotation, we were given a mission to defend a long valley that ended in a constricted pass. It was optimal for the defenders. The Krasnovians would have to run a gauntlet of several miles of narrow valley to reach the pass, which served almost as the stopper in a bottle. So to succeed, we only had to kill the enemy as they traversed the valley, then block the pass—how hard could that be?

We labored feverishly for more than forty-eight hours to prepare our defenses. Soldiers dug fighting positions, or foxholes, bulldozers worked round the clock carving lengthy tank ditches across the terrain, and miles of angry-sharp concertina wire was strung. Our bastion looked—and felt—impregnable.

To enable our movement during the frantically busy preparation phase, we left vehicle-sized openings in the ditches and concertina wire with the intent to rapidly close the gaps as the enemy's attack time approached. We'd heard stories about units that had prepared as we had and then inexplicably failed to close the openings, giving the enemy an open highway through their defenses. Nobody, we opined, could be that dumb.

Of course, that's exactly what happened to us. In the hectic preparation of defenses and positioning of units as the enemy advanced, the right hand failed to communicate with the left, gaps remained open (even though we'd positioned materials to close them), and the enemy drove past us unimpeded. We'd planned carefully, worked assiduously—and assumed stupidly. Now we lost completely.

After the training came the After-Action Review, a four-hour-long detailed postmortem of the action. In painful specificity, aided by then-cutting-edge computer-tracking technology, our observer-controllers, really evaluators and teachers, dissected the fight, identifying when and where we'd failed. Not surprisingly, we'd gotten the big-muscle movements right. It was in the little things, and in the places where the pieces of our "system" had to come together, that we came up short. Hopefully, we'd learned an important lesson.

As we shall examine in the following pages, the success of a military unit—indeed the success of any organization in its defense—depends on the multifaceted ability to **Detect** the enemy, **Assess** its strength and route of march, **Respond** with effective fires, and **Learn** enough in the process to prepare for subsequent attacks. This requires the function and interaction of a series of factors, or capabilities, that include things as obvious as communication and technology, as well as more discreet factors, like diversity and narrative, in order to produce a successful response. To the untrained eye, it looks like trenches and barbed wire, but to an experienced professional, the critical metric is the health of the unit as a "system."

In the Mojave Desert, the sad reality of our defense was that despite tremendous capabilities arrayed on favorable terrain, the interaction of a variety of factors led to our defeat. It wasn't a single idiot upon whom we could heap blame; it was the weakness of our system. A combination of shortcomings, none of them singularly fatal, did us in.

CHAPTER THREE

Communication

THE LIFEBLOOD OF THE SYSTEM

Lee's army will be your objective point.
Wherever Lee goes, there you will go also.

—LIEUTENANT GENERAL ULYSSES
GRANT'S ORDERS TO MAJOR
GENERAL GEORGE GORDON MEADE
ON APRIL 9, 1864, LEFT LITTLE
ROOM FOR MISINTERPRETATION . . .

Clear, concise, accurate, and timely
information is hard to come by.

THE LAST TO KNOW

The lifting of an early morning fog that had shrouded the plantation field east of New Orleans revealed thousands of British regulars advancing—an ominous sight. But the increasing daylight and improving visibility also exposed the veteran redcoats to the entrenched cannon and infantry of the polyglot force of US regulars, militiamen, local New Orleans businessmen, Choctaw Indian warriors, free Blacks, and Jean Lafitte's pirates assembled by Major General Andrew Jackson, "Old Hickory" himself.

The battle didn't last long. From earthworks reinforced with mud and cotton bales, the Americans decimated the British, whose casualties totaled more than two thousand. Only thirteen Americans were killed. It was a stunning, one-sided victory with backstories of heroism and buffoonery—as is true of most battles.

It was also entirely unnecessary. Fifteen days earlier, the Treaty of Ghent had formally ended the War of 1812. The combatants at New Orleans simply had not yet gotten the word.

Thirty-nine years later, in 1854, the British were on another battlefield, this one near Sevastopol during the Crimean War, when a lack of communication reared its ugly head again. At a point in the battle, Russian forces appeared to be moving to withdraw guns from positions recently captured from Turkish forces, Britain's ally. The British commander, Lord Raglan, ordered the Light Cavalry Brigade to move forward to prevent the Russian maneuver.

Almost two centuries later, the story, immortalized by Lord Tennyson's stirring poem "The Charge of the Light Brigade," remains controversial, fascinating, and for a soldier, almost painful to read. The order from Lord Raglan, who had a different, better view than the order's recipient, Lord Cardigan, was apparently ineffectively communicated by the officer who delivered it. The result of this miscommunication was the Light Brigade's charging the wrong Russian artillery battery, one that was well sited and prepared for defense — a mission bordering on suicide. The outcome was predictable. The Light Brigade lost more than 110 men and 375 horses. A stiff price for a page in history.

The simple act of communicating is anything but simple.

Alfred, Lord Tennyson's poem recounts the catastrophe of the soldiers: "Into the valley of Death / Rode the six hundred."
(PAINTING: *The Charge of the Light Brigade* BY RICHARD CATON WOODVILLE JR.)

THE FOUR TESTS

We likely spend more time, money, and energy on communicating than everything else we do—combined. We read, talk, text, chat, and Zoom. Occasionally we actually stop to think about what we're saying and hearing, but not always.

We prioritize our ability to communicate above most other things. Were Abraham Maslow to update his famous hierarchy of needs, battery power, cell signal, and bandwidth would likely compete with air and water—at least in our minds. It feels that important—and it might be. Absent the ability to communicate, individuals would function alone and accomplish very little. So, it is fitting that the first Risk Control Factor we examine is communication.

If we can ensure or facilitate the flow of information, and dial in the relevance, accuracy, and timeliness of that information, we can increase the effectiveness of our ability to deal with threats. Therefore, it is essential that we think about communication—not only at the most basic level but also on a more nuanced plane.

In the simplest terms, communication is passing information from one individual or organization to another. For that to happen, there must be someone transmitting the information, the physical means to move it from one point to another (e.g., voice, telephone, radio, mail), and a recipient.

For communication to be effective, the message transmitted must be accurate and timely, and the recipient must understand it. There are a host of other factors that must be dialed in to be effective, depending upon the context and the recipient—like the format and speed of the message—all metrics that have spawned an entire industry of consultants.

Let's first focus on the basics. There are four key "tests" that determine if communication is effective. We'll begin with two:

1. The physical ability to pass the information (can or can't)
2. The willingness to pass it (will or won't)

These first two tests capture many situations:

> If the means of transmission don't exist or have been interrupted in some
> way (e.g., loss of cell service or electricity, cyberattack) we either can or
> cannot physically communicate with the methods we desire or require.

> If either party, sender or recipient, is unwilling to participate, we cannot
> communicate.

But analysis must go further—ability and willingness are not enough to
capture the complexity of communication.

3. The quality of the message (accurate, complete, timely, relevant)
4. The receipt of the information (able or unable to digest and understand the message)

We've all experienced times when this has gone wrong: either the quality
of the message or the recipient's ability to understand it gets in the way of
effective communication.

> If the "quality" of the information is lacking, it is often meaningless, or
> worse, misleading.

If a message is in a foreign language, or couched in technical jargon under-
standable only to a few, it may have no value to its recipients.

Ultimately, this decision tree captures the reality that communication depends on a series of "tests," all of which must be positive. If there is a
single "no" in this chain, communication is either not happening or
flawed. The implications—for this most fundamental of all Risk Control
Factors—are significant.

Communication's importance, while notable in and of itself, highlights the interconnected and interdependent nature of the various Risk
Control Factors. Every other factor depends on communication to function effectively. In the same breath, communication *without* the other
factors is largely devoid of focus, balance, accuracy, as well as follow-
through to action.

We've likely all faced the challenge of passing all four tests.

In the fall of 2003, as I led a Special Operations Task Force against
Abu Musab al-Zarqawi's al-Qaeda in Iraq, we found that the intensity and
scope of the campaign demanded unprecedented levels of collaboration
and intelligence sharing within our force, and also outside it—specifically
with the CIA and other parts of the intelligence community.

Inside our Task Force, I discovered (to my frustration) that the technical setup of our information technology systems precluded our Army and
Navy special operators from sending each other emails. Absurd as that
was, it meant that our Task Force failed the can/can't test. And we had to
fix it.

At the same time, we quickly learned that among our partners outside
the Task Force, the perceived risks of communicating were huge, and resistance was fierce. Organizations, and the individuals who had spent
their professional lives in them, protected agency information and equi-
ties as though they were the last bastion of their castle. It wasn't a question
of whether they could share—they could. It was whether they *would*—a
will/won't problem—and a big one.

The resistance was understandable, but for the overall effort against
al-Qaeda, unacceptable. Occasionally, I would rail against agency operatives, arguing that I was not getting the full intelligence picture. Their

response was frustrating in the moment, though with time, is undeniably humorous: "What are we not telling you?" Of course, I couldn't know what I didn't know, and in the moment, it was galling.

To be fair, there is a culture in the military, informed by agency policy and habit, that discourages open sharing of information, and it took a conscious effort to overcome this long-held hesitation. There was an element of risk in sharing information that might find its way to unauthorized people, to the media, even to the enemy. Unintentionally, individuals might find themselves the original source of an embarrassing or painful leak. Also, even among people and organizations theoretically pursuing a shared goal, information is power. And most everyone likes power.

With great effort, we got over that hurdle—but it took time.

The final two "tests" of communication, however, were more complicated. The quality of the information being shared and the ability of the recipient to understand and use it remained a long-term challenge. In some cases the validity of information, often sensitive intelligence like an agent's reporting, was dubious and, without a full contextual understanding of the situation, of limited value. In other cases, misinformation, intentionally crafted or manipulated, as in the case of propaganda or disinformation, increased the challenge of recognizing the reality, or, as soldiers would say, *ground truth*, of the situation.

SYMPTOMS OF COMMUNICATION CHALLENGES

Failure to Transmit. A failure to send information guarantees it won't be received. But how often do we as individuals or organizations fail to share key knowledge?

Failure to Receive. An inability or unwillingness to receive or "hear" information also negates its value.

Lack of a Pathway. More common in earlier days with less sophisticated technology, the physical inability to share information in a timely fashion often results in uncoordinated efforts.

Misunderstood Message(s). A lack of clarity from the sender or insufficient knowledge or context in the recipient can render otherwise critical communication ineffective.

Overloaded Communications. An excessive volume of information can cause truly essential "signal" to be lost in the "noise."

Distorted or Corrupted Message(s). When key information is unintentionally misstated or misinterpreted, it is rendered potentially dangerous.

Intentional Misinformation. Information is intentionally corrupted to deceive or confuse, as in propaganda and in similar efforts.

This chapter explores the impact of our willingness and capability to communicate, and the ways that propaganda and misinformation corrupt our communication. We will learn how communication connects the other factors while at the same time being influenced by them. In the end, we will understand its special function and how the way we exchange information, and the quality of the information we exchange, helps or hinders our Risk Immune System.

THE RIGHT SIGNAL

On a pleasant Tuesday morning in September 2001, while I was at Fort Bragg, North Carolina, conducting a routine parachute training jump, al-Qaeda shocked the world with a devastatingly lethal act of terror. In the United States it was flashbulb moment—an intense burst that seared itself into the nation's memory. When nineteen hijackers passed unhindered through airport security, then successfully boarded and took control of four airplanes, subsequently turning the planes into weapons of death and destruction, it impacted the lives of every American.

No community, however, has changed more as a result of the events of 9/11 than the one most often blamed for the oversights that failed to prevent the tragedy: the intelligence community.

After the towers fell, the US government began thorough investigations and reporting on flaws in America's intelligence apparatus leading up to the attack. No study on the incident was more exhaustive than *The 9/11 Commission Report*. With more than eighty commission staffers writing some four hundred pages of detailed analysis, the report paints a damning picture of flawed structures, muddled processes, and disconnected efforts that proved ineffective in detecting and preventing an extensively coordinated terrorist operation within our own borders.

Working from what they described as the "benefit and handicap of hindsight," commission staffers wrote in frustrating detail about the inability of different components of America's web of intelligence collection and analysis to assemble pieces of the puzzle into a coherent picture that screamed *danger!* Repeatedly, relevant information was not disseminated nor analysis combined. Indeed, before that fatal morning, the United States possessed sufficient information to have indicated an imminent attack involving commercial aircraft. The dots simply needed to be connected—which required effective communication among those who had the intelligence, and could act upon it.

Despite those shortcomings, some intelligence reports predicting a terrorist event of this scale had in fact made their way to the desks of the most important decision-makers in the country. But the reports had not stimulated a response effective enough to thwart it. Why not?

As it had for years, the CIA selected between six and eight articles or short briefings each day on topics considered the most essential intelligence matters and amalgamated them into a single brief for the president, called the President's Daily Brief (PDB). In the eight months prior to planes slamming into the towers of the World Trade Center and the Pentagon, the PDB included entries related to Usama Bin Laden at least forty times.

American intelligence was aware that Bin Laden had plans for an attack. In June 2001, reporting "reached a crescendo," with at least six separate intelligence reports and one threat advisory forecasting imminent attacks. Reporting was not consistent on expected targets, however: briefings focused on potential attacks in Yemen, Saudi Arabia, Rome, Bahrain, Israel, Kuwait, and even the G-8 summit in Genoa. One report on June 28 summed it up, claiming Usama Bin Laden was planning "something 'very, very, very, big'" while seemingly not offering additional specificity, prompting the CIA to order all station chiefs to share al-Qaeda intelligence with their host governments.

Amid the confusion about Bin Laden's objectives in the summer of 2001, President Bush explicitly requested an assessment of al-Qaeda's capability and intent to launch a domestic attack. In response, two CIA analysts authored an article for the August 6 PDB titled "Bin Laden Determined to Strike in US." As *The 9/11 Commission Report* describes, this became the thirty-sixth PDB entry that year to mention either al-Qaeda or Usama Bin Laden—and the first to raise the prospect of domestic attack.

At that frequency, we can imagine what must have been a deafeningly loud cacophony of alarms. How could the al-Qaeda threat not have been front of mind—all the time?

Easily put into context by quick back-of-the-envelope math, in the eight months prior to 9/11, the PDB included a minimum of 1,400 entries, or short briefs, on specific intelligence subjects. This means that just under 3 percent of the PDB entries were devoted to Usama Bin Laden, with just a tiny sliver representing briefings pertaining to the likelihood of a domestic attack.

These percentages reveal another fundamental challenge with communication. It simply isn't enough to get a message to the intended recipient if the message is incomplete: reports have to be pieced together to create a coherent story that can be communicated and prioritized. As *The 9/11 Commission Report* states:

> [N]o one working on these late leads in the summer of 2001 connected the case in his or her in-box to the threat reports agitating senior officials and being briefed to the President. Thus, these individual cases did not become national priorities.

EVEN HIJACKERS STRUGGLE WITH COMMUNICATION

The air traffic controller couldn't get ahold of American Airlines Flight 11 for ten whole minutes on the morning of September 11, 2001; after instructing the pilot to climb to 35,000 feet, he hadn't heard back. At 8:24 A.M., he finally heard an unintelligible message over the airplane speaker:

> "We have some planes. Just stay quiet, and you'll be okay. We are return-
> ing to the airport."
>
> A few seconds later, the message continued: "Nobody move. Everything
> will be okay. If you try to make any moves, you'll endanger yourself and the
> airplane. Just stay quiet."
>
> The air traffic controller was stunned. Unable to fully discern the first
> message, he knew the implications of the second: American Airlines Flight
> 11 had been hijacked.
>
> When the teams on the ground rewound the tape, they discovered that
> the third and fourth words in the first crackled transmission were crucial: the
> hijacker said they "have some planes." The plural nature of this phrase—
> though initially unclear to the controller—foreboded the scale of a wider
> attack.
>
> The hijacker pilot evidently hadn't used a jet airliner's radios before, so he
> was unfamiliar with which signal was transmitted through which receiver. A
> simple communication error—on the part of the hijacker—was illuminating
> for air traffic controllers, who put their response efforts into motion, sending
> military airplanes to counter future attacks and ultimately grounding all planes.

Failing to bring together specifics of pending attacks, the US government neither understood nor predicted the exact timing and manner of
the assault until it was unfolding in front of our eyes. *The 9/11 Commission Report*, in its Executive Summary, presents a scathing review:

> The most important failure was one of imagination. We do not believe
> leaders understood the gravity of the threat.

While that may have been true, it didn't feel that way to me. Although
assigned to Fort Bragg, North Carolina, at the time, I spent the month of
June 2001 in Kuwait for a rotation as the forward commanding general of
US forces. Each day intelligence reporting highlighted al-Qaeda's threats
with security heightened and movement off the base strictly limited—
and it had been that way before and after my month in the saddle. The
threat of al-Qaeda felt very serious. But other noise in the system was also
deafening.

The noise in the intelligence system challenged analysts to identify critical information, or a signal, among the massive volume of interesting but irrelevant data. Additionally, the random nature of much of the information makes extracting accurate predictions—finding the *true* signal among the noise—much harder.

While reports like those included in the PDB are not random noise, the same idea applies. Non-al-Qaeda entries in the PDB—while likely accurate concerning an entirely separate topic (i.e., signal, but signal toward a different end)—drew attention from the intelligence subject that ended up being of most consequence. Because of the sheer amount of intelligence collected, relevant predictions can be lost in the noise.

There's no easy or obvious solution. The other assessments are likely essential to the president and other key leaders trying to understand critical issues—but they can drown out the signal of risks that will manifest with dire consequences. The signal was clear—but the danger of al-Qaeda's plan to strike the United States was lost in the noise. As George Tenet, the director of Central Intelligence, said, "the system was blinking red"—but the system was blinking red on several separate dashboards, each with hundreds of other flashing lights.

WAR ON TRUTH

Long ago, a quote often misattributed to Samuel Clemens, better known as Mark Twain, reminded us: "What gets us into trouble is not what we don't know. It's what we know for sure that just ain't so." Regardless of who said it, the statement's wisdom is proven time and again—with painful costs.

Beyond our ability and willingness to communicate lies the more subtle question of what we communicate. While candor and accuracy are routinely lauded, they are often in fierce competition with intentional and unintentional misinformation.

The 1935 Venice Film Festival awarded the Best Foreign Documentary title to *Triumph of the Will*, a stirring production by filmmaker Leni Riefenstahl that captured the previous year's Nuremberg Rally. In the picture, Adolf Hitler, in the beginning years of his twelve-year reign as authoritarian leader of Germany during what was known as the Third Reich, is depicted as a charismatic genius restoring the Fatherland to its former greatness. Part of a larger, aggressive influence campaign orchestrated by Paul Joseph Goebbels, a university-educated doctor of philology, the motion picture helped solidify the führer's place in the eyes of the world and in the hearts of Germans.

More than eight decades later, the film comes across as an over-the-top propaganda piece that we would hope could never connect with sophisticated audiences. But it did—and was another link in an unbroken chain of frighteningly effective Nazi efforts to shape public opinion. The former army corporal Adolf Hitler understood why:

> Effective propaganda must be limited to a very few points and must harp on these in slogans until the last member of the public understands what you want him to understand. . . . As soon as you sacrifice this slogan and try to be many-sided, the effect will piddle away, for the crowd will neither digest nor retain the material offered.

Hitler intuitively knew that it is human nature to seek out a signal and that simple, one-dimensional slogans could be used to appeal to people's emotions and convince them that "the fact is real, the process necessary, the necessity correct, etc."

Leni Riefenstahl's Triumph of the Will *captured Hitler's mastery of the power of propaganda.*

The Nazi use of propaganda was not a new phenomenon, but Hitler's rise to power coincided with the mechanical means to produce it at massive scale. As technology and media have evolved, so too has the reach and impact of propaganda and misinformation. We want to believe we are too clever to be duped by misinformation—but our habits of mind and tendency toward confirmation bias (which we will address again in Chapter 8) make us all too susceptible. Sometimes the truth can force itself upon us, but most often it is elusive. Too often we believe what is comforting and convenient. Too often we are unable or unwilling to put in the hard work to distinguish fact from fiction.

Let's consider the ill effects of smoking. The linkage between smoking and lung cancer had already been largely established by the 1950s, posing a threat to the lucrative tobacco industry. But instead of directly countering the idea that tobacco was harmful, the leaders of the industry waged a more subtle effort to raise doubt about the conclusions and offer the idea that perhaps the data could support a more benign message. In this way, *smoking kills* was weakened to *smoking might kill*, thus allowing the smoker to rationalize the risk as a mere possibility, not an inevitability.

The tobacco industry knowingly designed its message to encourage misinterpretation of scientific fact, and for a long time a great number of people went along with it. In retrospect, some of the industry's funded

If doctors smoke Camel cigarettes, why shouldn't you? The tobacco industry crafted its messages carefully to minimize the dangers of smoking.
(FROM THE COLLECTION OF STANFORD RESEARCH INTO THE IMPACT OF TOBACCO ADVERTISING [TOBACCO.STANFORD.EDU])

research and messaging seem preposterous, like the 1954 statement below. But the tobacco industry's efforts to minimize the dangers of smoking were remarkably successful because they told people what they wanted to hear.

> It is an obligation of the Tobacco Industry Research Committee at this time to remind the public of these essential points:
> 1. There is no conclusive scientific proof of a link between smoking and cancer.
> 2. Medical research points to many possible causes of cancer. . . .
> 5. The millions of people who derive pleasure and satisfaction from smoking can be reassured that every scientific means will be used to get all the facts as soon as possible.

But irrationality and self-deception are not limited to smokers. Nor are they limited by political persuasion, age, race, gender, or education—it's open to all comers. And despite its initial promise to bring a new era of knowledge and transparency, the internet has made misinformation decentralized and more widespread.

While some of it seems too far-fetched for any reasonable person to believe, in total it represents a form of communication that is as pervasive as it is uniquely dangerous. For just as a failure to communicate can be fatal, falsehoods can be equally toxic. Its causes and its symptoms are different, but the patient dies just the same.

Maintaining a healthy Risk Immune System depends not only on our ability and willingness to communicate in a timely manner but also on the quality and veracity of what we communicate. We must be able to effectively deliver and receive relevant, verifiable information, and we must be able to identify and filter out propaganda.

We must pass *all* the tests.

JOIN OR DIE

A famous slogan of the American Revolution reminded both the thirteen colonies and the widely spread colonists that successful opposition to

States were cut from one giant snake—one missing
would leave the entire entity dead.
(CARTOON: BENJAMIN FRANKLIN'S *Join, or Die* [1754])

Great Britain demanded unity. The graphical depiction of a snake cut into pieces poignantly communicated their individual vulnerability.

It was an apt warning. The British recognized early on that separating and isolating colonies or regions from each other was the most effective way to defeat the budding revolution. The defeat of General "Gentleman Johnny" Burgoyne's army of redcoats, loyalists, and hessians at the Battle of Saratoga in 1777 blocked an attempt to cut off New England from the rest of the colonies. Stop the Americans' ability to communicate, British strategists correctly reasoned, and they are defeated.

Just as a snake cut into pieces cannot survive, our organizations—if separated by gaps and failures of communication—cannot endure. We are weakest when we are not connected, when information fails to move from point A to point B. When we lack unity our communications crumble; when our communications crumble, we are vulnerable to risk.

When all is said and done, communication is the essential enabler— the most critical factor. The remaining Risk Control Factors can be dialed to perfection, but absent the ability and willingness to communicate and receive accurate, timely information, the system fails to function.

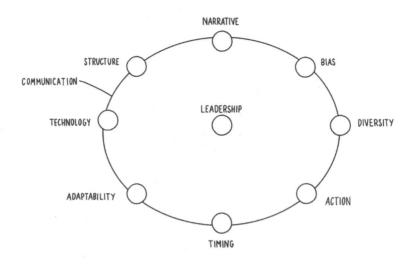

But even the strongest communication must function in conjunction with the other Risk Control Factors. Like many things, communication is essential, but, by itself, insufficient.

YOUR TURN

What types of information does your organization exchange? In what formats? Does it pass the four tests? Where does it fail, and why? Where are the fail points?

How do you measure if your information is accurate, reliable, and verifiable?

What forms of internal propaganda or misinformation are present within your organization? How about external?

As an organization, what measures can you take to weed out what is comforting and convenient so that what you rely on is objective, accurate, and verifiable?

THE BOTTOM LINE

Communication allows the Risk Immune System to work. Get this right or we fail.

CHAPTER FOUR

Narrative

THE MIND OF THE BEHOLDER

Be Silent, Friend
Here Heroes Died
To Blaze a Trail
For Other Men

—PLAQUE OUTSIDE THE ALAMO
MISSION, SAN ANTONIO, TEXAS

How we think of ourselves—and tell our story—
does much to drive our behavior
and determine outcomes.

LINE IN THE SAND

On a still-chilly March afternoon in 1836, twenty-six-year-old Lieutenant Colonel William Barret "Buck" Travis drew his sword and carved an uneven line across the dirt of the compound courtyard.

Many of the Alamo's roughly 180 defenders watched carefully. With characteristic drama, the South Carolinian turned Texas patriot invited the ragtag soldiers to cross the line and join him in defending the decrepit fort against overwhelming odds—and signal their willingness to die for the idea of an independent Texas.

The Battle of the Alamo is a special moment in American history, and nothing less than sacred in Texas. The old mission where the defenders fought valiantly to the last man is hallowed ground in San Antonio. Many generations have been inspired by the image of former congressman Davy Crockett and his fellow heroes fighting bravely to their final breath.

The truth is that what the Alamo's small garrison did was courageous but not strategically significant. The narrative they created, however, has

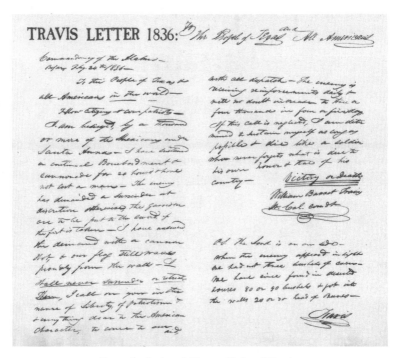

*From the besieged Alamo, Colonel Travis
exhorted Texans to "Victory or Death."*

been powerful out of proportion to any other metrics of the battle. The line-in-the-dirt story is likely apocryphal, an effort to describe the commitment of the diverse band of rebels who opposed the Mexican army's General Antonio López de Santa Anna to "Victory or death." "Remember the Alamo" became a rallying cry for the Texan victory at San Jacinto. Descriptions of stalwart Texans resisting a tidal wave of Mexican soldiers have been shorthand for patriotic heroism ever since.

Dismissing the fight for the Alamo as a popular but heavily romanticized story is to miss the forest for the trees. The importance of the Alamo lies entirely in its narrative—in the story it tells about who we are and what we do. The crumbling old mission communicates values of selfless sacrifice and unwavering commitment to a greater cause. It reflects brightly how Americans *want* to see themselves, and to be seen by the world, and has carried almost magical force for nearly two hundred years.

I first became fascinated by the Alamo when Fess Parker's 1950s portrayal of Davy Crockett on Walt Disney's television program ended at the climactic battle. Later as a young boy visiting relatives in LaFayette, Alabama, I saw John Wayne's epic 1960 version and was hooked.

Although I'm now fully aware of the more complicated aspects of the "Texicans" and their successful war for independence, each time I travel to San Antonio, I go to the Alamo. I envision the exhausted defenders and the equal courage of their Mexican opponents. I'm no longer young or naive, but even now the narrative embraces and envelops me. It's powerful stuff.

SEMPER FIDELIS

Narrative is the story we tell ourselves—often about ourselves—and it has a defining quality. Built on a foundation of stories and related values and beliefs, narrative gives shape and meaning to individuals and organizations and transcends sterile structures. It drives *who* we are, *what* we do, and *why* we do it.

Central and essential to defining individuals, teams, and causes, narrative gives an organization an identity. Where narratives are weak or contradicted by facts or perceptions, organizations become threatened; when narratives provide motivations or identities that are not congruent with objectives, they can be problematic.

From an organizational standpoint, narratives set norms and standards that do much to drive behaviors. Although a soldier in the Army, I spent a lifetime admiring the United States Marine Corps's brilliantly effective use of narrative to define the Marines, all the while creating expectations to which new recruits are rapidly indoctrinated. From day one at boot camp, new Marines are stripped of much of their previous persona and are taught to self-identify with a set of values to the cause, such as *Semper Fidelis*—Always Faithful.

Commanding the combat-hardened veterans of a Special Operations Task Force, I learned that a complex weave of personal and organizational narrative lies behind the commitment and performance of each operator. Some soldiers fought with an intense patriotism—carrying small American flags and couching our effort against al-Qaeda as another version of the two world wars. Others viewed Islamic fundamentalists as a threat to our religious beliefs. Some considered themselves a version of the hard-bitten soldiers of fortune who fight because they believe they are warriors to the core. For most, it was a combination of narratives together that provided them with the purpose necessary to maintain their commitment.

It was never about the paycheck.

PERSPECTIVE MATTERS

In 1957, Vice President Richard Nixon, representing the United States at a ceremony celebrating independence for the West African nation of Ghana, approached a Black guest and asked him:

"How does it feel to be free?"

"I wouldn't know, sir," the man responded. "I'm from Alabama."

Though Nixon intended his question to be little more than a social pleasantry, the man's no doubt jarring response spoke volumes. The second-ranking official in the United States, which was near the apogee of post–World War II power, was on a mission to demonstrate America's commitment to independence, democracy, and opportunity—and was bluntly confronted with the uncomfortable reality that the legacy of slavery in the enduring form of lynching, Jim Crow, and segregation continued to undermine the United States' credibility as a bastion of human freedom.

Nixon's question to the Black man rested on a correct understanding of America's narrative: our nation did indeed define itself by freedom and democracy. At best, however, the narrative was incomplete—it did not reflect the reality of millions of citizens for whom the story line of freedom and progress was only a frustrated aspiration.

The ideals advocated in the Declaration of Independence, though celebrated in Ghana, were stunted in the American South. In that moment, the American Declaration of Independence's "self-evident" truths that "all men are created equal" seemed to apply more directly to Ghana, now unfettered from imperialism, than at home in the United States.

Through a lifetime of observation, I've learned a pretty simple truth: what individuals and organizations believe about themselves drives their values, beliefs, and actions. Narratives are fully mental concepts. Just as beauty is in the eye of the beholder, narrative—the resounding message that explains purpose, meaning, and mission—lies in the mind. And it is under our control.

In the following vignettes, we will look at Google's Project Maven and the US Army's recruiting campaigns to highlight how narrative misalignment around an ethos produces existential risk. A unifying narrative, we'll discover, boosts a Risk Immune System by imbuing an organization with shared consciousness and common purpose—enabling a team to undertake effective action.

SYMPTOMS OF NARRATIVE MISALIGNMENT

Cynicism. Team members conclude that the organization's narrative does not adequately or accurately describe what they are actually asked to do.

The "Say-Do" Gap. Leaders espouse one thing—and then do another. Lofty values sound good, but employees know when the bottom line and other interests trump ideals. And most resent it.

Muddled Priorities. When we aren't clear on who we are or what we're trying to do, it's hard to prioritize actions.

Tensions. Misunderstood or conflicting narratives can undermine confidence and committment.

Brand Damage. Untrue or ineffective brand narratives can destroy the credibility of our products and businesses.

DON'T BE EVIL

Paul Buchheit, Google's twenty-third employee, had a sense of humor. He was sitting in a meeting in early 2000 to discuss and choose the company's values, and he recommended a simple three-word phrase: "Don't be evil."

Buchheit applauded Google for turning away from the malevolent temptations of some advertising agencies. These companies would pay search engines, like Google, a pretty penny to stealthily sneak ads into users' searches, but Google resisted. This was a noble decision that, while not as lucrative from an advertising standpoint, made the experience more pleasant for the user. Buchheit acknowledged this to say:

> It just sort of occurred to me that "Don't be evil" is kind of funny. It's also a bit of a jab at a lot of the other companies, especially our competitors, who at the time, in our opinion, were kind of exploiting the users to some extent. They were tricking them selling search results—which we considered a questionable thing to do because people didn't realize they were ads.

Though initially his recommendation was humorous, Buchheit stood behind it, reflecting later that the phrase was not just your "typical meaningless corporate statement or platitude." Though some of his teammates were initially hesitant, they ultimately capitulated, and "Don't be evil" became one of Google's core values. The phrase took this fledgling start-up to new moral heights beyond the advertising space, inspiring Google to try to use its services for the common good.

"Don't be evil" was easy to remember, comforting in tone, and noble in purpose. When the company aimed to go public in 2004, Google's IPO registration incorporated the phrase—serving as a central message about the kind of company Google was, where it would sit in the market, and more important, what it would do for the world. The company wrote, "Don't be evil. We believe strongly that in the long term, we will be better served—as shareholders and in all other ways—by a company that does good things for the world even if we forgo some short term gains."

The IPO was successful, and the tech start-up grew rapidly. Revenue skyrocketed from nearly $3.2 billion in 2004 to $10.6 billion by 2006. The world had invested in this growing company that was committed to using technology to better the human condition. This ethos also did a fantastic job of attracting employees. Larry Page, one of Google's founders, specifically highlighted this fact in the IPO prospectus, arguing that "talented people are attracted to Google because we empower them to change the world." Google employees seemed to be able to have it all, pairing their "staggering incomes" with the feeling they were doing "good" in the world.

But Google's narrative would soon be challenged. In September 2017, Google entered a contract with the Department of Defense (DoD)—

Google's "Don't be evil" narrative was closely tied to their company's brand.

uniting in an effort they'd call Project Maven. Per the contract, Google would provide the DoD with artificial intelligence services that would take footage from unmanned aerial vehicles (UAVs), commonly called drones, and help track people and vehicles. Typically, remote video feeds were only monitored for a segment of time, such as when aircraft were in flight over a target area. Now, artificial intelligence (AI) software could scour footage that humans didn't view for useful information.

The DoD engaged with Google for two main reasons: to acquire these AI capabilities, and, more broadly, to increase the department's artificial and machine learning capabilities. The DoD knew that its competitors were changing and that it was entering an "AI arms race"—and it believed Google could provide the capabilities it needed to compete.

Google eagerly signed the contract. Now identifying as an AI company (*not* a data company, as it had been formerly known) Google would create a "customized AI surveillance engine" to scour the DoD's massive amount of footage. Google's computer vision, which incorporated both machine learning and deep learning, would analyze the data to track the movements of vehicles and other objects. As they quietly engaged with Project Maven, Google's AI services showed initial progress—Google's software had greater success than humans in detecting important footage.

AUNT JEMIMA

Aunt Jemima is a brand of syrup and pancake mix and other foods, whose packaging features the image of the eponymous character originally appropriated from nineteenth-century minstrel shows. In June 2020, Quaker Oats announced it would be replacing the name Aunt Jemima more than a hundred years after its introduction because of its racist history. With changing cultural tides, it became increasingly apparent that the "mammy" character was racist, contradicting the brand and values the company espoused. The brand's new name, Pearl Milling Company, was released in February 2021.

Some jumped to the brand's defense, going so far as to claim that the first woman hired to play Aunt Jemima, Nancy Green, was one of the nation's first black millionaires. In fact, this was not the case. Born into slavery, Green became a housekeeper and a Baptist missionary. Eventually the company hired another woman to portray Aunt Jemima. Green was buried in an unmarked pauper's grave.

The Aunt Jemima image used on pancake-mix and syrup bottles celebrates white nostalgia for an imaginary past. Rather than celebrate Black progress, the brand's narrative minimizes it—and soon will be a relic of the past.

Was the Project Maven contract in line with the "Don't be evil" value? Many Google employees didn't think so. Encouraged to "act like owners" of the company and speak up when issues arose, it was "Googley" to voice concerns, relay worries to leadership, and to be an active member whose skills and opinions shaped the company.

As rumors spread about this new project, uneasy Google employees put out feelers to investigate. They dug through lines and lines of computer code to learn more about this controversial project that would potentially use Google's AI tools as weaponry. Liz Fong-Jones, then an engineer at Google, caught wind of the company's secret Project Maven—and, in Googley fashion, posted her concerns on a blog post that garnered support from others in the company.

In 2018, emboldened by their culture of sanctioned activism, a group of employees gathered to write an open letter to CEO Sundar Pichai to express their concerns over his new project. Arguing that "Google should not be in the business of war," they had two principal requests: that Google would end its participation in Project Maven, and that the company would "draft, publicize and enforce a clear policy stating that neither Google nor its contractors will ever build warfare technology." The employees, in this letter, and in their conversations, expressed frustration about how Google's actions directly contradicted the company's underlying narrative of not doing evil. Their letter reads:

> Google's stated values make this clear: *Every one of our users is trusting us. Never jeopardize that. Ever.* This contract puts Google's reputation at risk and stands in direct opposition to our core values.

In signing the Project Maven contract, some employees worried that Google had stooped to the level of competitors, and that its use of AI would betray the trust of the public. They argued that this direct, palpable contradiction to the company's narrative would "irreparably damage Google's brand and its ability to compete for talent"—which had been a great focus in the 2004 prospectus. At least a dozen employees quit as Google pursued its work with Project Maven through May 2018.

Google's leadership heard these protests from within the organization loud and clear. In June 2018, after continuing pushback from employees, Google announced they would not renew the contract with the Department of Defense, which was picked up by Palantir, a data software company.

The narrative misalignment and associated corporate churn didn't stop there. Google went on to work with the Chinese government to censor search results and, presumably, monitor its citizens, in efforts known internally as Project Dragonfly. Eventually, the investigative news site *The Intercept* exposed Google's dealings in another serious blow to its "Don't be evil" narrative. To complicate matters even further, the project was also scrutinized by Congress.

What could Google have done differently? First, it's important to understand that evil is in the eye of the beholder. I, for one, would not consider a partnership with the Department of Defense evil—but that's bringing my own biases to the table. With biases and perspectives like these in mind, Google should have defined the scope of its "Don't be evil" narrative from the beginning—to apply to advertising, to company culture, and more broadly to contracts with third parties. Left unfettered, the "Don't be evil" value took on its own meaning in the minds of its employees, which became increasingly at odds with the contracts Google pursued. With clearer narrative precision, the misalignment could have been prevented.

Google's dealings with Project Maven and Project Dragonfly lend us a helpful warning: a contradiction baked in our own narratives invites unforeseen risk, and when our uniting ethos isn't aligned, the threat may even become existential. Narrative drives purpose, meaning, and mission—individually and collectively. You create a narrative, and your actions must be consonant with that narrative, or the narrative must change.

WHAT'S YOUR WARRIOR?

Look now—in all of history men have been taught that killing of men is an evil thing not to be countenanced. Any man who kills must be destroyed because this is a great sin, maybe the worst sin we know. And then we take a soldier and put murder in his hands and we say to him, "Use it well, use it wisely." We put no checks on him. Go out and kill as many of a certain kind or classification of your brothers as you can. And we will reward you for it because it is a violation of your early training.

—JOHN STEINBECK,
East of Eden

I come from a family of soldiers. My father was a soldier, my father's father was a soldier, my four brothers were soldiers, my sister married a soldier, my wife's father was a soldier, her brothers were all soldiers, and her sister is the widow of a soldier. Unsurprisingly, by the time it came for me to

Uncle Sam sternly pointed his finger at eligible soldiers to enlist.

apply to college, I applied to West Point, embarking on a well-trodden path. I too would be a soldier.

As you'd expect from my family background and love of history, I had a relatively clear expectation of a soldier's life. Yet many people, especially young people and their parents, develop their views largely through movies they've seen, and through the Army's own recruiting campaigns.

Military recruiting is anything but new. The effort to interest, cajole, even shame healthy military-age Americans to enlist in the service has a long history. The most famous of all Army recruiting campaigns is arguably *I Want YOU for U.S. Army*, featuring James Montgomery Flagg's depiction of a stern Uncle Sam forcefully pointing his finger. Against a backdrop of foreboding signals of war with Germany, the iconic picture was initially published on the cover of *Leslie's Weekly* magazine's July 6, 1916, issue bearing the title: "What Are You Doing for Preparedness?" The US Army then adapted the image for its own purpose, printing more than four million copies between 1917 and 1918.

These slogans have shifted over time — and demonstrate how a variety of narratives can encourage young men (and later, young women) to don the uniform. For example, a recruiting tactic throughout the 1950s was

An advertisement in the 1959 Recruiting Journal of the United States Army *shows potential soldiers their range of choices after enlisting.*

Choice, not Chance, which highlighted the many options potential enlistees could choose from, by using cartoons that highlighted the different vocations within the Army to give them a sense of agency. As this 1959 advertisement captures, they could *choose* their vocation before enlistment, *qualify* via aptitude and physical exams, and *know* generally what they'd be doing before departing for their assignment.

The United States changed from conscription to an all-volunteer force in 1973, so no American could be forced to join the services any longer. To attract new recruits, the Army tried a spin-off of Flagg's earlier *I Want You for U.S. Army* depiction with *Today's Army Wants to Join You,* in an attempt to convince volunteers that the Army was interested in a recruit's needs, interests, and ideas for the Army and recruit's "mutual gain." Later, from 1980 to 2001, *Be All You Can Be* was a popular slogan that emphasized military service as an opportunity to fulfill an individual's untapped potential. Post-9/11 recruiting recognized the reality of likely combat with an edgier message: *An Army of One* came next, from 2001 to 2006, followed by *Army Strong*, which lasted for more than a decade.

In 2019, the Army launched a new campaign: *What's Your Warrior?* that highlights both combat and noncombat roles. A video advertisement is full of computer-generated images, bolstered by energetic electronic music, highlighting all the potentials of service: "Cross Mountain Ranges" for the adventurers, "Split Cells" for the science-minded, "Master the Elements" for the curious, "Speak New Languages" for the savvy, "Command the Tools of Tomorrow" for the ambitious, and "Turn a Global Challenge into Your Daily Mission" for the action-oriented. Viewers see a service member completing laboratory work, watching as the contraption they use to collect samples transforms into a weapon. The advertisement concludes with a question for the viewers to answer: "What's Your Warrior?" Where recruiting campaigns of the past had emphasized "Army" and "Soldier," focused on the concepts of responsibility and opportunity—this reference to "Warrior" was a thematic change.

On the surface, this new campaign evokes images of strength, intrepidity, and other admirable traits associated with those traditionally designated to fight for the larger group. It also implies a visceral simplicity of purpose and identity: *warriors fight, that's what they do.*

But considered historically, the term *warrior* has a complicated history. It's a Middle English term that comes from a variant of the Old French *guerrier*, which translates to "make war." As Jim Gourley argues, the word hearkens to tribal societies, the warrior classes of the Stone Age, a "military anachronism" that has since been replaced with the narrative of the soldier. As our societies have become less tribal and more modern, focused on industries like politics, medicine, and trade, "soldiers [have] replaced warriors, states [have] replaced tribes." The use of the word *warrior* reminds us of a more barbaric, more aggressive, less civilized age—and has the potential to send the wrong message to those interested in joining the Army.

I was taught from an early age that the difference between an army and a dangerous mob is discipline. Being called a warrior does not automatically equate with a lack of discipline, but the soldiers, airmen, Marines, sailors, and Coastguardsmen of US forces are not *just* warriors—they are warriors tempered by the rigor of law, fine-tuned by ethics, and lifted by a strong sense of morality. Dismiss or bypass law, ethics, and morality, and you are left with terrorists, bandits, mercenaries, and barbarians.

The dangers of permitting narrative drift like this were exhibited by the 2019 presidential pardons granted to four military personnel accused of serious misconduct: First Lieutenant Michael Behenna, Major Matthew Golsteyn, First Lieutenant Clint Lorance, and Chief Petty Officer Edward Gallagher. Their crimes ranged from mistreatment of detainees to killing civilians and prisoners—all prohibited by the military. Although judged and found guilty by panels, or juries, of military professionals, their pardons were accompanied by rhetoric from quarters describing them "as dedicated warriors battling enemies who wear no uniforms and follow no laws of war."

Whether or not these men are guilty can be hotly debated, but the larger question about the essence of "warriors" remains. Described as "'warriors' and not traitors," these men were celebrated in some accounts for acting outside the normal bounds of military conduct. The implication that warriors cross boundaries that timid military bureaucrats shy away from should have a dangerous resonance. Those rigorously enforced constraints on the military are what keeps the force from drifting into serial misconduct. History proves that the erosion of discipline and constraints leaves military forces in a dark and dangerous place.

Clearly, I'm not saying the choice to use the term *warrior* to entice young women and men to enter the military automatically signals that American service members will devolve to bands of pillaging marauders. But words matter. As new Marines mold their values and behavior to meet the *Semper Fidelis* narrative provided for them, so too will the young soldiers interpret what being a warrior is—and act accordingly.

The same holds true for organizations. A business's narrative will create expectations for its employees—guiding their behavior, reactions, commitment to teammates, and investment in their work. In a world that requires naming and meaning, *how* we define ourselves is important—and promises to have large and lasting effects on our actions.

NARRATIVE GHOSTS

In the United States, our initial reaction to the coronavirus's emergence in China was largely muted. We had seen viruses of its kind before and didn't believe it would cross oceans and come to the United States.

We were wrong.

The respiratory illness it caused, COVID-19, soon spread to the United States. Called a "hoax" by the unconvinced, a "calamity" by the panicked, a "disaster" by citizens and leaders who sensed the impending disruption—the names we gave it helped guide our response. Some scoffed at the "China virus" or the "Kung Flu," while others geared down for the ordeal to come. Political rhetoric bumped heads with scientific prediction, as varying descriptions of the virus dictated reactions to the disease. A lack of a coherent narrative meant a lack of unified response.

On March 11, 2020, as worldwide infection reached 118,000 people, with eight countries, including the United States, each reporting more than 1,000 cases, the WHO declared COVID-19 a "pandemic," a distinction usually reserved for horror movies, evoking images of the bubonic plague and dead bodies piled in the streets. The virus was now a worldwide problem—nations began to lock down their cities and close their borders.

The names given the virus—from a Public Health Emergency of International Concern, to a hoax, to a pandemic—were narrative choices that gave the public an organizing principle from which to understand this noxious disease, and a narrative baseline for the world to follow to guide its response. The virus *itself* didn't change, but the reaction did—as the case numbers increased and the perceived threat grew. Like throwing baking powder on a ghost to see where the specter stands, COVID-19's narrative helped the world see, appreciate, and respond to the threat.

The lesson is clear. A shared narrative allows us to unite around a common purpose that is required to undertake effective action. What is true for governments is true for organizations: we must take care in defining the problem, naming the issues and complexities, and crafting solutions. This will be an iterative process. Narratives are *not* static—quite the opposite. Teams will constantly have to alter their understandings of the world, sharpen their own stories, and calibrate their norms and expectations as conditions shift.

Iteration, coupled with a constant commitment to shared values and goals, is vital—and what defines a strong Risk Immune System.

YOUR TURN

What story do you tell about yourself? Does it accurately reflect your ethos and values?

Are your culture and actions in alignment with your narrative, and are they consistent across the organization?

Is the way that you are perceived externally in alignment with the way you perceive yourself internally?

What steps can you take to avoid narrative drift and keep your teams aligned?

THE BOTTOM LINE

When our narrative is misaligned to our purpose, values, or strategy, we invite risk into our organization.

CHAPTER FIVE

Structure

PUTTING THE BUILDING BLOCKS TOGETHER

Bureaucracy is the death of all sound work.

—ALBERT EINSTEIN

Ultimately, organization matters. An improperly assembled weapon will not fire.

THE BIG GREEN MACHINE

"Dutch, where's your division?" raged Lieutenant General Walton Walker, the American Eighth Army commander. Standing opposite him, Major General Laurence "Dutch" Keiser was pointing to an acetate-covered operations map marked with grease pencil showing unit locations. He attempted to give an answer—but his efforts were fruitless.

Walker had just arrived after overflying Keiser's 2nd Infantry Division's embattled sector—which ran along the Naktong River and formed the western side of Walker's Pusan Perimeter in South Korea—and knew things were in a shambles. The map was wrong. Keiser's information on his troops' locations was wrong. It felt on September 1, 1950, as though just about everything was wrong.

The Korean War—initially called a "police action" by the Americans—was still in its infancy. The ten weeks since North Korea had suddenly invaded its southern neighbor on June 25 were a disorienting maelstrom for US Army leaders. Within days of hostilities, the southern Republic of

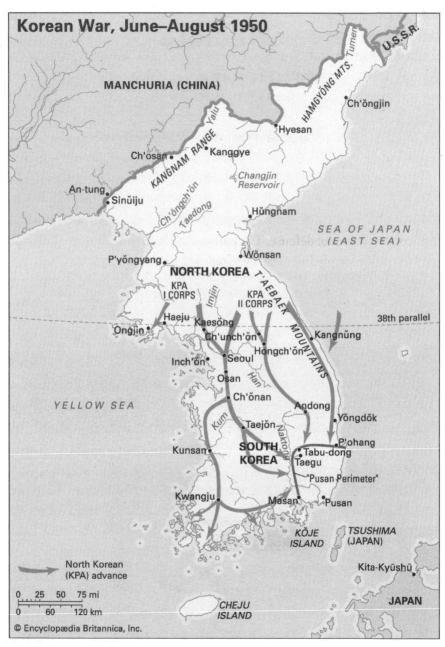

Korean War, June–August 1950

MANCHURIA (CHINA)

KANGNAM RANGE

Yalu

HAMGYŎNG MTS.

Tumen

U.S.S.R.

Ch'ŏngjin

Hyesan

Ch'osan

Kanggye

An-tung

Sinŭiju

Ch'ŏngch'ŏn

Taedong

Changjin
Reservoir

Hŭngnam

SEA OF JAPAN
(EAST SEA)

P'yŏngyang

Wŏnsan

NORTH KOREA

KPA
I CORPS

Imjin

KPA
II CORPS

TAEBAEK

Haeju

Kaesŏng

Ch'unch'ŏn

Kangnŭng

38th parallel

Ongjin

Inch'ŏn

Seoul

Hongch'ŏn

MOUNTAINS

Osan

Han

Ch'ŏnan

Andong

Yŏngdŏk

YELLOW SEA

Kum

Taejŏn

Naktong

P'ohang

Kunsan

SOUTH
KOREA

Tabu-dong

Taegu

"Pusan Perimeter"

Kwangju

Masan

Pusan

KŎJE
ISLAND

TSUSHIMA
(JAPAN)

North Korean
(KPA) advance

Kita-Kyūshū

0   25   50   75 mi
0   60   120 km

CHEJU
ISLAND

JAPAN

© Encyclopædia Britannica, Inc.

*North Korean forces race down the Korean Peninsula, forcing United Nations and
Republic of North Korea units into a perimeter around the port of Pusan.*

Korea forces were routed by the North's military, which included units bloodied in combat during China's civil war and equipped with Russian T-34 tanks—which overwhelmed anything the South possessed.

In an effort to stem the South's collapse, the United States deployed forces stationed in Japan to Korea. Many policymakers and military leaders assumed the appearance of American units would intimidate and then drive back the North Korean invaders, but the first US Army units, undermanned, poorly equipped, and grown soft in the years of occupation duty since World War II, were pushed back to the southern tip of the peninsula. What followed was a hard-pressed effort to hold onto the vital port of Pusan.

Backs to the wall, American and allied forces doggedly sought to establish coherent lines of defense. They aimed to have flanks tightly connected, and to secure supply lines from the rear to bring forward ammunition and food and backhaul casualties.

In the opening weeks of fighting, US forces struggled with a loss of cohesion.

These were often hopes unrealized. North Korean tactics used highly mobile infantry that moved across seemingly impassable hills to get behind American positions, disrupting resupply, communications, and above all, confidence. Time and again units lost effective command, control, and cohesion—and GIs "bugged out," or retreated in panic. It was dangerous to the force, and it was embarrassing to the nation.

It was against this backdrop, in a frightening moment of possible defeat, that three-star Lieutenant General Walton Walker, formerly one of General George Patton's World War II commanders, stormed into Major General Keiser's canvas HQ tent and erupted at his subordinate. The forces had lost cohesion, and their fragmentation added risk to an already challenging fight.

Considering the circumstances, neither the US Army's difficulties nor Walker's frustration were entirely unexpected. Like almost every kind of soldier ever fielded, Americans function best as part of a whole, within a structure that operates like a gigantic machine—each piece dependent on the others.

Complaints about Army bureaucracy and the "big green machine" are likely as old as militaries themselves. Regulations, formations, uniforms, "hurry up and wait," and other constraints on individual liberties are often maligned. But the cohesion and strength of unified action by a group—a team—is powerful. As a result, commanders are comforted when maps reflect unbroken lines and signal officers report reliable communications.

By tradition, soldiers in the ranks are outspokenly frustrated by the discipline that corsets them. But those same troopers, particularly those huddled at night in lonely foxholes, depend on a belief that they are part of a larger whole—part of an organization that is focused on and committed to their well-being.

Structure, we know from personal and historical experience, is simultaneously essential and dangerous. The connections, processes, and resulting cultures that provide strength and integrity to the overall organization can also induce sluggishness and rigidity. But the aphorism "can't live with them, can't live without them" applies—so we have to try to get our structures right.

WHOSE MAP IS IT ANYWAY?

Often our structural problems are systemic. Just as often they are self-inflicted.

The 9/11 Commission Report uncovered some harsh truths about the US government. One of the most startling realities was the inability of the agencies and organizations tasked with our protection to connect the dots and block lethal threats.

This inability stemmed from a mundane but deeply consequential reality that persists to this day: the American federal government lacks a common structure for the way it views and organizes the world. In essence, the organizations that make up the federal government have different maps—though geography is agreed upon, each divides the world differently.

Take Israel, for example. The State Department considers Israel to be a part of the Near East, but the Department of Defense treats Israel as part of Europe. The contradictions continue: Egypt can be considered part of the Middle East and part of Africa, depending on who you ask in government—and both answers would be correct. India is part of what the Department of Defense now calls Indo-Pacific Command, and at the same time its chief regional rival, Pakistan—across one of the world's most perilous strategic fault lines—falls into the Department of Defense's Central Command. In the event of a conflict between the two countries, the Department of Defense would default to two separate teams managing the situation.

Dizzy yet?

Different structures lead to inevitable gaps in communication processes, information sharing, and situational awareness—which lead to painful consequences. Our own structures often exacerbate, not alleviate, already tricky national security dangers. This is a tension all bureaucracies share: structures that guide us can all too often be those that lead us astray.

As I took command of the Special Operations Task Force in 2003, I assumed that the structure I had to worry about was that of our adversary, al-Qaeda in Iraq. So I focused the efforts of my force on understanding, locating, and then destroying it. But ultimately, to win, I found I had to spend more time and effort on another structure: our own. That was unexpected.

I'd spent much of my career in our Task Force, a purpose-built organization designed to accomplish the nation's most difficult counterterrorist missions. Composed of specially selected, exquisitely trained professionals, the units of the Task Force boasted unparalleled capabilities, impressive histories, and cohesive, almost tribal, cultures. Each unit was comfortable functioning independently, but interaction between units inside our Task Force was plagued by rivalries. Collaboration with outside entities across the US government was a struggle on the best of days.

The challenges did not leap out when looking at an organizational chart. Reflected in neat boxes and clear lines, the nation's counterterrorist capability appeared orderly and effective. If only that were the case. In practice, relevant authorities were often redundantly competitive, and yet there were also gaps in oversight. Our ability to wage a coordinated campaign was far more modest than would have been expected given the resources the nation had invested, far less effective than the neat little lines on the org chart suggested, and most consequentially, our ability to defeat al-Qaeda in Iraq was compromised, even questionable.

SYMPTOMS OF STRUCTURE PROBLEMS

Unclear Roles and Responsibilities. Individuals and subordinate organizations are unsure of who is supposed to be doing what. And so much gets left undone.

Duplicative Efforts. An ill-defined organization leads to multiple parties attempting to accomplish the same tasks.

Gaps Where Seams Should Be Tight. Everyone thinks someone else was supposed to bring the beer to the party.

Tortured Communications. Information travels painfully slowly through the labyrinth—typically too late to address the need.

The Longest Chain. You have to get approval from your boss's boss's boss—and you're not even sure who that is.

Structural issues like these are frustrating and commonplace, but they are not a legitimate excuse for failure. They are within our control. Because our Task Force was committed to success, we doggedly worked our way through the problem.

A formal reorganization effort was a tempting response, but the bureaucratic hurdles associated with the process were daunting. And because we lacked a clear view of what kind of structure would work (much less be optimal), I opted instead for making changes "provisionally," implementing constant adjustments and improvements. We iterated this process continuously as the requirement, and our understanding of it, evolved.

Additionally, we designed the provisional organizations to be cross-functional so they included a range of both capabilities and representatives of multiple units—to help build cultural cohesion across the wider force. It didn't always function smoothly, but we changed anything that didn't work and tried something else. We never stopped making improvements.

Ultimately, the structures we create are incredibly important, and they are often doubled-edged swords: for an army, the strength of its battle line can become vulnerable to inflexible rigidity. In a similar way, an elegantly structured organization can provide great organizational clarity—but can easily function as a lumbering bureaucracy that's unable to adapt.

As *The 9/11 Commission Report* illustrated, the autonomy of each federal government office having a worldview that works for them can, in the same breath, stall multibranch government responses—obfuscating a clear response and getting away from the mission at hand. The structure of an organization exists in a paradox: it needs to work independently, but *also* in conjunction with other related structures. A steady brick is good and well alone, but it needs to stack upon others to build a sturdy tower.

Tied up in the issue of structure is that of power—of who sits at the top of the hierarchy, nearest to the clouds, or closest to the crown. Structure *informs* power—who has the jurisdiction to lead, whose influence deserves respect or derision, who has the agency to make decisions. In this chapter, we will see this phenomenon in action as we examine White

House seating arrangements and the placements of risk officers in financial institutions. Structure can uplift—or it can render teammates powerless, thereby leaving you, and your organization, susceptible to more risks.

PROXIMITY IS POWER

The West Wing of the White House is smaller than you think. Chase Untermeyer, a former executive assistant to then vice president George H. W. Bush, described it as a "cushy, high-end funeral parlor," with flowers, thick carpets, and nice furniture, no bigger than a "prosperous" suburban house. Tiny, sometimes windowless offices line the historic hallway and are so small that the Reagan administration's communications director, Patrick J. Buchanan, received a real window with glass from his staff to lean up against his office wall, poking fun at his small work space. Staffers, however, vie for the cramped spaces in order to be closer, and hopefully closest, to the commander in chief.

George Stephanopoulos, a Democratic operative turned journalist, famously whined about the location of his new office in the West Wing. His description of why it mattered is insightful.

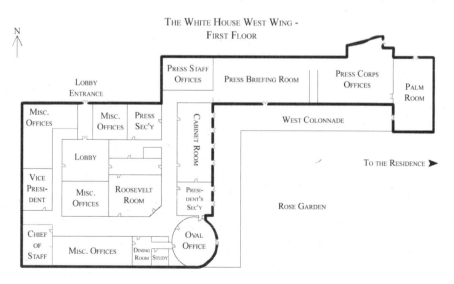

The West Wing has a small hallway, and staff rooms, part of the small blocks of "Miscellaneous Offices," can be no bigger than a storage closet.

Proximity . . . is a source and sign of power. The closer you are to the
president, the more people believe he listens to you. The more people
believe he listens to you, the more information flows your way. The more
information flows your way, the more the president listens to you. The
more the president listens to you, the more power you have.

Stephanopoulos had just been assigned a new role in the Clinton administration, where he was working "more closely" with the president. His
new office, then, had to reflect this shift, being closer to the Oval Office
"even if it were a matter of inches." He anxiously awaited his new room
assignment, dramatically likening the Old Executive Office Building
(across the street with eighteen-foot ceilings) to "Siberia." He was ultimately assigned to a tiny study with a peephole that faced into the president's private dining room—giving him full, "protected" access to the
president. As real estate agents endlessly preach, location is everything.

While Stephanopoulos may seem to have been needlessly obsessed about
where he sat, his anxiety illuminates a stark truth: by losing influence, you
risk losing effectiveness. The structure of an organization informs who can
work with whom, who exerts influence, and who is subject to power. Healthy
Risk Immune Systems acknowledge this very fact, and leaders do well to
recognize the ways in which structures impose power dynamics that may
determine how effective individuals are—and how successful teams may be.

BURYING RESPONSIBILITY

The collapse of Lehman Brothers in 2008 is a well-known story of corporate mismanagement: Lehman Brothers made some ill-fated investment
choices for a good part of the first decade of the twenty-first century, accu-
mulating high-risk mortgage-backed securities. Andrew Ross Sorkin's ex-
cellent account, *Too Big to Fail: The Inside Story of How Wall Street and
Washington Fought to Save the Financial System—and Themselves*, presents a startling truth: Lehman Brothers couldn't manage risk properly because its risk management functions were buried in corporate hierarchy.

Make no mistake: the team's risk assessments were *not* incorrect because they disregarded the idea of risk management entirely—in fact,

Lehman Brothers had several formal mechanisms to **Detect**, **Assess**, and **Respond** to risk—they were simply rendered ineffective and powerless by the organization's structure.

Before we dive into the details, and what we can do to prevent making similar mistakes, it's important to recognize that Lehman Brothers wasn't alone in its practices. An economy-crashing series of events like the one we saw in 2008 was only made possible through similar behavior across the financial industry: Merrill Lynch, American Express, Morgan Stanley, and Goldman Sachs all had structural risk management challenges that elevated risk. In fact, burying responsibility for risk management was a cultural norm on Wall Street in the early years of the 2000s—and when the bill finally came due, it was paid by the entire global economy.

Wall Street had plenty of evidence that its risk management systems were broken. One notable example was in 2001 and 2002, when the country witnessed the collapse into insolvency and eventual bankruptcy of Texas-based energy-trading giant Enron. Enron's failure was just one of many events that spurred Congress and the Securities and Exchange Commission to enact new regulations that encouraged financial institutions to create chief risk officers (CROs) and enterprise risk management functions to prevent similar issues on Wall Street.

ENRON: THE FOX WATCHING THE HENHOUSE

While enjoying unprecedented growth in the 1990s, Enron created a "Risk Assessment and Control Department." This department, tasked with evaluating and signing off on proposed investments, was presented to the outside world as proof of the company's diligent and cautious approach. Within Enron, however, the department was a joke. Their concurrence on a potential investment was treated as a mere administrative formality, not credible due diligence on the fundamentals of a potential deal. Indeed, what the outside world deemed worthy of celebration was, for the decision-makers at Enron, nothing more than a "hurdle" to overcome in pursuit of greater investment returns. The structure was one of deception, and they got away with it—until they didn't.

Like the post-9/11 reforms undertaken at the federal level, these actions were designed to prevent a Wall Street catastrophe by enabling an accountability mechanism for its risk assessment processes.

This seemed to solve the problem: rather than simply expecting the senior leaders of a firm to assess financial risk, companies now had dedicated officers and teams responsible for monitoring hazards. These new positions would consistently ensure companies' investment strategies did not expose them to unreasonable market risks. We can safely assume, then, that risk management could no longer be ignored, right?

Wrong. While firms did name CROs and gave them important responsibilities, they failed to account for a psychological concept known as moral licensing. To put it simply, if you were a trader or an executive at a firm with a CRO and a risk management structure, you could assume that someone else was responsible for monitoring risk and so you didn't need to worry about it individually. It's similar to the bystander effect: when someone, for example, falls ill and a first responder asks a group of bystanders to dial 9-1-1, nobody calls—assuming someone else has.

What this meant in practice at banks was that if a risky investment was under evaluation, traders could assume that an authority figure charged with risk management would intervene if the proposal put the firm at risk. In the absence of intervention, they assumed the investment was responsible—and would proceed accordingly. Assuming silence equaled consent was irresponsible and costly. Misaligned incentives often prompted this behavior, as traders were rewarded for taking risks with the hope of higher returns, while the risk management functions—supposed to rein in this behavior—were sidelined from doing their jobs.

CROs weren't the only ones assessing risk, however—traditional management could still ensure a bank made wise risk assessments. The next-in-line risk assessors, however, were often unequipped to make informed judgments. Corporate leaders, like Joe Gregory at Lehman Brothers, lacked the technical expertise to comprehend the risk their companies assumed as financial derivatives, especially mortgage-backed securities, became increasingly complex throughout the early 2000s. Even the CROs, who did have a better technical understanding, were often outpaced by market innovation.

The failure of Lehman Brothers was the tipping point that ushered in the Great Recession. On paper, the iconic firm was well equipped to respond to risk: the bank's board of directors had a dedicated risk-management committee. Furthermore, the company's CEO hired the best of the best: an accomplished CRO from Goldman Sachs.

But the CRO was often asked to leave meetings with the firm's executive committee when risk-related issues were under consideration. By 2007, Lehman's leadership stopped inviting the CRO to executive committee meetings altogether. The CRO was rendered powerless in not being able to attend—the institution's structure thwarted an exhaustive risk assessment.

Lehman's board of directors could have possibly intervened to ensure the CRO was properly employed, but the board—even within its risk-management committee—did not fully understand the complex derivative and securitization decisions and failed to act as a result. Even after Lehman's collapse, a member of the board's dedicated risk management committee stated in shock: "This is a day of disgrace! How could the government have allowed this to happen? Where were the regulators?" Lehman's own risk-management committee took part in moral licensing.

Had Lehman simply not thought about risk, perhaps its collapse would be a simpler story to understand, but that wasn't the case. Lehman hired a talented CRO, who made risk management a priority for the business through the early 2000s, but then "sidelined" her, isolating the CRO from decisions on risk. Additionally, Lehman's board was ill-equipped to understand contemporary financial instruments, so even though there was a "risk-management committee," it existed in name only, convening only twice in both 2006 and 2007. Power was buried in the structures of the organization. This was made worse by increasing risk-appetite limits and minimizing the organization's Global Risk Management Division, challenging the risk management protocol that had once been one of the "core competencies of the firm."

In hindsight, it is clear that before the financial crisis, risk wasn't a uniform concept on Wall Street. Each bank thought about risk and managed it (or failed to manage it) differently. There is a clear pattern—from

Enron onward—of establishing risk-assessment functions but then preventing these teams from checking unnecessarily risky behavior.

The lesson boils down to this: hanging a RISK sign on offices is irrelevant if they lack the influence to shift organizational decision-making. Our structures are not effective in name alone—accountability and authority have to be operationalized to best posture ourselves against risk.

IT TAKES A NETWORK

From foxholes to the offices in the West Wing to the desks on Wall Street, every organization offers us a singular truth: structure matters. Structure defines decision space, informs reporting channels, establishes communication networks, creates organizational cultures, and allows for checks and balances. And at the end of the day, although structures *seem* unmovable—associated with physical elements like concrete and steel—they are far more fluid. Our organizations always expand and bend as requirements change—increasingly so, as we become more connected than ever in the digital age.

Over the course of my career, I've learned that while structure provides guidance, safety, and routine, it can potentially weaken our Risk Immune System. Structure can limit and entrench decision space, stopping the flow of information or preventing decisions from being made altogether. It can also create the illusion of decision-making; for example, designating a department to carry out a function critical to your organization and then expecting it to do so without any support or oversight. Beyond this, structure can bury power and render contributors voiceless, so it must be used carefully as a tool to elevate the capable and assist the struggling.

With this vulnerability comes an opportunity to align your organization around priorities, clarify decision space, and establish clear expectations for your team to be best equipped to **Detect**, **Assess**, and **Respond** to risks. A critical question is: Does your structure make sense for what you're trying to do and for the environment in which you are operating? Beware the reflexive temptation to restructure to provide the illusion of progress.

I've long believed that restructuring is often just an exercise in deception: titles and parking spaces change, but everyone operates the same way. It's imperative to address the fundamental processes and be willing to admit the possibility that the supporting culture is dysfunctional—and make necessary changes from there.

YOUR TURN

Does your organization's structure function as envisioned? Does it help your team achieve its goals?

Where is power located in your organization? Who benefits from being close to this power?

Where in your structure is responsibility for risk? Is this responsibility understood and respected?

THE BOTTOM LINE

Structure enables or inhibits the effective functioning of any organization's Risk Immune System.

Understanding structure's impact on our processes and culture, positive or negative, is critical.

CHAPTER SIX

Technology

THE TURBULENT MARRIAGE
OF MAN AND MACHINE

*We live in a society exquisitely dependent on science
and technology, in which hardly anyone knows
anything about science and technology.*

—CARL SAGAN,
ASTRONOMY PROFESSOR,
SCIENCE WRITER, HOST OF
THE PBS TELEVISION SERIES COSMOS

*Technology raises a new question:
Who or what is in control?*

SITTING ON A HOT FRYING PAN

Rule breaking makes for great storytelling: American children know the tale of the Boston Tea Party and lunch counter sit-ins of the 1960s from a young age, just as Chinese citizens know the story of Chairman Mao and the Long March. But the name Stanislav Petrov is at most a historical curiosity, despite his world-changing act of disobedience.

Arguably, September 26, 1983, witnessed the single most important act of insubordination in the history of human civilization. On that fateful day, Lieutenant Colonel Petrov of the Soviet Union's Air Defense Forces was stationed at a command center outside Moscow. The facility was responsible for monitoring automated reports from Soviet satellites that tracked American and NATO nuclear forces, and it was a crucial part of the total Soviet defense network.

In his role, Lieutenant Colonel Petrov occupied an essential position in the Soviet Union's decision-making structure. If surveillance systems identified a series of missile launches, it was Petrov's duty to make an im-

Lieutenant Colonel Stanislav Petrov's bravery wasn't publicly known until after the Soviet Union's collapse.
(NIKOLAI IGNATIEV / ALAMY STOCK PHOTO)

mediate judgment about whether or not they were hostile and inform headquarters of an incoming attack. While he had no direct authority to initiate a counterstrike, his position gave him considerable control over whether or not the Soviet Union considered itself under attack. A single phone call of warning to the Soviet high command would likely cause the gears of nuclear war to turn, potentially culminating in the launch of thousands of missiles and bombers, tens of thousands of targets struck, and many millions dead. Petrov was an essential human link in an otherwise automated decision chain.

It was during his Monday watch, amid escalating tensions with the United States, that Lieutenant Colonel Petrov's computer systems changed their indicators rapidly and without warning from "launch" to "missile strike." The signal indicated that the United States had launched five Minuteman intercontinental ballistic missiles from their silos and they were bound for the Soviet Union. Now it appeared that the unthinkable had become a reality: President Ronald Reagan had launched a surprise attack.

For fifteen seconds Petrov's team paused in shock, but then their training kicked in. They understood well that following any such "missile strike" warning, they were to immediately notify high command, which would effectively initiate the Soviet Union's response to the American attack. Their process was supposed to be rapid and straightforward—and the computer's unequivocal indicators made it a nearly reflexive exercise.

It was a surreal moment. Lieutenant Colonel Petrov was an experienced professional, but he'd never experienced this. Still, he knew the time it took for a Minuteman to complete its mission—from launch to the impact of multiple nuclear warheads—was about twenty-five minutes. So, rather than immediately picking up the phone and issuing the warning his computer dictated he make, he waited. Instead of acting immediately, and without consideration, he looked to other sources of information. Petrov stunned the command center with what could have been viewed as indecision, incompetence, even disloyalty. But something told him the computer wasn't telling him the whole story.

Five agonizing minutes passed. Hundreds of personnel at the command center stared at their leader, waiting for him to notify his headquarters of an imminent attack. Petrov later explained the moment was like "sitting on a hot frying pan," but he "had a funny feeling in [his] gut." He knew it would be strange for the Americans to launch a surprise attack with only five missiles. Petrov—and every other student of American attack capability—expected hundreds in that scenario. Even though the computer indicator was flashing "missile strike," what his systems alerted made little strategic sense.

Petrov also considered the fact that the blaring "missile strike" warnings were coming from a single source: Soviet satellites. For the threat to be authentic, Soviet ground-based radars, while slower to detect an attack than satellites, should have been serving as a second source confirmation—but they remained silent. Finally, Petrov remembered that the computer system signaling an incoming attack was new, had been hurried into service, and was therefore not entirely reliable.

With conflicting factors to consider, Petrov defaulted to his experience and judgment. He concluded that they were witnessing a system failure, not the start of a new world war. While machines screamed at him to do otherwise, Petrov communicated no alert to Moscow and reported a technical malfunction instead. For the remainder of the twenty-five-minute calculated flight time, he likely assessed and reassessed just how sound his "50-50" estimate of probability had been.

With the armchair comfort of hindsight, we know now that no Minuteman missiles slipped loose of their silos in America that day, and no bombs fell on the Soviet Union. The truth was that an early warning satellite constellation had picked up the sun's reflection on the clouds, and its automated systems interpreted the flare as an indication of a missile launch, setting Petrov's crisis into motion. That he made the correct decision is a testament to good judgment in a crisis—especially when compared with what the operators of the Vladimir Ilyich Lenin Nuclear Power Plant at Chernobyl, Ukraine, did 943 days later—but it is also illustrative of how technology changes decision space in a complex world.

Until Petrov's moment, it's unclear whether anyone in the Soviet leadership fully understood the stark reality that they had ceded control over their most grave responsibility. Every element of Petrov's dilemma—the Minuteman missiles, the Soviet satellite array, the ground-based radars, the computer warning technology, and even his communications system—pushed a decision of war and peace away from the Soviet Politburo and into the hands of a fairly junior officer, and even this young officer's control was limited. For Petrov was largely dependent on technology, and while satellites and ground-based radars both provided valuable information, it was too often incomplete, even faulty.

FAIL SAFE

In this film from 1964, starkly shot in black and white, and without any musical score, Henry Fonda portrays a president forced into the unthinkable choice between dropping a nuclear bomb on New York City or entering into a thermonuclear war with the Soviet Union.

The culprit behind the hellish conundrum? A computer system designed to create a nearly perfect defensive system for the United States.

When the system malfunctions, humans are forced to step in to mitigate the effects—at tragic cost. In the film's final moments, Air Force Brigadier General "Blackie" Black, flying his aircraft over Manhattan, releases an atomic bomb on the city where his wife and children are living—then commits suicide in the cockpit.

Today, what was once the domain of speculative fiction has now become reality as AI-enabled systems are increasingly involved in time-sensitive, life-and-death decision-making.

Petrov faced a hellish dilemma. The speed of modern weapons necessitated employment of still-immature technologies that created hyper-empowered individuals who exercised de facto authority over the most fateful decisions the Soviet Union would ever face. Would the Soviet high command have second-guessed Petrov's judgment had he made the warning? With the clock ticking down, it seems likely that they would have ordered a retaliation.

Ultimately, this decision-making architecture—a complicated system designed to maximize speed and efficiency and minimize complexity in a moment of crisis—left a key question unanswered. Was Petrov a mere interpreter of computerized decisions, or was he a decision-maker expected to exercise individual and group judgment based on information provided by the computers? Petrov chose to be the latter, but it remains unclear if the developers of the system intended for a lieutenant colonel to make such strategically fateful choices.

We now know that Lieutenant Colonel Petrov was correct in waiting for more information—there were no missiles in flight. However, his judgment was not celebrated; in fact, he received a reprimand for his refusal to follow clear instructions during the incident. And Petrov's supervisors even faulted his improper note taking during the crisis. Petrov continued, and eventually ended, his career in relative obscurity. He also possibly saved the world, his exploits made public only after the Soviet Union collapsed.

DITCHING THE SLIDE RULE

In 1974, at the start of my junior, or "Cow," year at West Point, the Academy launched into bold new territory by issuing handheld calculators to every cadet—for which it promptly charged us about $105. For a number of "Old Grads," some of whom were our professors, this change amounted to heresy. The slide rule, which we'd been issued as Plebes, or first-year cadets, was relegated as useless, as we could now simply punch a few keys to unlock the secrets of mathematics.

This technological shift wasn't heretical to me—I never was able to figure out how to use a slide rule. And although the Texas Instruments miracle calculator never taught me much math, I could use it to add, subtract, multiply, and divide, and that was handy.

From then on, I was always a bit of a technology enthusiast. In 1982, as an Army captain, I paid $4,800 for a RadioShack desktop computer with a floppy disk drive and used it to "computerize" many of my infantry company's functions. The desktop was remarkably helpful, and a couple of years later, as a battalion operations officer, with my team, I

Slide rules are laughable contraptions today but were an integral part of the mathematics curriculum at West Point until my "Cow" year. Here, cadets carry them in their hands.
(ALFRED EISENSTAEDT/LIFE COLLECTION/GETTY IMAGES)

mounted a newer RadioShack machine onto my armored vehicle, again at my personal expense, and deployed with it to training exercises. It was a cutting-edge early version of a laptop, a groundbreaking innovation that at the time reinforced our excitement for what would soon become possible.

To be sure, I wasn't the first military leader to embrace emerging technology—leveraging advances has been a constant of warfare. From the then-revolutionary adoption of the stirrup (which allowed riders to sit more steadily in the saddle and employ weapons while mounted), to railroads, telegraphy, and more recently precision munitions, conflict has both driven and been shaped by every kind of technological development. My primitive computer was simply the latest generation.

Technological advancement moved with unprecedented speed throughout my career. The weapons my grandfather used when he entered the Army in 1917 were very similar to those wielded when he retired after World War II. But a mere twenty years after I put my first rudimentary computer into service, I found myself in command of a Special Operations Task Force empowered with vastly advanced and more prolific technology than earlier soldiers, including me, could ever have dreamed of.

Even at the most tactical level, the impact of new technologies was profound. By leveraging the capability of Predator drones to provide real-time full-motion-video overwatch of any activity—and then sharing that intelligence across the force—we dramatically increased our pace of operations. This is how it worked in practice: A force raiding an enemy target would typically include 100 to 120 commandos—organized into support, security, assault, and command elements—and would require eight to ten Blackhawk helicopters, which were always in limited supply. With the early warning and better targeting capabilities provided by the Predators' overwatch, we could often reduce our force to between twenty and thirty operators. The result? By using the drones we could conduct several times more operations with the same assets. (We'll return to the Predator again, in greater detail, in Chapter 9.)

Technology's contribution was even larger at the higher, more strategic plane. Operating from more than seventy locations worldwide, our force was able to maintain a constant, instantaneous connection by using secure video links to command, control, coordinate, and even lead. We reaped these benefits in 2006, particularly on the evening when Abu Musab al-Zarqawi, the leader of al-Qaeda in Iraq, was successfully targeted. That same night, we were able to *also* conduct a departure event for my deputy commander, linking elements of our force from across the world with spouses and comrades back in the United States for a heartfelt send-off—*while simultaneously conducting seventeen more combat raids hitting targets associated with Zarqawi.*

But that level of tech-enabled operations didn't come automatically, nor did it come easily. For example, in early 2004, we found that to be effective in the fight we had to disperse our force across twenty-seven countries yet maintain constant collaboration. In earlier times—even five years prior—that would have been both physically and technologically impossible. It took both a hardware and a cultural investment strategy to make it work. But over time, we were able to grow our daily Operations & Intelligence (O&I) briefing into a powerful venue.

It began with a tech backbone that made distributed communication possible, requiring email, chat, and video functions to work harmoniously, often from austere environments. Speaking of austerity, the amount of money we spent on satellite bandwidth alone would stun you, but it was an absolute requirement, no less important than ammunition or food for our forces.

Next, we had to make this interconnectivity valuable. I've described how I used the O&I in detail in previous books, but having an operating rhythm in which an entire team connected daily to discuss common problems wasn't necessarily intuitive. We had to force it at first. However, as time went on—and as participants knew they could derive value from both sharing and listening—the O&I gradually became an essential component of our organizational culture. More than fifteen years after bringing this forum together, it's still a vital function within elite Special Operations Forces.

Fear and apprehension are normal responses to new technology. That's why it's important to have a plan for incorporating new technology into your workflow in a way that's smooth and transparent, and that emphasizes the technology is intended to make everyone's life easier, not harder.

"LET ME SPEAK TO AN AGENT"

Sometimes technology sucks. You're anxious and irritated even before the phone stops ringing and your call is answered. Your lost credit card, canceled airline flight, or some other malady has injected an unexpected hurdle into an already hectic day. You want someone—anyone—to fix the problem. But when the call finally connects, the voice you hear isn't human. Now you're forced to navigate through a menu of "if your call is about this—press that" wickets until you arrive at something you *think* is correct. Then the automated voice informs you that wait times to speak to an agent will be more than thirty minutes. You curse, loudly enough that

There is no greater frustration than being put on hold when your car is broken down, or when you're trapped in an airport—and stuck wrestling with an automated agent.
(ZIVICA KERKEZ / SHUTTERSTOCK)

people nearby can hear you, and they smile, not cruelly, but in sympathy—
they've been there too. We all have.

Most client-facing firms celebrate values that place customer satisfaction at the center of how they desire to operate. But doing it well costs
money. Historically, companies have had robust customer service programs with employees dedicated to responding to requests and complaints. These systems were not perfect, the job was never glamorous, and
these staffs were expensive, but there were benefits. At each stage in the
process, there was a human exercising a degree of judgment. The decisions were hardly Petrov-scale, but to a frustrated consumer these interactions could mean the difference between anger and a lifetime of loyalty to
a brand. Often the exchange took place over a phone, but there was still
no sense that a technological system was exercising any control—the exchange remained fundamentally human.

Automated customer service—popularized in the 1990s—has sup-
planted many traditional client interactions. Humans are still involved
nowadays, but they've become almost incidental to the process. AI-enabled
computing systems are your first point of contact, and while they're supposed to mimic a human interaction, they're hardly seamless. Regardless,
our society has clearly dialed up our use of automated systems: by 2025 it's
possible that 95 percent of customer interactions will take place between a
form of artificial intelligence and a human customer. And who could
blame the companies who have made this shift? The shift to AI-enabled
automated systems is an easy one: there's no cost to train, no health-care
expenses, no vacation days, no morale issues, and there is uninterrupted
twenty-four-hour service.

In fact, AI-enabled customer service is so profitable—and investors assess
that the concept has so much potential—that AI-enabled automated services
have expanded to food preparation, delivery, and a slew of other tasks traditionally performed by a human. Technology is lowering labor costs so fast
that the gravity to adopt forms of automation is almost inescapable.

However, our collective experiences show us that this increased reliance upon technology carries serious risks. Indeed, the perceived benefits
of AI can often be a false economy: where decisions are unconsciously
shifted away from careful processes, or human interaction is impacted,

then added costs—financial, reputational, and otherwise—invariably arise. Ceding the ability to manage relationships to an algorithm, we've rolled a dangerous die.

SYMPTOMS OF PROBLEMS IN THE MAN/MACHINE RELATIONSHIP

Who's in Charge? There is a lack of clarity in whether man or machine is actually making key decisions. Lieutenant Colonel Petrov's case illustrates the malady.

Unintended/Unknown Dependence. An organization is unpleasantly surprised at a critical moment to find itself dependent on technology that is vulnerable to interruption or malfunction.

Vulnerability to Interruption. Loss of essential power, connectivity, or necessary operations/maintenance expertise can leave an organization unable to function.

Unintended Consequences. Decisions or actions performed economically by machines can alienate clients and customers.

Speed Kills. While we often assume that faster is better, a machine's ability to assess and respond to a situation often offers little time for reflection or intervention (as with Lieutenant Colonel Petrov). Hypervelocity missiles fired from shorter range would have left Petrov with few options.

While it's a given that we will increase our reliance on new technology, we must be thoughtful to dial in its usage to ensure its benefits outweigh its negatives. We must employ human judgment, like Lieutenant Colonel Petrov did, to navigate technology's effects. Whereas a professional customer service representative at baggage claim can help a distressed customer find their luggage with empathy, a nonhuman voice can't do the same—and it mustn't try. The technology Risk Control Factor requires a careful balance: loud, powerful radios are only enjoyable when tailored to the right frequency.

Part of the solution is acknowledging that contemporary AI is limited, and that in-person interaction may be needed to complement an AI-enabled system. While there's a segment of conversation that can likely be easily automated—the credit card cancellation, for example—more sophisticated transactions are going to require human intervention at some point, anyway. We cannot get so distracted while expanding our use of technology that we fully remove humans from all parts of the process. We must not entirely cede control to technology.

WFH

As a response to the COVID-19 outbreak, many companies in early 2020 sent their employees to work from home. While these efforts were an act of solidarity with social distancing initiatives to slow the pandemic, they were also an acceleration of a trend underway for more than a decade.

The changes to day-to-day work life were immediate and momentous. Workers often found themselves transported from a popular office open floor plan to makeshift offices in their kitchens and living rooms. The sound of background chatter from other cubicles and breakout rooms was replaced with barking dogs and the pitter-patter of feet from children who were also learning from home as their schools closed to combat the virus's spread.

Working from home produced some interesting developments. On one hand, organizations had to provide Zoom, Microsoft Teams, Skype, GoToMeeting, and other communication technologies to their employees, not all of whom were tech-savvy and none of whom had on-site, in-home IT support. And organizations had to do so in a matter of days.

For many firms the frightening transition was surprisingly smooth. Connections were quickly established, meetings shifted to being virtual, and thankfully the sky didn't fall. Many senior leaders soon adopted a nonchalant demeanor of confidence that they and their teams were "digital operators." Talk began of a "new normal," discarding "legacy" office space and the end of commuting and uncomfortable business dress.

It was that simple—and yet it wasn't. Connecting people proved technically easier than expected. An increasingly digitally proficient workforce (aided by the youngest generations) proved capable of leveraging the new tools—many while wearing a dress blouse or shirt with pajama pants.

But as time passed, a more subtle and fundamental question surfaced. What about productivity? Most employees value uninterrupted hours free of meetings and distractions to focus on assigned tasks. But a drumbeat schedule of video calls—many of which take longer than the brief hallway conversations used to address minor issues—as well as a lack of face-to-face opportunities to learn from teammates and receive guidance or positive reinforcement, produced a sense of isolation and diminished confidence. Additionally, many supervisors struggled to effectively lead teams without appearing overly invasive.

Operating in this new normal, organizations that were regionally or internationally dispersed found that a normal nine-to-five workday was no longer relevant and began working in twenty-four-hour cycles. Weekend work, once expected of a small segment of the workforce, now became an unspoken requirement for many more. There arose an uncomfortable trade-off: we work more, we work harder, but we burn out faster—like a candle with a large wick.

The repercussions of the pandemic-driven dispersion are still felt to this day and have arguably changed the nature of work forever. It's difficult to itemize every potential change WFH is bringing into organizations, but there's one certainty: your organization is, and will continue, transforming to the demands of a new, globally dispersed remote workforce. There is no turning back. To manage this world, we have to dial in how we are using technology—being deliberate in exactly how these changes are affecting our employees.

It's imperative to ask questions of your team about the transition to new technologies. Organizations need to know about employees' new stresses, challenges, and opportunities. Your team should study not only how you are adding technology, but more important, how you are relating to it. Acknowledge differences, limitations, and opportunities. Test your own assumptions, ask questions of your team about their perspectives, and then ask again.

Our organizational culture is shifting—it's up to you to figure out just how this change is affecting you and your teams. A healthy Risk Immune System becomes vulnerable when organizations fail to acknowledge and adjust to the changes taking place. Knowing that transformation is inevitable, we can ensure that we're asking the right questions of ourselves and our teams to calibrate to our new reality in order to be successful in an increasingly digitized world.

DEUS EX MACHINA

Technology, as we all are aware, requires constant updates. We can never arrive at a final technological solution—seemingly perfect products are often improved upon years, or even months, later. The technology Risk Control Factor works the same way—it requires frequent updates and recalibration on how *much* technology we employ, and how much human influence, through judgment and wisdom, we incorporate.

Like all Risk Control Factors, technology carries both risks and opportunities. Ineffective or inappropriate use of technology can produce unintended negative effects. But effective incorporation can be a game changer. It's in our power, and under our control, to make the necessary adjustments. Our Risk Immune System has to be constantly aware of new systems and devices and the risks they bring, and to survive in today's complex world, we must always be ready, in the face of increased automation, to rely on our own human judgment and wisdom.

YOUR TURN

Do you understand where and how your organization's operation incorporates technology?

To what extent do you rely on automated processes?

Where is your technology vulnerable to malfunction, interruption, or outside manipulation?

THE BOTTOM LINE

As technology continues to evolve, so must we. This means cultivating an active awareness of the ways in which technology shapes our processes and culture.

CHAPTER SEVEN

Diversity

BLIND MEN AND ELEPHANTS

*A man who is trampled to death by an elephant
is a man who is blind and deaf.*

—AFRICAN PROVERB

*If you don't see and address a problem from
multiple perspectives, you'll miss something—
and it may be the critical thing.*

SOURCE OF STRENGTH

The Edmund Pettus Bridge is 1,248 feet long with a distinctive steel arch rising over its center span. Completed in 1940 and named for Edmund Winston Pettus, a former Confederate brigadier general and later Grand Dragon of the Alabama Ku Klux Klan, the bridge secured a place in American history on March 7, 1965. On that day, a march to secure voting rights for African Americans ended in a brutal attack by two hundred state police and deputized whites led by Sheriff Jim Clark of Dallas County. Films of the melee show deputies, some on horseback and brandishing leather whips and clubs, beating the marchers, including future congressman John Lewis, in an attack later dubbed "Bloody Sunday."

The violence was followed by two subsequent marches, the last of which covered the entire fifty-four miles to Alabama's capital, Montgomery, highlighting the desire for fair access to the exercise of democracy—the right to vote. The goal of the movement was equality under the law, a basic right. If you look at the photos and films of the events, now more

Dr. Martin Luther King Jr. leading the fifty-four-mile march from Selma to Montgomery.
(PHOTO BY WILLIAM LOVELACE/EXPRESS/GETTY IMAGES)

than fifty years old, you are struck by the diversity of participants: men, women, old, young, Black, white—impressive, even by today's standards.

It is important to remember that the march and the entire civil rights movement were never about *diversity*; they were about *equality*—the idea that everyone is entitled to an equal opportunity, the right to succeed or to fail, and the right to select the political leaders who serve us.

Although early civil rights efforts represented a diverse coalition, more recent events are far more broadly representative. Diversity is held to be a source of strength.

We must remember, however, that diversity, unlike equality, is not a legal right. The leaders of the civil rights movement didn't seek wide representation to achieve *diversity*; they did it out of a clear-eyed determination to win their fight for *equality*. As long as truly equal opportunity is protected, the composition of teams and organizations will, and should, come out as it may.

But while diversity is not *a* right, it *is* right because it works. Assembling people with differing abilities, backgrounds, and perspectives has proven time and again to be a winning approach. The road to failure is strewn with teams that lacked diversity of thought and perspective.

Diversity can be a powerful strength for any organization and the difference between winning and losing. The more you aim for diversity in the perspectives you seek and incorporate, the stronger your Risk Immune System becomes. Just as the physical immune system gets stronger as it learns to fight off different kinds of threats, so too can we inoculate our organizations against groupthink. We can equip them with the ability to provide novel solutions to complex problems by incorporating diverse thoughts, backgrounds, and opinions.

But while achieving diversity is important, dialing in your actions is essential. Demographic diversity is an absolute necessity but insufficient on its own. Diversity is not limited to the obvious factors of gender and race. Rather, as we'll demonstrate in the story of John F. Kennedy's dealings with Cuba, diversity of *thought* is crucial in situations of great risk and uncertainty. Finally, we will argue—by exploring the topic of fusion cells in the Middle East and the United States—how the diversity of *capa-*

Protests against racial injustice following the death of George Floyd in 2020.
(PHOTO BY STEPHEN MATUREN/GETTY IMAGES)

bility must be sought in order to have the best posture to identify, assess, and mitigate risk.

SYMPTOMS OF DIVERSITY CHALLENGES

Stale Preservation of the Status Quo. People who have similar thoughts and abilities recommend the same actions—often sustaining the status quo.

Finger-pointing. When balls are dropped because new angles haven't been considered, organizations that lack diversity point fingers inward rather than look for fresh perspectives from the outside.

"Why Didn't I Think of That?" A classic indignant question asked when a diverse perspective *outside* the team breeds a better, more creative idea.

"Who Could Have Known?" A lack of diversity always increases the odds that those in charge will fail to identify possible risks because of their limited perspective.

Outpaced by Innovation. Diversity brings a freshness of ideas—organizations that lack diversity are slower to innovate.

Groupthink. When teams are pressured to accept the shared consensus, they're less likely to share new (or potentially controversial) ideas.

GREAT MINDS DON'T THINK ALIKE

The human brain is relatively standard in size and shape—about three pounds with four distinct lobes on each hemisphere. Our thoughts are shapeless outputs from these lumps of mass, and, unlike their physical host, vary between humans. Diversity of thought, born out of differing backgrounds, experiences, and perspectives, is crucial when interacting with risk.

Logically, organizations with members who share similar profiles will likely have more thought patterns in common than organizations that are more diverse in their composition, which may affect how vulnerable an organization is to blind spots and risk. In 1961, a lack of diverse thought proved problematic for a fledgling president—John F. Kennedy.

In the months after Fidel Castro overthrew the dictatorial regime of President Fulgencio Batista, Cuba's policies rapidly aligned with the Soviet Union's and became openly hostile to the United States. In response, the CIA developed a series of plans to overthrow Castro's regime, one of which leveraged Cuban expatriates, or exiles, as they were known, to enter the island nation and, with the help of a disgruntled populace, replace the left-leaning government. Dwight Eisenhower, nearing the end of his presidency, supported the planning process. The day before relinquishing office, the former five-star general recommended to President-elect Kennedy to do "whatever is necessary" to execute the plan successfully.

In the eyes of most Americans, the situation in Cuba was dire. At the height of the Cold War, a Soviet client-state only ninety miles from US shores was a frightening prospect. At the outset of his administration, the forty-three-year-old Kennedy was placed into a high-stakes drama from which there was no easy exit.

The options were not attractive. The CIA plan had started with the idea of training Cuban exiles, who would then be quietly infiltrated onto the island, where they would organize and lead a resistance movement. However, as planning and training progressed, the concept evolved to include a conventionally organized invasion force of 1,400 soldiers conducting air strikes with beach and parachute landings on the southern coast of Cuba. After establishing a beachhead and repelling Castro's inevitable counterattack, the effort would attract local support to the cause or, if that failed, move into the mountains to commence guerrilla operations. Ironically, the contingency to wage irregular warfare would have leveraged a strategy similar to that which Castro had successfully used against Batista, but it was unrealistic because it required the exiles to move eighty miles from the Bay of Pigs to the Escambray Mountains.

Kennedy was appropriately skeptical and reluctant to begin his administration with an operation that he worried was likely to fail. But to simply cancel it would have been costly. Rumors of the impending operation were already surfacing, and to appear weak on communism so early in his presidency would have invited attacks from the opposition, in the same way President Barack Obama would have faced vicious political rebuke if he had decided not to launch the strike that ended up killing Usama Bin Laden. An additional challenge would be what to do with more than a thousand trained Cuban exiles anxious to retake their country.

A week after his inauguration, the president met with his key advisers,

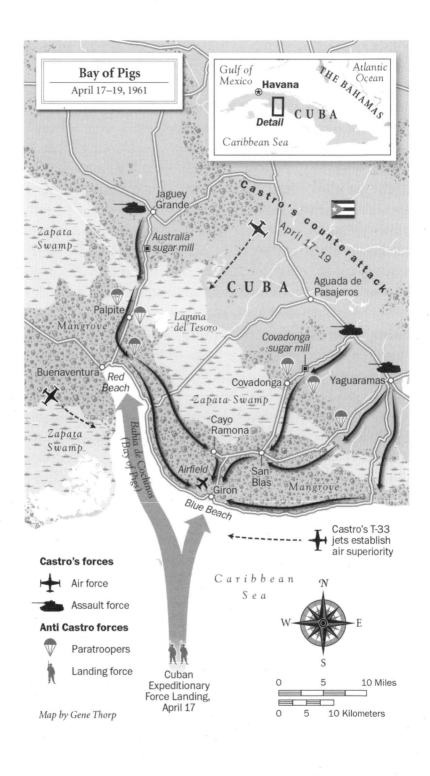

Bay of Pigs
April 17–19, 1961

Gulf of Mexico

Havana

THE BAHAMAS

Atlantic Ocean

CUBA

Detail

Caribbean Sea

Zapata Swamp

Jaguey Grande

Castro's counterattack April 17–19

Australia sugar mill

CUBA

Aguada de Pasajeros

Palpite

Laguna del Tesoro

Covadonga sugar mill

Mangrove

Buenaventura

Red Beach

Covadonga

Yaguaramas

Zapata Swamp

Zapata Swamp

Bahía de Cochinos (Bay of Pigs)

Cayo Ramona

Airfield

Giron

San Blas

Mangrove

Blue Beach

Castro's T-33 jets establish air superiority

Castro's forces

✈ Air force

🛡 Assault force

Anti Castro forces

🪂 Paratroopers

🧍 Landing force

Map by Gene Thorp

Caribbean Sea

Cuban Expeditionary Force Landing, April 17

N
W — E
S

0   5   10 Miles

0   5   10 Kilometers

including the Chairman of the Joint Chiefs of Staff, General Lyman L. Lemnitzer, a burly combat veteran, to review the situation in Cuba. In the meeting, Lemnitzer expressed his personal view that based on the strength of Castro's military forces the prospects for the operation's success to overthrow the Cuban leader were slim. But one of the intents of the meeting was to direct the Defense Department to more formally analyze the operations being proposed and report the results promptly to the president.

President Kennedy's inclination to seek the assessment of military professionals was sound. For, despite reflecting the scale and complexity of a conventional military operation, the Bay of Pigs mission was a secret plan developed by the CIA—not the Pentagon—where expertise in such operations traditionally lay. Furthermore, operational planning always faces a tension between maintaining security to prevent dangerous leaks that can advantage the enemy and including a wide-enough spectrum of participants to bring diverse perspectives. Security considerations dominated the CIA's planning process, so Kennedy rationally aimed to incorporate outside opinions.

But when the president *did* seek the experienced views of his military advisers, men who had spent major parts of their lives conducting just such operations, the Joint Chiefs of Staff failed to deliver. The young president had not yet learned what questions to ask, and the military leaders, skeptical of the CIA and feeling out of place to give their perspective on a plan that wasn't theirs, didn't point out the pitfalls.

Over the next two and a half months, until the operation was ultimately launched on April 17, 1961, there were multiple interactions in which the conclusions of the nation's most senior military leaders were solicited and received. In retrospect, it would be difficult to argue that the process served President Kennedy, the Joint Chiefs of Staff (JCS), or the nation well.

The Bay of Pigs invasion failed miserably and, as history tells us, ranks high among the most humiliating blunders in American foreign policy. The plan's underpinning assumptions were badly flawed, particularly the expectation of a popular uprising, and both operational and logistical shortcomings doomed the mission. The survivors of Brigade 2506, the

President Kennedy met with the Joint Chiefs of Staff before the Bay of Pigs invasion. Ultimately, he was frustrated they didn't stop a plan fated to fail.
(ABBIE ROWE. WHITE HOUSE PHOTOGRAPHS.
JOHN F. KENNEDY PRESIDENTIAL LIBRARY AND MUSEUM, BOSTON.)

invasion force, were captured and held for more than a year until President Kennedy negotiated their release.

The reasons for the mission's failure are as numerous as they are unfortunate. Although furious with the CIA's faulty plan that doomed the mission, President Kennedy was most palpably frustrated with the Joint Chiefs of Staff. Kennedy claimed that they had failed to communicate *what* the dangers were with this operation. Wary of their ability or willingness to provide advice, Kennedy reportedly said to an aide that the Joint Chiefs "just sat there nodding, saying it would work."

The reality was more complicated but still disappointing. The Joint Chiefs were equally mistrustful of Kennedy, doubtful of his military judgment and protective of their prerogatives. After providing a series of noncommittal evaluations and tepid validations of the invasion plan (most of the chiefs advocated for a more muscular approach including US forces), they argued later that it was a CIA operation and that their inputs were not welcome by the new president and his immature team. Regardless of where blame lay, the president lacked the diverse perspectives needed for an effective assessment.

Not surprisingly, the 1961 Joint Chiefs were not a model of diversity. In addition to Lemnitzer, the chairman, members included Admiral Arleigh Burke, chief of Naval Operations; General George Decker, Army chief of staff; General Thomas White, chief of staff of the Air Force; and General David M. Shoup, a Medal of Honor winner for his valor at the Battle of Tarawa in World War II and Commandant of the Marines. All were white males and long-service professional military officers whose views had been shaped by World War II, Korea, and the Cold War. The highly publicized youthful dynamism and thirst for innovation of Kennedy's incoming team did not resonate particularly well with them.

The invasion was a clear decision-making failure. It became obvious later that many of the decision-makers involved harbored significant doubts about the wisdom or viability of the operation, but those disparate views were never tabled and considered. Analysis that could, and should, have been provided for such a complicated military course of action was lacking.

It would have been a simple task to dissect the Bay of Pigs plan and red team, or identify, its vulnerabilities—but that didn't happen. In fact, a subsequent study of the failed process identified the problem of groupthink, a phenomenon that occurs when the pressure to conform within a group limits its ability to surface new and alternative perspectives.

WHAT IS GROUPTHINK?

Irving Janis spent two years examining the Kennedy team's planning of the Bay of Pigs operation, asking why the consensus-driven decision-making process led to disaster.

Janis's answer? A new theory: groupthink—a phenomenon that occurs when a group adopts a similar opinion and fails to appreciate or seriously consider other concepts or explanations. To prevent disunity, groupthink silences deviant thoughts to produce a group consensus.

Leaning on biology, Janis defines eight "symptoms" that members of an "in-group" often display on the road to groupthink.

Janis observes that Kennedy's team assessed they were **invulnerable** to danger and the threat of defeat, engaging in **rationalizations** to ignore warnings and protect themselves from falsifying their own assumptions. They perpetuated **stereotypes** and preserved the **morality** of their in-group, wrongly discounting the ability of Castro's air force to respond to the invasion.

Groupthink is not the comfortable arrival to agreement. Janis finds that victims of this phenomenon apply **pressure** to those who may disagree or shares doubts to preserve the cohesion of the group. He argues that the Joint Chiefs of Staff likely participated in **self-censorship**, intentionally keeping quiet about doubts so as to not break the consensus. Arthur Schlesinger Jr., historian and Special Aide to the President, allegedly reported his teammates blocked the president from hearing alternative opinions—or as Janis describes, they were acting like **mindguards**.

Finally, victims of groupthink appear to be **unanimous**: creating the "illusion" that all believe the majority view. This misperception of consensus increases the pressure to accept the view of the group.

The antidote to groupthink is diversity—including differing perspectives into the decision-making process. And the planning for the ill-fated invasion failed to do just that. Although the JCS themselves were hardly a diverse body, the failure to bring their candid viewpoints into the CIA's deliberations reinforced the vulnerability that groupthink produced. It is ironic that the absence of the unvarnished views of five "old white guys in uniform" highlighted a lack of diversity, but it is the failure to include a range of thought, including dissenting views, that is key.

Kennedy vowed to ensure that the mistake would not be repeated, and he got the opportunity sixteen months later, again involving Cuba. This time the process unfolded differently.

On October 16, 1962, surveillance imagery informed President Kennedy that Soviet medium-range missile sites were being built in Cuba. The USSR achieved a strategic advantage by basing weapons in Cuba, allowing them to successfully target a set of American cities, including Washington, DC. The missiles' positioning would reduce not only the missiles' flight distance, but also America's response time.

The timeline of the Cuban Missile Crisis was far more complex than the simplified version history remembers.

TIMELINE OF CUBAN MISSILE CRISIS

OCTOBER 16, 1962: Surveillance imagery informs President Kennedy that Soviet medium-range missile sites are being built in Cuba. This threatens the southeast United States with nuclear weapons with a short time of flight (and limited time for a US response).

OCTOBER 18, 1962: Officials receive intelligence that larger, fixed intermediate-range ballistic missile (IRBM) sites are also being constructed on the island that will range most of the continental US—excluding the Pacific Northwest. In response to the news, the Joint Chiefs of Staff support a full invasion of Cuba.

OCTOBER 19–20, 1962: The Joint Chiefs of Staff, the National Security Council, and other advisers discuss and debate options for the American response. President Kennedy settles on the "blockade-ultimatum" decision.

OCTOBER 22, 1962: The president formally convenes ExComm. President Kennedy informs Congress of his decision to initiate a blockade and addresses the American people on the crisis. He sends a letter to Chairman Khrushchev communicating his blockade decision.

OCTOBER 24, 1962: Chairman Khrushchev responds to Kennedy's letter, expressing grievance and frustration at the blockade. The Soviet premier hints at potential military retaliation for the blockade.

OCTOBER 26, 1962: Cubans continue to ready their missile sites. President Kennedy receives a letter from Khrushchev that says the Soviet ships headed to Cuba do not possess military armaments, and requests that the United States declare that they will not invade the island nation.

OCTOBER 27, 1962: President Kennedy receives a seemingly contradictory letter from Chairman Khrushchev, requesting that Kennedy remove American missiles from Turkey in exchange for the removal of Soviet missiles in Cuba. An American U-2 plane is shot down, and the pilot killed.

OCTOBER 28, 1962: The Soviets, aware of the potential escalation of the crisis, and threat of an imminent US attack, announce they will remove and dismantle their missiles in Cuba.

With the painful experience of the Bay of Pigs still fresh in his mind, Kennedy approached this new crisis differently, changing both the process he drove and the participants he included, with the aim of providing him viable options that reflected a range of perspectives.

To incorporate the different views he needed, Kennedy included a variety of officials (who, in the 1962 US government, were all men) he both respected and knew would bring diverse opinions, eventually labeling the collected body the Executive Committee of the National Security Council (NSC), or ExComm. Key members of ExComm were predictable based on their national security–related positions and included McGeorge Bundy, the national security adviser; Vice President Lyndon Johnson; the secretaries of defense and state; John McCone, the director of the CIA; and General Maxwell Taylor, "the new chairman of the joint chiefs and a much cooler head than his predecessor who showed deference to the president." Others were focused choices, including Assistant Secretary of State for Inter-American Affairs Edward Martin, as well as Llewellyn Thompson, an adviser on Russia. Beyond these, Kennedy included his brother Attorney General Robert Kennedy, and the secretary of the treasury, C. Douglas Dillon, people whose views the president valued.

Much has been written about the brilliance of creating ExComm, but this wasn't really a structural solution to a difficult problem. President Kennedy was ensuring he was getting diversity of thought by getting other perspectives and opinions, which gave him a broader range of options.

Because the crisis had a military aspect to it, the JCS were again a key component. Though there had been significant changes to the JCS since the Bay of Pigs invasion, including the addition of cigar-chomping Curtis LeMay as Air Force chief of staff, it should be no surprise that the nation's most senior military officers still favored aggressive military solutions to counter the threat Cuba posed to national security. Like hammer-carrying men looking for nails, they recommended that US forces conduct air strikes against the Soviet targets in Cuba and potentially move to invade afterward. As deliberations began, even President Kennedy regarded air strikes as the most viable option—aligning with the more aggressive approach.

This wasn't a scene from the dark comedy *Dr. Strangelove*. Nor was it confirmation that these World War II veterans were bloodthirsty warmongers. Instead, passionately committed to their nation's defense, they predictably reflected the perspective they'd developed over a lifetime. Kennedy respected (and initially agreed) with their recommendations, but he also wanted to avoid having his options prescribed for him as they had been for the Bay of Pigs invasion—and so he leveraged ExComm to diversify the views and options presented.

Kennedy understood that process matters, particularly in a crisis, and that diversity takes time. It's one thing to get all the right players in the room, but if the team doesn't have the process or time to swap ideas and challenge arguments, they fail to provide diverse perspectives to attack the problem. Fortunately, in a crisis remembered for the constant pressure of clock and calendar, President Kennedy managed the process to allow the team he'd assembled the time to thoughtfully consider and to debate.

At the outset, the thinking of his advisers coalesced into two major options: to conduct a blockade around Cuba or to prosecute more aggressive military action against the small island nation. To further the process, ExComm broke into separate groups to discuss the options, each group making "the strongest case possible" for their preference. The groups then exchanged what they had come up with, challenging and critiquing one another's assumptions and logic. As a result of these debates, the still-young president now had more than the painful binary choice of "do nothing," or "all-out war."

Interestingly, history reflects of ExComm that four members in particular, John McCone, the director of the CIA, Treasury Secretary C. Douglas Dillon, Llewellyn Thompson, and Robert Kennedy were notable and "atypical" contributors to the debate, ultimately recommending the "blockade-ultimatum" option. This compromise would quarantine all Soviet ships with military equipment headed toward Cuba—with the option to escalate force to air strikes as the situation demanded. In a more contained process, of these four, only the CIA director would likely have been included, and the critical diversity they brought would have been lost. President Kennedy ultimately selected the course of action these ExComm members advocated.

Kennedy also sought selected outside views and reached out to former president Eisenhower to solicit his opinion of the "blockade-ultimatum" option. The old soldier responded, "I think you're really making the only move you can." Soon after, Kennedy communicated the blockade plan to the American people.

After reaching the first decision to attack or blockade, the president had ExComm do another round of deliberations to help him decide how to respond to two seemingly contradictory letters sent by the hard-edged Soviet premier, Nikita Khrushchev. The advisers focused on how to respond to Khrushchev's request for the Americans to remove US missiles from Turkey in exchange for the removal of Soviet missiles in Cuba — judging whether it was fair, or if it would appear that the Americans had capitulated to Soviet demands.

Expressing the view that the blockade was too forgiving a reaction to the Soviet moves in Cuba, the JCS again recommended an aggressive military posture with action as needed. Kennedy took a less hardline position and insisted they identify options that address the problem, without making any quid pro quo arrangements with the Soviets. Tensions rose as a U-2 was shot down and its American pilot killed in Cuban airspace, and President Kennedy stressed that Khrushchev remove missiles and dismantle bases in Cuba or produce "grave risk to the peace of the world." Robert Kennedy shared this sentiment with Ambassador Dobrynin, with the promise that Americans would not attack Cuba.

Competing and conflicting versions of history describe how the crisis ended, but ultimately, the Soviets withdrew their missiles from Cuba, aware that further escalation in conflict might lead to nuclear war. Some months later, the American missiles were removed from Turkey.

The diversity of opinions that contributed to the Cuban Missile Crisis response, as well as these dealings, ultimately led to a superior outcome. If Kennedy *had* followed the initial suggestions from the JCS, the United States very well could have incited a nuclear Armageddon. Throughout the Bay of Pigs and Cuban Missile Crisis dealings, President Kennedy thought deeply about the issues, seeking to become somewhat of an expert himself so he could ask the right questions and balance the advice and competing perspectives he received.

To be sure, the process wasn't as perfect as some written accounts or films have portrayed it, but it got the job done. In the end, diverse views were considered, and a workable solution was pursued. And the world did not suffer a nuclear war—which was ultimately what mattered most.

Attorney General Robert Kennedy had been part of the deliberations. He speaks with some bias to preserve the memory of his brother and his presidency, and explained the president's approach this way:

> From all this probing and examination—of the military, State Department, and their recommendations—President Kennedy hoped that he would at least be prepared for the foreseeable contingencies and know that— although no course of action is ever completely satisfactory—he had made his decision based on the best possible information. His conduct of the missile crisis showed how important this kind of skeptical probing and questioning could be.

Leaders don't necessarily have to know all the answers, but they should be focused on asking the right questions, gathering a diversity of thought in the room to make the best decisions for their team.

OUTLIERS IN THE BOARDROOM

Diversity of thought is particularly important for boards of directors. I served on Deutsche Bank USA's board for two years as the only director without extensive banking experience, and I saw firsthand the necessity of diversity for boards of financial institutions. As Chris Clearfield and András Tilcsik argue in their book *Meltdown: What Plane Crashes, Oil Spills, and Dumb Business Decisions Can Teach Us about How to Succeed at Work and at Home*, the most successful banks are the ones with the most diverse boards made up of a mix of bankers and nonbankers.

There are three reasons for this. The first is the tendency of boards with only bankers to rely too heavily on personal experience, which rarely stimulates out-of-the-box thinking. Second, common banking experience can lead to overconfidence, since any recommendation will exist within an echo chamber of shared opinion. Finally, banker-only boards often fail to have "productive conflict" in which members can see things differently, debate, and disagree to produce more fruitful outcomes.

My personal experience with Deutsche Bank USA validated these conclusions. On the board, I was able to offer a very different, albeit less experienced, point of view. Although I often felt self-conscious asking "stupid questions," upon leaving, my fellow board members would send me off saying they valued those very queries. My questions—which reflected my own military training and leadership experience—helped to illuminate blind spots that long experience can produce. Deutsche Bank didn't place me on its board to red team or to intentionally function as the bank's devil's advocate, but my background—and, humorously, my ignorance—helped me function in that capacity.

While I'm fascinated by boards at large and have sat on a number of them, the board of Theranos—a Silicon Valley start-up that aimed to revolutionize blood testing—caught my attention for its time in the spotlight. Using lessons learned about bank diversity to examine Theranos, Tilcsik and Clearfield argue that the board's fundamental lack of diversity played a crucial role in allowing the company's fraud to go as far as it did.

It feels odd to pair an accusation of homogeneity with Elizabeth Holmes, who herself appeared to be a paragon of diversity—a young, standout woman who was only nineteen years old when she dropped out of Stanford and started the company. She garnered national attention within the male-dominated Silicon Valley world with an innovative blood-testing technology.

But the Theranos board members, such as Henry Kissinger, James Mattis, and George Shultz, "would have been more at home at a public policy think tank than at a cutting-edge medical technology firm"—"lack[ing] medical or biotechnology expertise"—which was crucial for a biotechnology company with ambitions to fundamentally change health-care testing. These board members couldn't appreciate the science behind the business; Holmes built her company, and scammed her customers, on technology that didn't even work. Ultimately, a *Wall Street Journal* article exposed Theranos, and the firm shut down in September 2018, fifteen years after it started.

While bringing in board members of varied backgrounds is important, it also requires the kind of diversity that naturally "makes the whole group more skeptical," invites pause, and opens the door for new viewpoints. Lacking this skepticism, the science behind Theranos went unchallenged. Paraphrasing Sallie Krawcheck, the former chief financial officer of Citigroup, Tilcsik and Clearfield contend that "diversity works because it makes us question the consensus. What the heck is that? Why are we doing it? Can you run that by me one more time?"

Theranos's great rise and tragic fall plainly show us that a Risk Immune System needs to be skeptical of the solutions we propose. This only becomes possible when we intentionally incorporate diversity of thought in our teams and processes. To ensure that no blind spots are missed, we need to both honor the counsel of our experts, who provide us with the soundest information, and incorporate the opinions of those who don't have in-depth knowledge of or experience with the subject.

FUSION CELLS

I was raised on the tale of the Blind Men and the Elephant. In the story, six blind men encounter an elephant. Each proceeds to "see" the animal the only way he can—by touch. One feels the leg and concludes the elephant is like a tree. Another finds the tail and describes the elephant as rather like a rope. And so on. Of course, none of the men were wrong, but neither were they completely right—so they never produced a reasonable description of the elephant.

I often described our initial challenge of "seeing" al-Qaeda as being similar to that of the blind men and the elephant. The Special Operations Task Force had to work with various members of the Department of State, the CIA, the National Security Agency, and the US Treasury in an effort to understand, and therefore defeat, al-Qaeda. Each organization could only "see" the enemy from a single perspective, which risked producing dramatically skewed conclusions.

Although we all received the same intelligence, our different experiences and biases led us to draw wildly different conclusions—resulting in some bitter disagreements and muttered curses. Like the blind men, none of us saw things clearly enough to identify the beast. We harbored too many unconscious biases.

How, you might wonder, could people (even from a range of organizations) given the same intelligence draw stunningly different conclusions? It was easy, only too easy.

Ultimately, the solution that worked for us was fusion cells. The name informs their function: fusion cells *fuse* intelligence across handfuls of personnel within different agencies and military units. In our case, the fusion cells were physical spaces—offices where two or more organizations could combine information, resources, and personnel—as well as organizational constructs, assembling representatives from a range of organizations. They were all part of a synergistic effort working toward shared goals.

Although fusion cells dealt primarily in intelligence as part of the broader Special Operations Task Force, they also drove *action* against enemy networks and served as critical nodes in liaison networks that connected our force internally and externally with a wider range of partner organizations such as embassies, intelligence agencies, and conventional military forces—with tremendous success.

The use of fusion cells to achieve connectivity, synergy, and, most important, diversity in a unified effort has been widely adopted by military organizations and governments alike. Functioning as a network of teams, fusion cells make it possible for organizations to leverage a range of capabilities and scale of capacities impossible otherwise.

For example, when American forces must engage in hostage recovery, the US Hostage Recovery Fusion Cell (HRFC) serves as the "operational focal point" to facilitate information gathering and planning in what is typically a chaotic process. The HRFC has five main hubs: an intelligence component from the intelligence community; an operational component from the Department of Treasury, the FBI, the State Department Diplomatic Security Service, and the Department of Defense, with representatives from Special Operations Forces and the Joint Personnel Recovery Agency; an external engagement team that coordinates with the media and legislature; a family engagement team that works directly with families whose loved ones are in crisis; and a legal team with an attorney from the Department of Justice. In total, by *fusing* intelligence and incorporating a diversity of capability, the HRFC has successfully brought numerous hostages back to their American homes.

The fusion cell model has been broadly adopted in different capacities. The Joint Terrorism Task Force in New York (JTTF-NY), formed in 1980, effectively connects capabilities across the nation by enabling local police to assist the intelligence community. JTTF-NY has enjoyed several notable successes: investigating a plot to bomb John F. Kennedy International Airport in 2007; another, two years later, that intended to attack the city's subway system; as well as an attempted bombing in Times Square in 2010.

Fusion cells aren't only helpful for hostage rescue and terrorism prevention: they can be invaluable for any team that needs to rapidly share information and feed off a diverse perspective. In response to the COVID-19 pandemic threat, the state of Missouri tried a proven technique of fusion cells to bring together sixteen state agencies to execute strategic priorities. Leaders and subject matter experts from across the state—in areas such as economic development, higher education, public health, and supply chains—partnered with local health authorities, infectious disease experts, and hospital and health-care organizations to produce a robust response to COVID-19. The ad hoc, cross-agency team seamlessly gathered, analyzed, and acted upon information to make swift, effective decisions during the crisis. Notably, the fusion cell helped to "shine light" on topics, making outstanding tasks and issues public. Participants had to routinely provide status reports, updates, and After-Action Reports to ensure the team was acting on time and moving effectively.

What can we learn from this? To bolster their defenses against risk, organizations should encourage their teams to incorporate fusion cells, ensuring that people with different roles and bodies of knowledge are involved in key decision-making processes and sharing information.

DIVERSITY IN PRACTICE

In the next chapter, I will warn that bias can prevent the accurate identification, assessment, and mitigation of risk. Diversity is an antidote to bias, and by providing a panoply of demographics, thought, and capability, we can reduce the likelihood of groupthink. More cooks in the kitchen may produce a bit of chaos—but in the long run, it can also expand the menu to offer a more varied selection of palatable options.

It's worth noting, however, that simply having the elements of diversity in place in your organization doesn't guarantee that your teams will *act* on it. Unless members of a group are positioned to challenge one another, think outside the box, ask tough questions, and provide thought-provoking answers, diversity comes to naught. Diversity is an *action*, not a possession: a constant effort to promote, consider, and challenge new perspectives and abilities on your team.

Diversity must be operationalized. In the Special Operations Task Force, we sought frank inputs from a variety of demographics and backgrounds and leveraged our daily command-wide video teleconference to ensure rapid synthesis and wide dissemination. President Kennedy's Ex-Comm met to discuss the formal exchanges of opinions before making recommendations. Healthy boards of directors include nonexperts and outsiders to help foster candid conversations. We can, and should, put structures in place to gather diverse responses to risk.

The risks we encounter in today's environment increase in speed and complexity, and our Risk Immune System must seek and operationalize diverse opinions to best compete and survive. We all know and appreciate the benefits of diverse teams—their importance not only in physical representation but also in thought and capability. "Seeing" only one part of the elephant is a risky habit.

YOUR TURN

What is the status of diversity in your organization? Consider race, gender, experience, and perspective.

How does the desire for consensus affect your decision-making?

Who is absent from the room when decisions are made? How can you include new, fresh perspectives?

How can you operationalize diversity in hiring, promotion, and assignment?

THE BOTTOM LINE

Diversity isn't a nice-to-do, it's a need-to-do. Different perspectives and skills increase our effectiveness. Achieving diversity requires deliberate action.

CHAPTER EIGHT

Bias

FILTERS THAT DISTORT

If slaves will make good soldiers
our whole theory of slavery is wrong.

— HOWELL COBB,
CONFEDERATE GENERAL
AND GEORGIA POLITICIAN

Just because we believe
something doesn't make it so.

SEEING WHAT WE WANT TO SEE

Patrick Byrne suspected a "Sith Lord" was stealthily threatening to undermine him. He claimed to be working with the FBI to pursue, on their orders, a romantic relationship with a woman accused of working as a Russian agent in the United States. He also claimed that he was "asked to set up Hillary Clinton" amid a "political fraud conducted by the deep state, against Democrats and Republicans." Once the truth was revealed, Byrne promised the story would be "100 times bigger than Watergate."

It was, at a minimum, unusual behavior—particularly because Patrick Byrne was the high-profile CEO of Overstock.com, a publicly traded company that had been shaping the way Americans shop from home since the early 2000s. And arguably, the body of people who should have been most interested in Byrne's erratic behavior—the group who was legally responsible for his actions, his board of directors—appeared not to notice, or care.

Why didn't they? Were they collectively stupid or negligently out of touch?

Neither was the case. This collection of experienced professionals responsible to represent shareholder interests naturally viewed their CEO through a lens of commercial performance. And under Byrne's leadership, the firm had been very successful. Furthermore, his Dartmouth/Cambridge/Stanford pedigree, paired with his successful business track record, led the directors to conclude that while undeniably eccentric, Byrne was still the right person to guide Overstock to ever-greater returns.

In one sense, the board was appropriately biased toward what they perceived as being best for shareholders. A bit of aberrant behavior might seem to pale in comparison to impressive profits and growth for Overstock. Byrne was unquestionably eccentric, but one can assume the board believed that his success was more impressive than his blog posts were concerning. It was a narrow, but predictably biased, view.

The public, however, assessed Byrne's behavior differently—they were aghast. After the CEO posted about his involvement with the FBI on his website, the stock price of Overstock crashed 36 percent within a few days. Institutional investors and other stakeholders eventually concluded that Byrne's curious behavior reflected more than harmless eccentricities, and that he was so out of touch with observable reality that he couldn't be trusted to serve as CEO. After a particularly concerning post about the "deep state" targeting Overstock, the underwriter of the firm's insurance for its directors and officers said it could no longer maintain the policy as long as Byrne continued to serve. As the team worked through the news of the threatened policy cancellation, Byrne announced his resignation. Following the news, Overstock rapidly regained 10 percent of its share value.

Weak boards failing to intervene with suspect CEO behavior is a familiar story. Take former Uber CEO Travis Kalanick—whose behavior and leadership went unchecked as the company soared to unprecedented heights. Since 2009, Kalanick had revolutionized the ride-hailing industry, and in 2017 the tech start-up operated in more than seventy countries, valued at nearly $70 billion by its private investors. Beneath the hood of the car, however, was an engine of toxic corporate culture.

PONZI SCHEMING

■

How much is a stamp worth?

In 1919 Charles Ponzi realized that there was profit potential in redeeming international postal reply coupons. Customers could exchange the international coupons for American stamps, and—if the country's economy was weaker than that of the United States—could make a profit. Ponzi sold this idea to investors with tales of agents buying exorbitant amounts of international coupons to trade for a profit in the United States. He promised that, in just ninety days, their investments would double. The number of investors grew rapidly.

The entire operation was a scheme. The international coupons, though used initially, fell to the wayside, as Ponzi used incoming investment money to pay the phony returns from past investors, pocketing enormous amounts of cash. The operation lasted only nine months. But in that time, from an investment of only $30 in stamps, Ponzi had defrauded $15 million from his investors. Thus, the famed "Ponzi scheme" was born—a version of which the infamous fraudster Bernie Madoff would use more than fifty years later.

Kalanick steered Uber to fourteen company-wide cultural values that arguably warranted poor behavior, including "Meritocracy and Toe-Stepping," "Always Be Hustlin'," "Let Builders Build," and "Principled Confrontation." Workplace harassment reportedly ran rampant, employees were seemingly encouraged to step on one another to achieve company success, and high-performing employees were often protected from the consequences of their inappropriate behavior. Uber's board, riding the waves of its success, had been hands-off in reacting to allegations, until protests internal to the company finally became public.

Only then did Uber hire a team of lawyers to investigate and recommend changes that included hiring a chief operating officer, changing the company's stated values, and, ironically, creating a stronger, more independent board of directors.

Leaders who are perceived as being successful aren't always given a crown, but often do get a hall pass. Bernie Madoff's fictional investing

Charles Ponzi, the namesake
of the "Ponzi scheme."
(PHOTO BY LESLIE JONES)

genius deceived some relatively sophisticated investors for years, and questionable behavior by corporate leaders like Patrick Byrne and Travis Kalanick was tolerated in apparent deference to their business successes. The Securities and Exchange Commission (SEC) assumed that Madoff—an experienced financier who played a part in launching the Nasdaq stock market and himself advised the SEC on trading securities—was acting responsibly. But Madoff was secretly running a multibillion-dollar Ponzi scheme that, once revealed, resulted in a 150-year prison sentence.

The SEC wasn't alone in assuming Madoff's good intentions: JPMorgan, who ran his bank account, did not raise any red flags about signs of money laundering, nor did accounting firms identify anything suspicious in their financial reviews. There was a demonstrated willingness for stakeholders to cover their eyes—to unquestionably accept something that was too good to be true, as long as it served their short-term benefit.

As we shall examine in more detail throughout this chapter, bias is an invisible hand driven by self-interest. Too often it contributes to and reinforces an unfair system. It foments willful blindness, creating narratives that achieve personal goals at the cost of greater equity and justice. We all live with biases—biases of those around us and biases of our own. Left unexamined and unchecked, they can skew our ability to respond to threats.

So, what can we do about them?

BREAKING DOWN BIAS

Biases are as old as humans, and in some ways have been essential to our evolution and survival. The ability to think in patterns, to categorize, and to draw inferences from past experiences aided hunter-gatherers long before humanity began establishing settlements, embracing agriculture, or creating boards of directors.

But the same biases that have helped us survive for millennia can pose challenges to successful decision-making in complex environments today. Identifying these biases, being honest with ourselves about how the lenses through which we view the world are often fogged or dirty, and doing our best to limit the damage they can do are fundamental to dealing with risk.

SYMPTOMS OF COMMON TYPES OF BIASES

There are countless biases that affect human judgment and decision-making. Here is a handful that can directly target your Risk Immune System. So as you are making decisions and seeking to **Detect**, **Assess**, and **Respond** to risk, consider if you are falling prey to any of these biases.

Common Information Sampling Bias. The bias to spend more energy and time on information everyone already knows rather than information that is new and could likely be helpful. (communication)

Confirmation Bias. The bias to lean on an existing belief and continually search for information to support it. (narrative)

Halo Effect. The bias to see someone favorably, regardless of actions. (leadership)

Status Quo Bias. The bias to believe the current state of affairs is the preferable option. (action)

Hindsight Bias. The bias to believe, after an event has occurred, that they would have predicted what the outcome of the event would have been. (timing)

Plan-Continuation Bias. The bias to not alter the course of action when situations change. (adaptability)

Ingroup Bias. The bias to think those within a group are superior than those outside of it. (diversity)

We won't try to plow new ground here. Bias, like risk itself, is the subject of study by psychologists, economists, sociologists, and experts in a variety of other disciplines. My goal is to leverage their work but try to keep things simple. So, we'll operate with the understanding that biases are an architecture of assumptions that affect our judgment and refract facts and realities in a way that can prevent the accurate identification, assessment, and mitigation of risk.

We'll also consider how bias impacts, and often complicates, how our Risk Immune System works. We'll show that increasing our awareness of existing or potentially damaging biases is critically important, and how dialing in to create checks and balances against racism, religious bigotry, and sexism is absolutely essential—and how we must avoid allowing what's known as "belief perseverance" to etch biases into thought patterns that shape our actions.

Before we continue, it is important to recognize that not all biases are created equal. A bias for a genre of literature, a type of food, or predictability (over spontaneity) is largely harmless. But when cultural or structural inequities are buttressed by mutually reinforcing biases, then the evil of racism and discrimination flourishes.

At the end of the day, we can't choose to have or not have biases—we have them. So we must identify and carefully consider them. We're no longer in a pre-civilizational survival mode, and it's imperative to identify biases and do what we can to limit and correct for their impact on our decision-making. A snap judgment that might have helped our ancestors avoid a predator can just as easily lead someone today to make a quick, evidence-free decision about their organization—or about a colleague—that causes long-lasting damage.

In this chapter, we'll dive first into the biases that underpinned both the reality and the myths of the short-lived Confederate States of America, and then we'll discuss how the more recent invasion of Iraq reflected more modern bias—at great cost.

CONSIDERING THE CONFEDERACY

In the United States, we live in an era of reexamining our biases. Monuments to Confederate soldiers are being removed from prominent locations, and the once-ubiquitous Confederate battle flag has been banned from NASCAR races. Even military bases, like Fort Hood, Texas, where I met my wife, and Fort Bragg, North Carolina, where I served for fifteen years, both named for Confederate generals, are, as of 2021, under review.

These moves are long overdue.

But before we continue, let's stop for a moment, because any thoughtful examination of bias, the derivative hatred of racism, and the ultimate evil of slavery risk being inappropriately softened by the comfortable jargon of theory. This is anything but theoretical—it is painfully real.

And we must confront its reality. Bias, even in its most extreme forms, is not limited to outlier individuals or organizations. It is a lurking cancer threatening us all.

In my previous book *Leaders: Myth and Reality*, I took a deep dive into my childhood hero, Robert E. Lee, recounting how time and events forced me to more closely consider my admiration for the officer who had graduated from West Point almost 150 years before I had. Though I had long respected General Lee, I came to more deeply appreciate that both during his lifetime and after his death, he supported, fought for, and represented concepts of slavery and white supremacy that I found abhorrent. After much reflection, on a morning in 2017, I took a portrait of Lee off the wall of my study—one that my wife, Annie, had given me when we were first married forty years before—and I placed it into the garbage.

Like many other Americans, I found myself face-to-face with the broader question of the Confederacy itself. My mother was politically liberal. But her family was rooted in the Deep South: her great-grandfather had been a brigadier general in the Confederate Army, and many of my southern relatives, who were neither irrational nor devoid of values, held views on issues that were very different from mine and my mother's. More broadly, the southern society of which they were a part had long-held biases that are often incomprehensible to outsiders.

How can that be? How can equally intelligent people arrive at diametrically opposed attitudes, which we are often prepared to defend vigorously, even violently? The reality is that our attitudes are less shaped by the quality of our intellect than by our perspectives, experiences, and, crucially, by our own self-interest. We've seen how even a nation founded on soaring concepts of liberty and equality can fail to adhere to those ideas in practice.

The United States is an instructive example. The first Africans were brought to bondage in the colonies in 1619, but slavery evolved differently in the northern and southern parts of the nation over the nearly 250 years that came after. The North developed an increasingly industrial and mercantile economy for which enslaved labor was unnecessary—and society's attitudes followed. In the South, however, Eli Whitney's cotton gin revitalized an agricultural and plantation-based model dependent on unpaid labor. Many people are surprised by the fact that in 1860, cotton-growing Mississippi was the wealthiest state per capita, but that fact is essential to understanding why most southerners, dependent on the "peculiar institution" of slavery, were so strenuous in their justification for and defense of it.

A Confederate statue commemorating Robert E. Lee in Market Street Park, Charlottesville, Virginia.

Their defense was anything but irrational behavior. Rather than accept the dubious premise that entire swaths of the United States were populated by malevolent bigots, it is easier to understand that our attitudes typically follow our perspectives—and our perspectives are aligned with our self-interests. Southerners didn't necessarily practice and defend slavery because they had deeply considered and believed fervently in its righteousness; they believed in it because they were dependent on it.

The disparity between how the Deep and Upper South approached secession is also illustrative of how biases are informed by perspective. In the Deep South, states such as South Carolina, Alabama, and Mississippi were wedded to "King Cotton." The white plant, laboriously picked by enslaved people, was spooled into fabric, dumping riches into the region. Slavery made cotton plantations viable: to outlaw slavery was to disrupt their economies and put their entire way of life into question.

In one sense, states in the Upper South, however, such as North Carolina, Virginia, and Tennessee, were less dependent on enslaved labor in their economies and as a result were more reticent to secede from the union. They ultimately joined the Confederacy's rebellion only when President Lincoln ordered seventy-five thousand troops toward the South at Fort Sumter—choosing to fight alongside their fellow southern states.

At the heart of southern biases stood an uncomfortable reality: southerners could not justify an economic model that was dependent on enslaved labor without being biased against the enslaved people themselves. Samuel A. Cartwright, a well-known physician in the 1850s, promulgated a false theory that African Americans were biologically inferior to whites, claiming that they had smaller blood vessels and brains, and a "tendency towards indolence and barbarism," and therefore had to be kept in an enslaved state for their own well-being. Scientific racism—a concept that went unnamed then but is clear to us now—gave southerners reasons, albeit untrue, to justify their biases against their enslaved workers.

Now, it's important to note that the majority of southern families were *not* slaveholders. But the fabric of the South's economy and lifestyle rested upon a superiority over African Americans held first in bondage and then at a segregated disadvantage. With this came a bias of white supremacy—one that was woven into the fabric of the South like the cotton threads that began in its fields. The words of the French political philosopher Montesquieu get to the heart of the relationship between religion, economic models, and white supremacy:

> It is impossible for us to suppose these creatures [enslaved Africans] to be men; because allowing them to be men, a suspicion would follow that we ourselves are not Christians.

If southern citizens had recognized that enslaved people were indeed equal to whites, they could not have justified slavery. Their biases, then, were the building blocks that supported the economic model upon which their worldview sat.

These biases did not stop after the Civil War ended. Romanticization of the "Lost Cause" narrative and institutionalized white supremacy justified Jim Crow, the brutality of Sheriff Jim Clark at Selma's Edmund Pettus Bridge, and the racist attitudes of countless people. More work remains to be done.

Biases typically reflect our interests and serve our needs. Once the Civil War transitioned from political disagreement to bitter combat, a new set of biases flourished. Now soldiers were biased toward the enemy simply because they were the enemy. Calling our enemies by epithets, racist or otherwise, dehumanizes them—and it is less difficult to kill an opponent once you have dehumanized them in your mind. In war, the biases become personal: we are quick to hate those who are hurting us. Biases prevent cognitive dissonance—supporting our thoughts and actions even when they are founded on destructive untruths.

"AT MY SIGNAL, UNLEASH HELL"

On March 14, 2003, General Tommy Franks, the commander of United States Central Command (CENTCOM), readied for war. Stationed at his headquarters in Qatar, he assembled his command team for a presentation on the upcoming invasion of Iraq, still waiting to receive the order from Washington to force Saddam Hussein and his Ba'ath Party from power.

Across the Middle East, hundreds of thousands of personnel and their equipment stood by, awaiting the order to march on Baghdad. It was the most technologically sophisticated force ever assembled, but inside, as in every army in history, was a heart that beat more quickly as passions rose.

In books, war can be a scientific process. But in practice, it is emotion brought to a boil.

At the CENTCOM headquarters that day, the assembled senior staff of American and allied officials waiting on the general's remarks quieted as lights dimmed and a video began to play on massive screens around the command center. The audience likely expected a statement from President Bush, or perhaps an intelligence assessment of the Iraqi military's conventional or assumed weapons of mass destruction (WMD).

The video showed neither. Instead, the staff watched footage of a clearing surrounded by trees, soldiers in armor bearing shields and swords, and the Australian actor Russell Crowe. It was *Gladiator*, the Oscar-winning film from 2000 that opens with a standoff between a Roman legion and Germanic tribes in a dark forest. Crowe's character seeks counsel from his staff, surveys the legionnaires under his command, takes note of the placement of his artillery, and, once aware that negotiations with the tribes would be fruitless, he orders an attack with: "At my signal, unleash hell."

And the Roman army does just that. In the scene that follows, the infantry moves into the attack, with centurions guiding the shoulder-to-shoulder formations of well-trained legionnaires. Engaging the Germanic tribes in pitched battle, Roman cavalry soon encircles the tribesmen, causing a panicked retreat. Crowe's character bests his tribal counterpart in combat, the legion completes its advance, and Rome's victory on its frontier is complete.

The film clip concluded, the lights of the CENTCOM headquarters went on once more, and the assembled audience returned to the PowerPoint presentation before them to discuss the upcoming war that they would likely have to fight.

But their hearts beat a bit faster and emotions ran a touch hotter.

It was a rousing introduction to the most serious discussions many of the participants would ever engage in. There were certainly attendees who enjoyed the clip for its masterful filmmaking, but others in attendance were confused, even aghast. Those who had seen war, especially recently in Afghanistan, knew there were few such moments of immediate triumph in

*General Tommy Franks wanted to
motivate his forces in advance of
an invasion of Iraq.*

modern conflict. What the legionnaires in the film achieved in a quick engagement—using well-organized violence to impart Rome's will on trou-
blesome outsiders—would not necessarily follow in Iraq.

With such a momentous occasion approaching in minutes, hours, or
days, the message the film clip sent through the command was simplistic,
but in a way matched the moment. The "Coalition of the Willing," those
who would follow the United States into war in Iraq, had sought negotiations but was ready for war. Iraq's Ba'ath Party "barbarians" across the border refused the offer—and so they would be destroyed. General Franks's
presentation, likely intended to inspire the force, also risked minimizing
the complexity of what was required to win the coming struggle or to hold
the lasting peace. CENTCOM was not entering a single engagement.
The effort to cross Iraq's southern border, America's Rubicon, with a massive Coalition army, would do much to upend and reshape the Middle
East.

Is confidence in the effectiveness of violence a form of bias? This
question might sound strange coming from me, but I believe it absolutely
is. For soldiers trained to master the employment of military force are
clearly prone to leaning toward its use. Their general attitude may be less

aggressive than that of someone like Curtis LeMay—the famed World War II Air Force general, who planned the bombing of Japan and later tussled with Kennedy during the Cuban Missile Crisis—but a man with a hammer is prone to look for nails. In practice, the idea that violence can solve complicated political problems alone is not substantiated by evidence or by my experience.

Next, is ignoring complexity a form of bias? Without question. I did not witness any successful effort to think critically about the underlying assumptions that guided the march to war. Indeed, neither of these reflexive responses—confidence in the effectiveness of violence and ignoring complexity—was helpful in the lead-up to the Iraq War.

At the outset of the Iraq War, I was working on the Joint Staff as the vice director of operations, part of the military bureaucracy that helped the secretary of defense and the White House cultivate responses to global crises. It wasn't a glamorous position, but it gave me an opportunity to observe the way the Pentagon and the White House thought about the prospect of war with Iraq.

This assignment also put me in the middle of a bureaucracy that was entirely ill-equipped to deal with either the forceful secretary of defense, Donald Rumsfeld, or the highly ideological proponents of action against Iraq—most notably Rumsfeld's deputy Paul Wolfowitz.

It was often a surreal experience.

My sense was that the Bush administration correctly judged that the regime of Saddam Hussein was dictatorial, brutal, and hostile to the United States. However, the Bush team diverged from the opinion of counterterrorism professionals and Middle East experts in its belief that Saddam Hussein was willing to tolerate the presence of al-Qaeda in Iraq. The expert assessment at the time was that Saddam Hussein and Iraq's Ba'ath Party were ideological opponents of al-Qaeda. We knew at the time that al-Qaeda targeted regimes like Saddam Hussein's Ba'ath Party. But despite experts agreeing that a Ba'ath and al-Qaeda partnership was highly unlikely, preparations for war continued unabated through 2002 and into 2003.

The Bush administration had a three-part risk assessment that shaped its decision-making. First, the administration assessed that Iraq remained in possession of WMD, despite its claims to have destroyed its stock-piles. This part of their assessment was only somewhat controversial—intelligence agencies across the world thought it was likely that the Hussein regime would have maintained part of its weapons program.

Next, the administration believed that Saddam Hussein didn't just have WMD, he was developing more dangerous WMD. Intelligence agencies' assessments were mixed on this point.

Finally, "hawks" on the Iraq issue, who strongly advocated for war against Saddam's regime, believed it was likely that the Iraqi dictator would cooperate with al-Qaeda against the United States. No senior intelligence professional or expert on al-Qaeda assessed this to be likely.

Ideology—here, a faith in the ability of American military might to achieve favorable political outcomes in Iraq quickly, and the idea that America's enemies would always find common cause—was a bias that elevated political commitment over expertise.

To me, and to many other professionals, the judgments about Saddam's capabilities, his intentions, and the likely outcome of his overthrow were weighted heavily with bias. All three components of the risk assessment were uncertain without more robust intelligence, but key members of the administration seemed willing to treat these unknowns as facts. They assumed that the string holding Dionysius II's sword was fraying, and that they had to act immediately to prevent it from falling and causing disaster. Simply stated, the decision was made to take Damocles's worst-case scenario to heart.

Other factors, like retribution for Saddam Hussein's foiled 1993 plot to assassinate President George H. W. Bush during a visit to Kuwait, and unrealistically optimistic predictions by anti-Saddam Iraqi expatriates, added to the complexity of the moment, but the United States had built an architecture of assumptions that channeled only two potential outcomes: safety from Iraq's WMD or eternal hazard from an alliance between al-Qaeda and the Ba'ath Party.

I didn't witness a check on the biases that enabled these assumptions, nor was there enough thoughtful consideration of a post-Saddam Middle East. In retrospect, difficult conversations at the Pentagon or White House could have led to a more competent invasion, and occupation—or perhaps even an effort to hold off invading altogether. But a nation traveling the road to war builds momentum that is difficult to slow or stop.

At the Pentagon, although there was only so much the uniformed military could do to shift the assessment of the Bush administration, it would also be disingenuous to claim that I saw significant military opposition to it. There were likely many who had doubts, but the uniformed staff largely focused on preparing the herculean task of deploying such a mighty force halfway around the globe for combat and—following the model of Samuel Huntington, a political scientist and director of Harvard's Center for International Affairs, from *The Soldier and the State: The Theory and Politics of Civil-Military Relations*—deferred policy decisions to civilian leadership. The assumptions and biases that guided the administration bracketed our decision space: we were asked to exist—and to execute our mission— within the limits the administration set out for us.

The assumptions I witnessed at the outset of the Iraq War weren't always irrational or baseless, but they could have all been tested with greater analytic scrutiny. Unfortunately, the administration's hawks, who wielded significant influence, treated war as a necessity. Their risk assessment was so dire—the grave compound risk of Iraq having WMD, working with al-Qaeda, and al-Qaeda employing these weapons against the United States— that any effort to think seriously about alternatives was suppressed. The National Security Council never even debated the need for the invasion at the time; it was just assumed to be necessary.

Entire books have been written on the lead-up to the Iraq War, so what I am doing here is simply putting my own perspective, undoubtedly burdened by personal biases, onto the story. As it prepared for war in Iraq, the Bush administration operated under a series of assumptions that infected its Risk Immune System, which ultimately led to an overestimation of the threat Iraq posed to the United States and a collective minimization of the difficulties involved in invading Iraq. These assumptions were the result of biases: ideology triumphed over expertise, and a bias toward military action rather than analytic reflection made the war an inevitability.

Natural biases led Confederate soldiers to fight bravely, and often die, for a cause that history finds difficult to justify. Were ours in Iraq any less powerful?

NO ZERO

Our goal in this chapter is not to outline ways to eliminate bias completely: that's impossible. But if we can examine our otherwise unchecked assumptions and increase awareness of the presence and potential impact of bias, we can mitigate many of its consequences. We must remain mindful that bias can be open and obvious, or an insidious infiltrator—and we must remain vigilant.

Political intrigue and war provide colorful backdrops to examine how bias can impact organizations' and individuals' decision space. It's important to remember that bias is universal and not bound to specific industries—business decision-making is just as impacted by bias as affairs of state, war, or political intrigue, and the effects of biased decision-making can be just as harmful and widespread. Organizations—from the most senior leader on down to the newest member of the team—have an obligation to constantly search for, evaluate, and take action to limit the impact of harmful biases.

There are some approaches that can help. First, organizations need a system for identifying inherent biases. Some of these are likely simple: if you're in Army Special Forces, chances are there's a bias toward asking a Green Beret to solve a problem. On the other hand, a formal analytic exercise like an Assumptions Check (a review of things assumed to be true upon which a plan is developed) is a good start. Red teaming (a process that uses an outside team to search for weakness in a plan or an organization) can also identify biases and assumptions that gird an organization's decision-making processes. We will examine these in Part 3, as well as other tactics organizations can use to strengthen their Risk Immune System.

Second, organizations must ensure there are appropriate accountability measures in place to limit the impact of bias on decision-making. I probably don't have to say it, but the examples in this chapter—"Sith Lord" blog posts, secession, and insubordination—trend toward the extreme. Still, these case studies demonstrate how corrosive bias can be if there is not a robust effort to limit its impact on organizations. Accountability, whether in the form of clear policies or values, can help organizations prevent their biases from corroding their decision-making.

Asking if our organizations have biases, or if we have them, is an easy question—we know the biases exist. The next step—taking decisive action to ensure biases are identified and decisions are adjusted accordingly—is much more complicated, but it is crucial to maintaining a healthy Risk Immune System.

YOUR TURN

What biases are endemic to your organization and its culture? To your industry?

What are the sources of your biases?

What are the structural or cultural factors that create or reinforce biases in your organization?

How can you mitigate the impact of biases?

THE BOTTOM LINE

Biases are the lens through which we see the world. Often rooted in our experiences and self-interests, they are largely unavoidable—but can dangerously distort our perspectives.

CHAPTER NINE

Action

THE COEFFICIENT OF FRICTION

The United States did not act early enough in mobilizing a federal response to COVID-19, and the delay increased both the human and economic toll of the disease.

—COUNCIL ON FOREIGN RELATIONS,
INDEPENDENT TASK FORCE ON PREPARING
FOR THE NEXT PANDEMIC, "IMPROVING
PANDEMIC PREPAREDNESS: LESSONS FROM
COVID-19," OCTOBER 8, 2020

> *Typically, for anything to get done, someone has to actually do something.*

Will the Block Slide?

At West Point, I took physics in my "Yearling," or sophomore, year and, as my final grade reflected, I didn't like it very much. My course was a version informally called Physics for Poets and Lovers. I wasn't a poet or a lover and was even less a physicist. Still, I was struck by the concept of inertia, defined as:

A property of matter by which it remains at rest or in uniform motion in the same straight line unless acted upon by some external force.

At the time, the United States Military Academy had operated for 171 years without changing very much, so if any place would know inertia, it was West Point.

After surviving the test (thanks to tutelage from my roommate Rick Bifulco) where I had to calculate whether a block would slide down a sloped surface and, if so, how far it would slide (and who cares?), I moved on to junior year—unaware of how much I would encounter inertia in the decades ahead. There is hardly a more powerful force.

I learned there is no action until inertia is overcome. And without action, not much gets done. But there was also another, less familiar factor in the calculation—the *coefficient of friction*.

Simply put, the coefficient of friction is a factor derived from experimentation that reflects how much force is required to either move an object that is at rest or continue moving an object already in motion across a given surface. Because it is the product of the interaction of the materials of the object and the surface it would move along, as well as a range of conditions such as temperature and moisture (remember how much easier it is to slide something heavy across an ice-covered street than dry pavement), there are specific coefficients of friction for an endless range of possible situations. To Cadet McChrystal it felt like pretty serious physics, and I was more interested in the real world.

But in a sense, individuals and organizations aren't hugely different from other objects. When something is static, overcoming inertia to begin movement can require significant force, and when you can control or manipulate other factors (affecting the coefficient of friction), you have the ability to facilitate or prevent movement. That's where the secret lies.

A NATION AT REST

In 1998, al-Qaeda orchestrated the bombings of US embassies in Dar es Salaam, Tanzania, and Nairobi, Kenya, that killed 224 people, including 12 Americans, and injured more than 4,500. Estimates of the threat posed by Usama Bin Laden, al-Qaeda's cofounder, rose yet again, and he was soon in the sights of US intelligence. There were multiple efforts to target the terrorist leader, including an August 1998 missile strike against al-Qaeda-related targets, but a year later Bin Laden was still alive.

By the mid to late 1990s, the Central Intelligence Agency possessed a new capability—an armed unmanned aerial vehicle (UAV) that could potentially strike with near-surgical precision. We briefly discussed the small drone, which came to be aptly named Predator, in Chapter 6. It was a relatively slow, prop-driven unmanned aircraft powered by a small engine. Up close, it was an almost laughable contraption compared with the sleek jet fighters the world's foremost superpower was famous for.

During my first on-site exposure to Predator, I was amused to find that the people flying the aircraft, fully qualified US Air Force pilots frustrated not to be in a conventional cockpit, did so from control panels mounted in what looked like a shipping container, all while wearing flight suits and colorful scarves. As a ground-pounding infantry soldier who enjoyed, but also resented, cool-guy Tom Cruise in *Top Gun*, I was almost embarrassed for them.

But the Predator was a deadly serious innovation. Initially developed to provide real-time, long-term surveillance of targets in enemy territory, the drone allowed analysts located hundreds of miles away to watch full-motion video (the equivalent of live TV) of target areas and individuals. It was a hugely valuable and tightly held capability.

When technicians figured out how to mount precision missiles that could be fired from the same distant base where the analysts watched, it was a game changer. This meant that unlike a sophisticated and very expensive cruise missile—which must be fired from afar with a significant flight time, during which the target might move—the US military could now watch a target in real time. They could then attempt to reach positive

The Predator didn't look menacing—but it became an invaluable tool for surveillance.

identification (PID) of the target, verify it's who they intend to kill, avoid hitting innocent civilians—and strike when the moment is right.

With this technological advance, the risks associated with striking terrorist targets had dropped dramatically. And critically, neither pilots nor ground raid forces needed to go in harm's way. Action became easier and less risky.

Still, despite extensive surveillance, revolutionary technology, and multiple opportunities to strike, no shot against Bin Laden was taken.

There were likely many reasons: concerns over another perceived failure, reputational risk to decision-makers, and a rationalization that the unsuccessful 1998 missile strikes would deter Bin Laden from future attacks, although there were no indications of that being the case. On any given day, not striking might have been the right decision, but if inertia was the underlying reason, the implications of this inaction could be significant.

In the end, Bin Laden's own momentum would continue uninterrupted, and American inaction would become a source of regret.

A Company in Uniform Motion

In 2000, the year after decision-makers chose not to strike the Saudi terrorist, Blockbuster CEO John Antioco strode into the company's Dallas boardroom to greet executives of Netflix, an online movie rental start-up. (At its inception, Netflix subscribers selected films online and were sent DVDs by snail mail.) Though the Netflix team donned informal attire consisting of tie-dye and Hawaiian T-shirts after being invited to the Blockbuster headquarters on short notice, they made a very formal offer: to sell their still-small firm to the behemoth Blockbuster for $50 million.

It would prove an awkward but historically significant gathering.

Blockbuster, the video rental giant, was the movie store you loved to hate. Though it boasted a wide range of titles, its service didn't rate even one Michelin star, and it typically smelled strongly of buttery popcorn. Customers, already frustrated when they couldn't find the movie they wanted, became even more irritated by late fees, which were a dominant

*Blockbuster stores always smelled like popcorn, but there were
plenty of movies for you and your family to watch and enjoy.*
(PHOTO BY RYAN HARDING)

part of Blockbuster's revenue. Profiting off human forgetfulness miffed so
much of its customer base that the movie giant had "managed dissatisfaction" within its business model.

As Marc Randolph, cofounder of Netflix, recounts, Netflix was David
and Blockbuster was Goliath. Randolph explains that Netflix's revenue
target of $5 million was pennies compared with Blockbuster's goal of
$6 billion. And the upstart's real estate, a two-story headquarters, paled
next to Blockbuster's nine thousand storefronts — its 350 employees
dwarfed by Blockbuster's 60,000. Rather than *beat* Goliath, however, Netflix wanted the teams to unite so the combined organization would have
the most competitive position in the watch-at-home movie marketplace.

Netflix had presciently concluded that for Blockbuster to survive in
the increasingly digital landscape, the movie store would have to expand
beyond its brick-and-mortar model. The physical stores, with their yellow
and blue logos and strip-mall locations, would be the hare in the race,
dominating the early days of the contest for the in-home movie market.
Although digital competitors would begin with tortoise-like sluggishness,
they would soon accelerate into exponential growth and ultimately prevail.

Netflix believed it was the right partner to steer Blockbuster into the
digital fast lane.

If Blockbuster acquired Netflix, the smaller firm reasoned, the two media companies would each contribute their unique skill sets. Blockbuster could manage the storefront, while Netflix could run the online arm of the organization. Netflix would focus on back-cataloging items so that Blockbuster could focus on new-release inventory—where its business thrived. Additionally, Netflix could save Blockbuster the cost of converting VHS into DVDs, escorting it into the new realm of digital rental.

To establish this partnership, Netflix offered itself up for purchase—arguing that Blockbuster would benefit from buying out the competition instead of entering into a lengthy and expensive contest.

Exhausted but well-rehearsed, the Netflix team delivered their pitch. Randolph recounts watching Antioco's face as he digested the offer, "his earnest expression slightly unbalanced by a turning up at the corner of his mouth." Though his look lasted only a second, Randolph recalls that "Antioco was struggling not to laugh." The Netflix team left Dallas disappointed.

The Blockbuster executives had decided that the opportunity to own Netflix was not worth the price, the churn of an acquisition, or the risk of a failed one. Coming on the heels of the very public dot-com crash in the spring of that year, Blockbuster claimed that e-commerce would have an uncertain future, and, as Randolph summarized, that the "business models of most online ventures, Netflix included, just weren't sustainable. They would burn cash forever." The choice to forgo the purchase was a business calculation, but it was also a decision to stick to the seductively safe path of inaction in a disorienting time.

It wasn't an irrational judgment—but it was a colossally wrong one.

Blockbuster simply couldn't appreciate the customer appeal of Netflix's model. Wasn't movie renting, as John Antioco himself wondered, an act of "spontaneity"? Netflix's slow process of selecting movies online and waiting for them to arrive in the mail removed the immediate gratification that had made Blockbuster so profitable in the first place. Besides, Blockbuster felt streaming was the natural evolution of the market.

As Gina Keating, author of *Netflixed: The Epic Battle for America's Eyeballs*, explains, media industry analysis conducted by Kagan Research, a company Blockbuster trusted, calculated that only 3.6 million users were interested in the world of online rental. Compared with Blockbuster's current 100 million renters worldwide, the juice, it was reasoned, was not worth the squeeze. And Blockbuster's success to that point had bred a measure of hubris.

But as events transpired, the two companies quickly became competitors. A year after the unsuccessful sales pitch, Blockbuster instituted its own in-store subscription model in 2001 to compete against the smaller start-up, putting advertisements on buses throughout Los Gatos, California, Netflix's hometown. Netflix, now identified publicly as a competitor, was on pace to hit one million subscribers in 2003.

Beyond the subscription model, Antioco also began to reconsider Blockbuster's assessment of digital rentals—that previous media industry analysis may have underestimated the public's interest in renting movies online. Blockbuster moved again in 2004, creating its own online platform which largely copied Netflix's form and content, and a hybrid program called Total Access in the fall of 2006 that united the tech arm of its business with its long-standing brick-and-mortar model. Through this program, customers could exchange the titles they rented online with ones in stores, creating an arrangement that would be hard for Netflix to beat.

It was a powerful and popular idea.

Seven years after Blockbuster rejected the Netflix offer, its 2007 analyst report highlighted what Blockbuster interpreted to be its strengths versus Netflix's weaknesses (Figure 1). Blockbuster's capabilities—ranging from Total Access, to in-store rentals, to the Blockbuster Movie Pass—far outnumbered Netflix's meager offerings of By-Mail and Digital services. This graphic seemed to confirm that its decision to *not* merge with Netflix was the right choice.

The irony of the scoreboard is obvious in retrospect: in a league that would soon be dominated by digital accessibility, the slide depicts Blockbuster fielding a large team while only two players take the field for Netflix—but they are 300-pound linebackers with Super Bowl potential.

Also shared in the same 2007 analyst report (Figure 2) was Blockbuster's interpretation of the "New Competitive Landscape." Blockbuster is up against a strong team of other players that include Redbox, Amazon,

New Paradigm

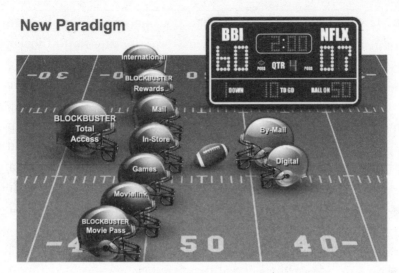

FIGURE 1: *Blockbuster believes it has a stacked field facing the far inferior capabilities of Netflix.*

New Competitive Landscape

FIGURE 2: *Blockbuster regards Netflix as one of many competitors—not a significant threat.*

and Best Buy. Blockbuster did not deny the presence of competitors from these other emerging threats but simply regarded Netflix as a small and insignificant part of its opposing army.

In both of these images, Blockbuster positions Total Access as its quarterback—a new introduction to the business that did, in fact, give the store an edge. And there was great initial success: Blockbuster attracted three million subscribers to Total Access, gaining 70 percent of new subscribers—an accolade that Netflix had received since Blockbuster tried its hand at the online business. Blockbuster's Total Access program had seemingly "reversed" the split, garnering the majority of new customers.

But it had been a tough, expensive road. Keating recounts that Antioco had spent "three years of gambles, sacrifices, and bravado" and more than $500 million—ten times more than the $50 million price tag Netflix had first offered ten years before—to produce the Total Access package that gave it an advantage over Netflix.

That year, Netflix CEO Reed Hastings, nervous about Blockbuster's new offering, made a proposal to purchase Blockbuster's subscribers. Netflix was no longer offering *itself* up for purchase, as it had seven years before—now the company had its wallet out to make an acquisition of its own. Hastings presented the final offer: Netflix would pay $200 for each of Blockbuster's subscribers, totaling up to $600 million, and cover other fees. Again, Blockbuster denied Netflix's proposition to join forces.

Although Blockbuster appeared to be in the driver's seat, there was a catch: Blockbuster's Total Access model was flawed. Each time a customer exchanged a movie in-store, it cost Blockbuster money. So, while popular, the program wasn't financially sustainable. Paradoxically, the success of Total Access created a "liquidity crisis" for Blockbuster—with an ever-increasing volume of interested customers, the company's debt would quickly grow.

While thrilled that Netflix admitted it couldn't compete with Total Access, and reluctant to sell the very subscribers that underpinned the program, Blockbuster "battled the dread of keeping the cash-burning promotion going indefinitely." Still, it chose to maintain its existing trajectory in the hope that Total Access would eventually prove profitable.

THE HOUSE IS ON FIRE

On the first day, Greta Thunberg sat alone outside the Swedish Parliament—holding her small sign and eating her packed lunch. She remained the length of the school day, until her father picked her up to bike home. This was the first day of the Fridays for Future movement that would spread across the globe as young students protested climate change.

Though a small act, Greta Thunberg's first school strike had ripple effects—prompting an international conversation about climate change. Her cause is for our world leaders to *act*—she shames those who do not, who willingly continue the status quo as the world continues to warm up.

"We are in the beginning of a mass extinction, and all you can talk about is money and fairy tales of eternal economic growth. How dare you!" she said, speaking at the UN Climate Summit. Brutally honest and often harsh, her words damned their resistance to action.

Thunberg stresses that the clock is ticking—only by "cutting our emissions in half in 10 years" does the world stand even a chance of preventing irreparable damage. She implores leaders to "act as you would in a crisis. I want you to act as if the house is on fire. Because it is." A year later, she lamented to world leaders that their "inaction is fueling the flames."

The determined Thunberg has gained celebrity and followers—her biographers in her spotlight for *Time's* Person of the Year in 2019 describes her success in transforming "millions of vague, middle-of-the-night anxieties into a worldwide movement calling for urgent change."

But the crisis remains—inertia is a powerful force.

It didn't. When a new CEO took over, Blockbuster defunded the Total Access program and increased its Blockbuster Online subscription price to keep its head above the water. As a result, many customers switched back to Netflix, which continued to grow in 2008 as they launched partnerships with Roku and Xbox to stream their services.

Blockbuster moved to closed down its remaining stores in 2013. Meanwhile, Netflix "announced that it had thirty-one million subscribers in the United States, three million more than HBO, and that its stock was at an all-time high."

Greta Thunberg holds a SCHOOL STRIKE FOR CLIMATE
sign outside the Swedish Parliament.

In 2020, twenty years after the two CEOs had first met, there is only one remaining Blockbuster store operating in the United States. Despite the failure of his decision not to acquire Netflix in 2000, Antioco was no fool. Shrewdly, in 2011, after leaving Blockbuster and observing the company under new leadership, he sold his Blockbuster stock and purchased a mass of Netflix shares.

AN EXCUSE FOR INACTION

Periodically, I'll awake in fright—a dream has transported me back to Bartlett Hall at West Point, into my old physics section room. It's an unnerving experience as I'm peppered with questions I can't answer. Inertia, I recalled, said that an object at rest or in uniform motion would continue to do that until something moved or stopped it. One question I never get in my dream, and don't remember ever hearing in class, is "*Should* the block move?" Or, if it's moving, "*Should* it change direction?"

In my physics class at West Point, we learned that, in the most basic terms, inertia tells us that absent external forces things will *keep doing whatever they're doing.* That's true not only if what they're doing is brilliant and successful but also if what they're up to is silly and destined for failure. An oft-used military axiom is: *Never interrupt your enemy when they're making a mistake.*

But shouldn't we interrupt ourselves?

The Blockbuster team, like all organizations facing risk, had two potential responses to choose from: to *act* and accept some variation of the conditions that Netflix proposed, or to choose *inaction* as the more agreeable alternative and reject the proposal altogether. Arguably, Blockbuster's initial response to not purchase Netflix was simply a bad business decision based on an incorrect guess at the future of home viewing trends.

Did Blockbuster succumb to inertia? And is inertia really a form of bias?

For our purposes, inertia can be defined as a bias toward inaction or changing course. Blockbuster may have decided to maintain the status quo with the brick-and-mortar movie rental model because it had been so historically successful—who could blame them? But that's not all: the power of inertia likely influenced Blockbuster's decision to stick with its model. The perceived risks associated with taking a more active step out of its comfort zone prompted Blockbuster to *not* take the risks that would have potentially saved the company.

We often stay where we are because it's easier not to move—and then rationalize that the choice to "stay put" was ultimately the right decision. While overconfidence can generate inertia, organizations also face a natural aversion to taking extreme measures. There are times when each of us fails to take action, even when we know we should—getting cold feet from fear or sweaty palms at the thought of defying the status quo. But in order to avoid the risks that come with missed opportunity, we must resist this bias for inaction, widening our aperture to act to better our businesses and teams.

SYMPTOMS OF ACTION—OR INACTION

Slow Reaction Time. Organizations that are biased for inaction tend to be slower to react and sluggish to adapt.

Missed Chances. Teams plagued by inertia fail to take advantage of opportunities, too set in their ways to change.

Contradictory Efforts. Teams experience whiplash when actions conflict and distract from a goal.

Playing Catch-up with Competitors. Teams that don't act quickly and effectively are rapidly surpassed by more aggressive and decisive organizations.

Analysis Paralysis. We fail to act at all when we are laser-focused on identifying options and paralyzed by the number of choices available to us.

Reactive Posture. We tend to react (sometimes emotionally) when we are not properly positioned for action.

The power of inertia makes it much easier to justify staying put even when our comfort zone is a painful place. During the civil rights movement, the potential for violence and confrontation gave white clergymen an excuse for inaction, though they knew better.

"Letter from Birmingham Jail"

In April 1963, two years before crossing the Edmund Pettus Bridge in Selma, Alabama, Dr. Martin Luther King Jr. pulled out his pen in the prison lighting, next to a copy of *The Birmingham News*. Dr. King had been arrested for leading a protest without a permit in Birmingham, placed in solitary confinement, and then criticized by white clergymen in one of the newspaper's editorials for the movement's nonviolent protests.

Though uncharacteristic of Dr. King—who typically didn't send long letters to his critics—he crafted a reply to the white clergymen once he had access to paper. In cramped script on margins of a newspaper, the thirty-four-year-old minister wrote his now-famous "Letter from Birmingham Jail."

Dr. King's missive, carefully carved on the thin newsprint, addresses the white moderates' bias for inaction. The eight white clergymen who wrote the caustic editorial give shape, voice, and form to the hesitations of inertia. Wanting to eliminate the risk of a radically altered status quo, these white moderates claimed that King's actions were too dangerous and timelines too aggressive, and advocated instead for a more careful, moderate approach to achieving equality.

Dr. King's letter constitutes a profound critique of white participation in the civil rights movement. Written clergyman to clergymen, it is rich with biblical references but also serves as a decisively strong case for action:

> I have almost reached the regrettable conclusion that the Negro's great stumbling block in his stride toward freedom is not the White Citizen's Counciler or the Ku Klux Klanner, but the white moderate, who is more devoted to "order" than to justice; who prefers a negative peace which is the absence of tension to a positive peace which is the presence of justice; who constantly says: "I agree with you in the goal you seek, but I cannot agree with your methods of direct action."

Unlike Blockbuster, whose hubris and lack of foresight prompted inaction, the white moderates theoretically supported racial equality, but their allegiance to the status quo, and fear of upending a caste system that directly favored them, made inaction the safer alternative. Inaction would protect them from violent pushback from other white citizens, shield them from excessive force in the form of police officers with attack dogs and water hoses, and preserve their reputations.

In his letter, Dr. King asserts that the white clergymen's piety belies their zeal for racial equality; as they "mouth pious irrelevancies and sanctimonious trivialities," they claim that segregation is not a religious issue but a social one that does not require their participation to correct.

Acknowledging the dangers of action, Dr. King writes that action should not be taken for action's sake alone but should be the result of careful thought, planning, and negotiation. Dr. King explains that activists collect information about an injustice and then negotiate—when

Dr. King was incarcerated nearly thirty times
as he fought to secure civil rights for Black Americans.
(PHOTO BY DON CRAVENS/THE LIFE IMAGES COLLECTION
VIA GETTY IMAGES/GETTY IMAGES)

their efforts are unsuccessful, they consider the possibility of nonviolent direct action. Before acting, protesters are encouraged to self-purify and attend workshops on nonviolence that teach how not to retaliate and how to tolerate jail when necessary.

In the case of the Birmingham protest, Dr. King and his supporters only turned to action when they were repeatedly unable to negotiate with city officials. Action would be taken to create "crisis" where negotiation *could* occur, and "dramatize the issue [so] that it can no longer be ig-nored." Their action wasn't impulsive but rather a fully thought-out and deeply considered strategy.

Dr. King intuitively understood that the effects of segregation would take decades to fix. The longer society waited, the longer they'd push seg-regation's effects into the future. Education would continue to be delayed.

Economic progress and equality in society and under the law would be needlessly slowed. With every generation, Dr. King understood citizens were renewing the decision to keep African Americans in subjugation. The risk of inaction—the continued segregation of African American citizens, the *probability* of continued degradation, and the *consequences* of never-ceasing segregation—warranted a response.

"Letter from Birmingham Jail" was circulated in 1963 as a mimeographed copy and was ultimately published as an article in the *New York Post*, *The Christian Century*, *Christianity and Crisis*, and *Ebony*. Dr. King expanded on the ideas of "Letter from Birmingham Jail" in *Why We Can't Wait*, recounting the activism of the Birmingham campaign and the March on Washington for Jobs and Freedom that year. The letter became a manifesto for the civil rights movement—the case for action in a world stifled by paralysis, a cause for participation in an era where so many white moderates stood idly by—and remains relevant for this pervasive bias for inaction we face today.

STANDING OPERATING PROCEDURES

As history shows us, the US military's decision not to strike Usama Bin Laden in the late 1990s had repercussions. On September 11, 2001, a carefully constructed operation unfolded in the skies over the United States, and seared into the minds of Americans with unforgettable power.

In the aftermath of 9/11, US Special Operations Forces came into vogue. Capabilities that had been created in the 1980s in response to rising terrorism worldwide seemed perfectly suited for the upcoming "Global War on Terror." Night-vision-equipped commandos delivered in the dark by blacked-out helicopters appeared to be the perfect antidote to violent ideologues. Embracing the mantra of the leather-jacketed police detective played by Sylvester Stallone in the 1986 film *Cobra*—"You're a disease, and I'm the cure"—the United States would use special operators to target this emerging threat. And we did—relentlessly.

Almost every night in Iraq and Afghanistan, teams of Army Special Forces, Rangers, or Navy SEALs, often accompanied by their Iraqi or Afghan counterparts would conduct raids. Approaching under the cover of darkness by helicopter or by ground, units would surround locations where terrorists were suspected of operating, then maneuver their way into the target area, prying open doors or breaching walls to reach their targets. Once inside, the commandos would gain control of all the people in the compound, search them and the location itself, take the wanted individual(s) to detention, and collect as much intelligence about the position as possible in the process.

Often, particularly in Iraq, actions on the target would involve a violent firefight in which night-vision-equipped operators, using M4 carbines equipped with infrared laser aiming lights, would identify and engage enemy fighters with stunning speed. From overhead surveillance platforms, like the Predator, the fighting had the look of exterminators cleaning out an infestation of vermin. Up close, bodies torn by high-velocity bullets bled as they have in wars in every age.

The forces conducting these missions to decapitate enemy opposition (al-Qaeda, Taliban, or Haqqani network operatives) reflected a traditional component of counterterrorist and counterinsurgency operations. Through countless iterations, these missions were honed into well-oiled standing operating procedures. In Iraq, at the height of the violence from 2005 to 2008, we conducted several hundred raids every month—at painful cost in casualties to our force, but with devastating effect against al-Qaeda in Iraq. It was necessary, brutal work.

But these operations, though valuable, were also a two-edged sword. Particularly in irregular warfare (typically defined as unconventional or guerrilla warfare), violence can create as much opposition as it destroys or suppresses.

For instance, in Afghanistan the primary mission of International Security Assistance Force was to support the elected government. Landlocked, less developed Afghanistan was very different from Iraq. In the traditional "graveyard of empires," we conducted counterterrorism efforts to target, kill, or capture the enemy while maintaining an overall focus to provide stability and secure Afghan sovereignty. Aggressive raids normally associated with counterterrorism weren't directly in opposition to stability operations, but the two types of operations were inherently in tension with each other.

The "night raids," as they were known in Afghanistan, became a critical political challenge because the operations were antithetical to the Afghan culture. Outside Kabul, Afghans often lived in large, multigenerational homes (called *qalats*) with high walls that resembled fortresses, and to enter uninvited was a cultural taboo, especially at night. I would hear numerous Afghan officials tell me that not even the Soviet Union or its allied government in Kabul would enter residences at night, simply out of respect. Afghans would firmly remind Americans that "not even my own brother could come into my home at night; I would have to kill him." More than a few Afghan men died rushing with a rifle (almost every Afghan home had at least one weapon) to defend against intruders—having no connection with the insurgency.

If these operations caused casualties among women or children, or a perception of disrespect toward the Qur'an, violent public demonstrations would often break out in protest to our actions. If our forces used dogs to aid the search, or if men searched Afghan women for weapons during the course of the operation, the insult was exponentially worse.

Soldiers would conduct "night raids" in compounds—
walled to provide residents security and privacy.

Afghans also believed these operations were haphazard, punitive, even random acts of violence, not intelligence-driven uses of force. That wasn't the case, but the perception became part of our operational reality.

"Night raids" were a subject of extraordinary political controversy from the president of Afghanistan down to the lowest civil servant in the Afghan government. No matter how essential they were to the overarching campaign against terrorists in Afghanistan and around the world, they inflicted a serious toll on the credibility of the International Security Assistance Force. Fundamentally, *the process we employed to improve our security directly challenged Afghan concepts of security*—in other words, our response to mitigating risk instead augmented the dangers we wanted to avoid.

Furthermore, these aggressive raids often conflicted with our own counterinsurgency efforts. The bulk of the International Security Assistance Force in Afghanistan was responsible for aiding the Afghan government in its attempt to secure the country from insurgent groups. These units would certainly fight, but they also sought to build roads, electrify towns and cities, aid agriculture, and assist the government in responding to the people's needs. Conventional units were often left to explain the rationale behind "night raids" that Special Operations Forces conducted.

Even well-intentioned and, from one angle, very effective actions can be detrimental to an organization's overall effort. The United States allowed itself to fight two different military campaigns in the same country, at the same time, and accepted that the results of the counterterrorism campaign complicated the efforts of the program to support the Afghan government. Commanders had ample evidence that this contradiction existed—so why did we do it?

The answer is not as simple as you'd expect.

When mitigating risk, organizations can also suffer from the effects of *velocity*—another physics phenomenon. Velocity is defined as "the rate of change of position along a straight line with respect to time," or, more simply, the speed of an object as it moves in a particular direction. Just as it can be hard to resist inertia, or a bias toward inaction, so too can it be challenging to stop once we've started on a set course.

This became painfully true in Iraq. On the one hand, the value of strike operations was undeniable and, in many cases, essential, but on the other hand, the reality is that organizations tend to operate a certain way, and from the early 1980s Special Operations Forces had honed the skills of raiding. The fact of inertia is that an object in uniform motion will tend to remain in motion—in the same direction—unless something stops it. And stopping men with hammers from looking at everything like nails is tough.

Common Denominator

It is easy to accept the premise that at some point action is essential. And it follows that the action we take must be appropriate to the need. But *doing something*—and in particular, *doing the right thing for the situation at hand*—isn't always easy.

Terrorists, counterterrorists, video executives, and white clergymen were all inhibited by inertia—and it doesn't stop there. The reality is that we all tend to maintain the status quo and "keep doing what we're doing." This is something we have to recognize and often work to overcome. In organizations inertia can be a reason for retaining positive habits, and it can also be a reason for continuing behaviors that were never consciously started. Similarly, velocity can be the explanation for why we speed ahead and keep moving in the direction we are currently going—even when our course is more destructive than helpful.

Effective action begins when we overcome inertia. It demands recognition of the need to act and the courage to take the step—absent that, inertia rules. Once in motion, we must constantly surveil our actions to determine if they are contextually appropriate, or if their intended effect backfires.

Action and other Risk Control Factors are invariably interconnected. For example, communication is often necessary to act, while narrative and bias either enable or inhibit our ability to act effectively. It's a complex system, but ultimately, if we can't overcome our coefficient of friction, the gears won't turn.

YOUR TURN

How do you overcome a team's natural bias for inaction?

How do you assess if your actions are appropriate in their context? How can you discern if you are overly cautious? How do you know when to change course?

What prevents you from shifting the status quo?

THE BOTTOM LINE

Ultimately, what we do (or don't do) determines the outcome.

CHAPTER TEN

Timing

SLOW BUSES AND FAST CARS

You can ask me for anything you like, except time.
—NAPOLEON BONAPARTE

> **When** *you do something is often*
> *as important as* **what** *you do.*

EARLY AND FAST

In an instant, cell phones lit up all over Taiwan. The Public Warning System (PWS), typically dispatched to warn citizens about natural disasters, sent text messages to selected cell phones around the nation. The alert—reaching phones in purses, in pockets, on kitchen counters, and in grocery baskets—offered a visible warning about the seemingly invisible threat of the COVID-19 virus, tagging the recipient as a potential carrier.

On February 5, 2020, Taiwanese officials had received word that ten passengers on the *Diamond Princess* cruise ship—which had visited Taiwan's Port of Keelung five days before—had tested positive for COVID-19. Concerned that passengers who had disembarked onto Taiwanese soil had carried and potentially spread the virus, officials immediately began an investigation, tracking the movements of the passengers through CCTV footage, credit card transactions, shuttle bus data from GPS, and mobile positioning information.

Moving quickly, Taiwanese officials instructed all 627,386 citizens who had possibly been within 1,600 feet of the passengers for more than five minutes to quarantine at home.

Taiwan's rapid response to the threat of infection posed by the *Diamond Princess* passengers is representative of its overall effective effort to limit the pandemic's impact. Officials made timely decisions to act and then leveraged technology to execute their responses rapidly. As a result, though Taiwan was expected to have a painfully high density of cases because of its proximity to mainland China and the numerous travelers between the nations, it kept the number of COVID-related deaths remarkably low: only seven as of May 2020.

How did they pull off such a successful response?

The truth is, Taiwan had begun to prepare for the possibility of a pandemic early on, more than a month before deploying the PWS, while concerns of COVID-19 were still quiet murmurs in most areas of the world. On December 31, hours before 2020 began, Taiwanese officials boarded planes flying from Wuhan to observe and track any presence of pneumonia-like symptoms. Before the World Health Organization—whose declarations typically speed up global response efforts to viruses—confirmed that the virus could spread human-to-human, the Taiwanese government surveilled all citizens who were arriving from Wuhan. Then, on January 20, Taiwan activated its Central Epidemic Command Center (CECC), which quickly wrote and deployed 124 action items that addressed school closures, resource allocation, business relief, and more. Taiwan was way ahead of the curve.

At first, the United States also seemed to react rapidly to the emergence of the virus, making quick decisions as early as January 17 to enforce medical screenings of passengers at designated airports who were returning from Hubei Province. American officials, however, decided not to enforce domestic social distancing measures or recommend against gatherings of fifty or more people until almost two months later, on March 15, long after Taiwan's initial interventions had helped prevent COVID-19's lethal spread.

So what? Did a few weeks really matter?

It turns out they did. According to an analysis conducted by Columbia University, 36,000 deaths could have been avoided if social distancing and other control measures had been adopted just one week earlier. And if these responses had been initiated *two* weeks earlier, on March 1, the United States could have avoided 83 percent of deaths by the beginning of May.

In other words, more timely decisions, accompanied by rapid execution, could have dramatically reduced the number of COVID-related deaths in America and spared us not only much of the carnage but also lasting memories of parking lot funerals, overwhelmed hospitals, and rationed personal protective equipment.

So, can we conclude that *acting early* and *moving fast* guarantee success? Not necessarily.

Anyone who has ever cooked a meal, shot at an elusive clay pigeon on a skeet range, or attempted to coax a three-year-old into a nap knows that acting too early can be just as ineffective as acting too late. The truth is, there is both a moment when an action should begin and a speed at which it is best executed.

Think of a baseball player at bat. At the professional level, pitchers routinely throw ninety-plus miles per hour, so hitters have less than a second to gauge the ball's trajectory and decide whether or not to swing, and if so, where they should place the bat. Hitters who, out of an abundance of caution, swing early too often don't last long in the game.

In the same way, we too often fail to decipher a problem or the actions required to solve it. We eagerly eye the ball and swing, but miss as the baseball sails into the catcher's mitt.

Flaws within our own Risk Immune System can also adversely affect our ability to make our responses to risk as timely and effective as they should be. Sometimes we succumb to inertia and resist taking action, or our leaders incorrectly speed up or slow down decision-making. At other times, our teams are unable to communicate the right information at the right time, and our structure's reporting channels slow down urgent messages.

Actions taken to mitigate risks must account for appropriate timing, or else even the most well-crafted decisions will fail. Achieving effective timing requires an understanding of when an impact is needed and how long it will take to implement the response. Think of hitting the baseball at just the right instant: we have to decide when and how to swing, then execute the action, to finally observe the impact of our response.

The process may appear linear and straightforward, but it actually warrants careful consideration. To achieve effective timing, we must first understand how long execution, or the implementation of our action, will take (think the speed of the batter's swing), and before that, we must determine how much time our decision-making process, including communication across channels, requires.

With the baseball leaving the pitcher's outstretched arm only about fifty-five feet from home plate, our baseball batter is required to assess the pitch, decide, and execute in about a quarter of a second. That explains why even professional ballplayers, most of whom have been on the diamond from an early age, are proud of batting averages that are still far closer to zero than a perfect 1.000.

Although every baseball pitch is subtly different, hitters have likely faced hundreds of thousands of them through their careers. In the same way, the stakes and conditions we confront are *always* in flux. Even the most experienced, carefully trained leaders are not always prepared to face unknown and unprecedented risks. Wars, recessions, and pandemics appear regularly throughout history, but occasionally enough so that most decision-makers encounter each once—if at all. And risks are sufficiently varied to defy a rigidly templated response. Our Risk Immune Systems must be sensitive to time, reacting quickly, and appropriately, as the conditions demand—whether it be in the eye of a hurricane or on the starting grid of a Formula 1 race.

A baseball swing is equal parts skill and timing.
(PHOTO BY DAVID MADISON/PHOTODISC/GETTY IMAGES)

"THE IMPOSSIBLE BUT INEVITABLE CITY"

In 1976, Peirce Lewis named New Orleans "the impossible but inevitable city." On the one hand, the city was impossible "in light of the region's inhospitable climate and challenging geography." It was inevitable because of its location so close to the mouth of the Mississippi River. The moniker forebodes storm damage.

Hurricane Katrina hit the height of its fury on Monday, August 29, 2005. Although technically a Category 5 storm with winds hitting 140 miles per hour on land, to everyone in its path, it was simply a terrifying monster. For those sheltering in New Orleans's Superdome, it was a frightening, exhausting, and often disgusting experience. That night, up to twelve thousand citizens watched a small hole in the Superdome's roof, ripped open by the unforgiving power of water and wind, grow larger and larger as rain poured into their refuge.

The storm passed, and soon the holes in the roof were filled with bright beams of light as the summer sun peeked in. But the ordeal was far from over. Though intended to be a makeshift shelter of "last resort," the number of Superdome occupants swelled as tens of thousands more sought refuge after the storm had passed—with reports of twenty-five thousand Americans staying there for at least a few days of shelter. Crowded with men, women, and children of all ages, the Superdome's plumbing couldn't keep up—the arena started to smell. Elderly citizens who sought refuge there often sat "unattended . . . not moving" for days at a time.

The world outside the Superdome was even grimmer: floodwater covered the roads after the levees had been breached. Residents, sitting on their scorching roofs, waved desperately to helicopters for rescue. Shards of wood crisscrossed in morbid piles of crushed homes as debris, dead animals, and human bodies floated in the streets. More than a million people who had escaped the city saw their homes on television, many unrecognizable after the storm's unfortunate transformation. Estimates of the damage cite between 1,200 and 1,800 deaths. Destruction to the city's infrastructure, environment, and psyche would take decades to repair.

Was this the unavoidable wrath of Mother Nature—or did human error add to the tragedy that unfolded?

It was a bit of both. The external risk of the fourth most intense Atlantic hurricane ever to strike the continental United States at the time was by itself huge. But ultimately, Hurricane Katrina was a failure in risk management. Weaknesses in the Risk Immune Systems at almost every level of government, complicated by personalities and the inevitable complexities of such an event, multiplied the costs in blood and treasure. Structural issues of jurisdictions, failures to communicate, biases, and other key factors all proved damaging to what should have been an effective response.

Examining those issues has already filled volumes, so here we'll focus more narrowly on the question of timing. Although many of the rescue responses were imperfect, and some badly flawed, had officials improved only the timing of their actions, the impact of Hurricane Katrina would have been far less painful. Dilatory pre-storm decision-making led to sluggish responses, as actions taken by New Orleans, the state of Louisiana, and the federal government came too late to provide the necessary aid.

But let's be realistic—it's impossible to make perfect storm predictions. Still, Katrina appeared during the Atlantic's traditional hurricane season, had been preceded by eleven other hurricanes or tropical storms that year alone, and emerged relatively slowly. Beginning on August 23 as a tropical depression, Katrina had achieved hurricane status on the twenty-fifth as it made landfall in Florida, to then pass through the Gulf of Mexico and pivot toward New Orleans.

While storms wax and wane in intensity and are notoriously fickle about changing course, there was ample time to take the appropriate steps to deal with the potential risk. However, Louisiana governor Kathleen Blanco and New Orleans mayor Ray Nagin were painfully slow to declare a mandatory evacuation of the city of New Orleans. Though these leaders were aware of the power of the impending storm fifty-six hours before it hit, they declared a mandatory evacuation only nineteen hours before landfall—at 11:00 A.M. (CST) on Sunday, August 28.

From the start, the evacuation orders went poorly, beginning with the mundane issue of buses.

Bus stops are often synonymous with timing: customers wait patiently by bus stops for their ride to predictably roll in. The bus, on a familiar timetable, lurches to a stop, audibly exhales—and the doors open for the passengers to embark. For Hurricane Katrina, there were two stages of busing: one to transport citizens *into* the Superdome for last-minute shelter, and another to move the Superdome's hungry and tired inhabitants *out*, to a safer and more permanent place of refuge. Both were ill-timed: the former suffered from leadership hesitation, the latter from a lack of preemptive decision-making.

When the belated evacuation order was finally declared, those who were unwilling or unable to leave the city were transported to the Superdome. But by this time, a large portion of the bus drivers the Regional Transit Authority (RTA) depended on had heard the concerning weather reports and already left the city—unable to do the work the city required of them. The plan for the buses, therefore, was canceled by midafternoon—the buses responsible for the evacuation were filled with gas and parked in a lot on a wharf near the city's downtown area, where they'd be parked when the storm hit. The city's other expected bus services that could have provided one last hope for remaining citizens had similarly been canceled.

But this wasn't even the most troubling timing challenge of the Hurricane Katrina response. When it was time to transport citizens *out* of the Superdome after the storm had passed, there was a lack of coordination between federal organizations like the Federal Emergency Management Agency (FEMA) and the Department of Transportation (DOT). The DOT, responsible for procuring buses in the event of a natural disaster, had to formally request permission from FEMA to do so. But by the time the storm made landfall, that authority had still not been given. This seemingly ludicrous bureaucratic snafu likely cost lives as citizens waited for a place of safe refuge beyond the Superdome. The FEMA director, Michael Brown, "could not explain the delay other than to say that the 'logistics system in FEMA was broken.'" This wasn't a logistics issue, however: it was a question of timing. Had FEMA granted the DOT permission *earlier*, there would have been less delay in procurement.

Eventually, the buses arrived, but not without further delay—illustrating that not only decision-making but also *execution* determines the timing of a response.

The general and military theorist Carl von Clausewitz has a famous reminder about war: "*Everything is very simple in war, but the simplest thing is difficult.*" The same can be said about the Katrina aid efforts. After flying over the highways to assess the damage of the city, Governor Blanco personally redirected the buses to the thousands of men and women she saw were stranded on highway overpasses—against the intent to first evacuate those inside the Superdome. Furthermore, bus drivers were often concerned for their safety in entering the city, as media sources had portrayed New Orleans as overrun with looters and murderers.

This hesitation prompted Governor Blanco to mandate in an executive order that members of the National Guard protect the buses, a process that necessarily made a sluggish process even slower. The last straw of the timing delay occurred when the bus drivers got lost trying to find the Superdome, presumably overwhelmed at having to navigate an unfamiliar city, where water blocked off normal traffic.

By Friday morning, September 2, five days after Hurricane Katrina ravaged the city of New Orleans, eight hundred buses evacuated fifteen thousand people from the Superdome. On Saturday, the last three hundred evacuees left the Superdome—finally clearing out the place of refuge that had turned from a temporary haven to a site of human desperation. The nearby Convention Center (a smaller makeshift shelter) was cleared through the weekend as well. Six days after the storm had hit, New Orleans was nearly evacuated.

What can we learn from this? The failures of timing during Katrina fall into two categories. The first, and most obvious, was a hesitation, even an unwillingness, to make difficult decisions early enough to ensure their effective implementation. The second, and almost more damning for bureaucrats, was a lack of understanding of the mechanics and interdependencies involved in the execution of the rescue efforts. Both failures were preventable, inexcusable, and fairly common.

Thousands of stranded citizens attempted to get on buses that would evacuate them to safety.
(AP PHOTO/DAVE MARTIN)

SYMPTOMS OF TIMING CHALLENGES

Hurry Up and Wait. Poorly timed decisions can often cause some parts of the plan to be rushed, and others to be painfully delayed.

Undercooked Cake. Taking a cake out of the oven too early means a soggy, unappetizing mess. Cutting corners and speeding up processes can compromise the end result.

Jumping the Gun. Sprinters who take off before the starting gun are disqualified from the race. Acting too early (though often in eagerness) can prevent the successful execution of a plan.

Too Little, too Late. We often don't know how long processes take until we're knee-deep in them. Thinking ahead can save you time overall.

Creating More Work. Those who make decisions *too* quickly will often have to make *new* decisions once the conditions inevitably change.

Although we treasure the opportunity to excoriate officials for their failures, we must also appreciate the pressures and forces that can cause delay or undisciplined execution. For instance, the financial and political costs of an unnecessary evacuation are steep, and there can be a strong impulse to respond to pressing needs that can undercut broader priorities. Acting early and making decisions promptly are within our control. Though we can appreciate the many reasons why people *might* delay action, it's imperative to get ahead of our hesitation, and act before it's too late.

THREE PIT STOPS

The Ferrari was not in a favorable racing position. Michael Schumacher, the famed German racing driver competing for Ferrari, stepped into the bright red vehicle donning a red helmet and jumpsuit—his physical confidence belying his position on the starting grid. For this 1998 Hungarian Grand Prix, the two McLarens in the race boasted faster qualifying times and had better starting positions. The Hungarian course was not conducive to overtaking—or passing other vehicles on the track—so the Ferrari would have to reconsider its strategy to best compete.

What strategy?

On its face, Formula 1 racing is pretty straightforward—it's all about time. The car that finishes first wins, so you want to sit in the fastest car and drive aggressively. It's a simple concept and the racing culture seems to embody it. Whizzing at maximum speeds of more than 200 miles per hour, weaving on the track in an attempt to overtake vehicles, Formula 1 drivers like Michael Schumacher regularly appear on billboards and in magazines advertising gasoline and car brands. Not surprisingly, Formula 1 is a sport of loud cars and big egos—with sizable cash prizes. In 2018, the total prize payout for the Grand Prix was $913 million.

This speed-obsessed sport is also dangerous—fifty-two drivers have died because of Formula 1 injuries since the 1950 World Championships at Silverstone in England. But interestingly, most Formula 1 teams assess the most pressing dangers to be the financial and reputational risks of losing the race.

The paradox at the heart of Formula 1 racing is that faster isn't always better; raw speed on the track isn't always enough to win the race. Ross Brawn, Ferrari's technical director in the 1998 Grand Prix race, understood that the difference between winning and losing in a Formula 1 race lies as much in decision-making as in motor power. With this in mind, he recommended a nonconformist strategy for the Ferrari car: a three-pit-stop approach, even though most of the competitors were banking on only two.

Anyone who's taken a family road trip with hungry children would ask the obvious question: How would the Ferrari car get to the finish line first if it stopped more often?

Pit stops are a crucial part of any Formula 1 race—a dance that's choreographed, drilled, and executed as quickly as possible. As soon as a car pulls into the pit stop, more than twenty teammates surround the car, changing the tires, adjusting the wings, and cleaning the driver's visor for visibility. Each decision, from the selection of tires to the amount of time spent in the pit stop, matters. Stopping in the pit the least number of times, for the shortest amount of time, would seem to be the obvious winning strategy.

For this reason, a three-pit-stop strategy in the Hungarian Grand Prix appears all the more ludicrous. Why would Ferrari, with a less favorable position on the starting grid, want to spend more time in the pits?

But the full reality was more complex.

In this 1998 race, and until 2009 when the practice was banned from the sport for consideration of cost and safety, the amount of fuel pumped into the car was a critical decision for each pit stop. It began with the fueling process, which was relatively slow, taking between six and nine seconds. But fuel is also heavy. Around this particular race track, each additional twenty-two pounds of fuel cost a car about .365 seconds per lap in speed. By making an additional pit stop, the Ferrari was able to run with approximately 66 pounds less fuel load, enabling it to drive 1.1 seconds faster on every lap.

Ferrari's three-pit-stop strategy, Brawn reasoned, would provide other advantages as well. First, as Ferrari's strategist said, it would put the Ferrari car "out of phase" with its competitors. Brawn recounts that three pit stops "wasn't quite the fastest strategy, but it gave us free track time." When the track was open, Ferrari could engage its fast motor without any needless holdups to make up lost time.

Second, the Ferrari team made an astute tire choice. Tire selection is a part of race strategy: teams predict which tires will be fastest on the track

Pit stops are tightly practiced and choreographed events
that can make or break Formula 1 strategy.
(IMAGINECHINA VIA AP IMAGES)

(given weather conditions, tire degradation, etc.) between pit stops. Thanks to the team's tire choice, Ferrari ran 0.6 seconds faster than competitors in early stages of the race. Though on paper the McLarens appeared faster (due to their quicker qualifying times), Ferrari was performing better thanks to the tire selection. Brawn was confident that Ferrari would race well as they gambled with their three-stop strategy.

And, of course, because the car didn't require as much fuel between pit stops, it would be lighter, and therefore faster, on the track.

The race began in typical fashion, with the Ferrari accelerating from the starting grid as if it were conducting the typical two-stop strategy. The Ferrari even made its first pit stop at an expected time, one that other drivers would deem reasonable for a two-stop race.

But, unexpectedly, at lap forty-three, the Ferrari pitted for the second time, refueling for only 6.8 seconds before racing ahead. The McLaren lead car pitted right after Ferrari, but took much longer to fill up on fuel to last the rest of the course. When the McLaren returned to the track, it was now *behind* the Ferrari. The red car was at the front of the pack.

APOLLO 13

As made famous by the critically acclaimed film *Apollo 13*, the badly damaged spaceship had a unique timing challenge in reentering Earth's atmosphere. If the command module came in too shallow, it would bounce off the atmosphere (to likely never return), but if it came in at a too-steep angle, the astronauts would be killed by the fire and heat of reentry. Earth's gravitational pull sped up this process: Apollo 13 accelerated as it approached Earth's surface. The team had to make course corrections *quickly*.

Coupled with this concern was that of battery power. Apollo 13's critical command module (where the pilots sit for takeoff and landing) had suffered a power shortage early on in the journey, so the team would have to rely on battery power to enter Earth's atmosphere. They had to carefully calculate *how long* they'd rely on the attached lunar module for power, and when to activate the battery supply to safely make it home. They switched to the battery power a nail-biting two and a half hours before splashdown, which, much to the world's relief, led to a safe arrival back on Earth.

The McLaren cars, however, didn't perceive the Ferrari's tactic to be a real threat: the Ferrari would have to retain a massive lead to be able to squeeze in a third pit stop and hold on to the winning position. The two McLaren racers would take back the lead while the Ferrari was refueling in the pits. There was *no way*, the McLaren cars assumed, that the Ferrari could get that far ahead, so they did not make any adjustments to their strategy.

Brawn, however, knew that the Ferrari could hold on to the lead if the car raced "19 qualifying laps." Qualifying laps—completed during the preliminary races as cars vie for a spot in the race—are typically faster than racing laps. Ferrari would have to push the car to its limit to hold its advantaged position.

The last ten laps before the Ferrari's final pit stop were pivotal. The Ferrari took advantage of its lighter fuel load while the McLaren vehicles, 66 pounds heavier due to their fuel load, lumbered behind. They were further slowed by their softer tires, which weren't able to grip the road and propel as easily in the heat as the Ferrari's heavier and sturdier tires could. One of the McLaren cars experienced a handling problem, which gave the Ferrari car an advantage as well.

Brawn's gamble paid off: the Ferrari remained in the lead. Even when the red car stopped in the pits for a tire change and refueling for a third time, it retained enough of an advantage to hold off the McLarens. In the end, the Ferrari was the winner of the 1998 Hungarian Grand Prix.

The story of the Ferrari's unlikely winning strategy shows us how a carefully thought-out action plan can make all the difference between a lengthy process and an efficient one. In our organizations, adding what feels like an extra step—whether to vet an action plan, communicate with other departments, or get buy-in from stakeholders—to our decision-making process can help us be more effective and save time in the long run.

"Slow Is Smooth, Smooth Is Fast"

There's a popular saying in the special operators' world: "Slow is smooth, smooth is fast." When operators move more slowly, carefully, and methodically, they don't make as many mistakes. By not acting too quickly to clear and search a house, for example, these operators increase effectiveness and save lives—often their own.

As we've learned so far, timing is not entirely about being early or acting quickly—it's about making the right decisions at the appropriate time and executing rapidly and efficiently for the most favorable results. As our batter in baseball knows, one swing, if executed milliseconds earlier or later than it should be, can produce an entirely different outcome. Similarly, any response to risk that otherwise accounts for Risk Control Factors—such as bias, diversity, or adaptability—but is ill-timed may be insufficient.

In this chapter, we began by looking at Taiwan's successful response to COVID-19, a case in which swift decisions united with equally rapid execution. The late decision-making efforts during Hurricane Katrina told a more cautionary tale. Finally, we saw how a counterintuitive strategy to stop more often during a Formula 1 race proved to be the right use of our most precious commodity: time.

While timing is, in all cases, important, the political courage to act coupled with effective levers of management is essential. In the case of COVID-19 and Hurricane Katrina, HHS and FEMA conducted two separate exercises that predicted the risks of an imminent global pandemic on the one hand (Crimson Contagion) and a hurricane that would hit and devastate New Orleans on the other (Hurricane Pam).

Both exercises were conducted *before* the respective crises occurred—and eerily predicted the circumstances that would later arise when COVID-19 droplets dispersed across the globe, and when Hurricane Katrina's winds whipped on New Orleans's famous Bourbon Street. The imminent nature of the threats, as well as the requirements of making decisions and executing actions, were both understood after the exercises were completed—but in both cases, political courage was lacking, and there was weakness in management to react as the situations demanded.

When thinking about timing, it's often helpful to work backward and identify exactly when your organization would like to see the impact of actions. Teams should then zoom out to determine *when* to execute the appropriate response. This way of thinking can challenge organizations to recognize the lag between decisions and execution—to speed up reactive processes and prevent needless delay.

Oftentimes, we make decisions without enough data—firing from the hip to act when the time isn't right—which I don't recommend. Conversely, we must not wait until we have all the information available to make decisions and execute our responses, because when we do, the pandemic has already spread, the hurricane has already made landfall, the competitors have lapped your car. Timing is a careful balance that we need to strike—the most robust Risk Immune Systems enable organizations to achieve the timeliest response to risk.

YOUR TURN

What determines the timing of your decisions?

What outside factors or constraints inhibit your ability to act at the right time?

What decision-making processes need to be recalibrated to improve timing?

THE BOTTOM LINE

A correct response to a threat can be entirely ineffective if poorly timed. Acting too early can be as wrong as acting too late.

CHAPTER ELEVEN

Adaptability

WILLING AND ABLE

*Fosbury goes over the bar like a guy pushed out
of a 30-story window or like a reluctant parachutist out
of a plane's hatch.... The crowds were laughing
so hard they didn't notice he won.*

—JIM MURRAY, *Los Angeles Times*

| *If it's stupid and it works—it isn't stupid.* |

THE FOSBURY FLOP

Dick Fosbury took a series of deep breaths. Wearing a blue shoe on one foot and white on the other, he pitched forward to run the circular route toward the high-jump bar, set at an intimidating 7' 4¼". He'd failed on his first two attempts but now shocked the 1968 Mexico City Olympic Games, and the entire high-jump world, by clearing the bar to win the Gold Medal.

Fosbury's victory was *itself* a surprise; he was not the favorite to win, and he was in one of the Olympics' most competitive high-jump fields. More shocking than his win, however, was *how* he won. Rather than use the popular straddle technique to haul himself horizontally over the bar, Fosbury cleared the height by taking his lanky 6' 4" body over *backward*.

It is still a sight to behold. Fosbury soared through the air headfirst and belly-up, arching his back over the thin bar, as his legs, tipped with spiked shoes, flew until his body collapsed into the foam pit. The crowd was

*Dick Fosbury was an engineering student who experimented
with new high-jump forms—and found great success.*
(AP PHOTO/FILE)

stupefied watching the success of this nonconformist technique. Fosbury
not only won but also set an Olympic record.

The "Fosbury Flop," as it is informally known, is a fascinating demonstration of adaptability. Dick Fosbury, a twenty-one-year-old Oregon State
civil engineering student athlete, struggled for years with the more popular
jumping techniques, studying and experimenting to find a better way. He
realized that by arching his back he could keep his center of gravity *below*
the bar—an advantage that would give him better control to clear it.

In an earlier time, his approach would have been dangerously imprac-
tical. But the hard landing grounds of the past—gritty sandpits, piles of
sawdust, heaps of wood chips—had evolved into cushiony foam pits in the
1960s. Now that it was safer to try bold maneuvers without great risk of
inducing head or neck injury, high jumpers like Fosbury adapted their
techniques to compete.

Adaptability connotes both the willingness and the ability to change.
Fosbury knew he couldn't win using the conventional techniques, so he
had a clear incentive to try something different. Because he was *willing* to
push the boundaries (other coaches would frantically read the rule books

to see if his new technique was allowed) and *able* to execute the new approach due to safer landing pits, he adapted.

At the next Olympic Games in 1972, twenty-eight out of forty jumpers competed using the Fosbury Flop. In 1988, all but one jumper used the technique. Fosbury's daring maneuver is now the standard in the high jump.

The willingness and ability for individuals or organizations to adapt to changing conditions is central in determining who wins; in the face of risk, adaptability decides who survives and who doesn't. Our Risk Immune System must be capable of determining when adaptation is necessary and then execute the changes required to meet emerging risks. We must maintain our willingness to change but be thoughtful of how we do so—always dialing in to take a closer, more critical look at what the impacts of change will be.

Whenever we talk about adaptability and change, we often refer to Charles Darwin and his theory of evolution: the "survival of the fittest." But the comparison is not really correct. Darwin defines adaptability in terms of survival—much higher stakes than successfully clearing a bar at track practice—and those who have the desired traits within an environment survive. Species of flora and fauna, his theory argues, can change and adopt new structures, behaviors, and physiology over time to best survive, but the individuals within the species cannot *themselves* adapt within their lifetimes. Organisms that have advantageous traits pass them

1. Geospiza magnirostris.
3. Geospiza parvula.
2. Geospiza fortis.
4. Certhidea olivasea.

Darwin observed how different species of finches developed variations in their beaks, arguing later that species survive in their environments based on fortunate mutation.

down to their offspring; adaptation, then, is a natural by-product of reproduction.

This is a slow and brutal way to adapt. For better or worse, Darwin argues, *you are what you are*, and adaptation in the moment is not an option. For organizations and individuals, it implies a fatalistic outcome.

Thankfully, we are not bound by the gifted Englishman's model of evolution. As both individuals and organizations, while we are often impacted or constrained by outside factors, much of our ability to adapt to the myriad risks that emerge lies within us. We can assess and consciously improve our system's adaptability—and live to see the results.

SYMPTOMS OF ADAPTABILITY STRUGGLES

Two Beats Behind. Teams that do not adapt lag their more agile competitors—with predictable results.

Frozen by Fear of Failure. Frightened by the specter of failure (or accepting responsibility for an adaptation that didn't work), leaders and their organizations remain unchanged as failure overwhelms them.

Supercharging a Losing Engine. Teams that rely on a relentless pursuit of maximizing an approach they have long used—unwilling to adapt to changing conditions and competition—watch the ship of progress sail by. Soon after Fosbury's win, competitors who didn't do the Fosbury Flop were weeded out of the competition.

Unable to Innovate. Organizations so set in their ways fail to look up, see what the new world demands, and innovate accordingly.

"Why Didn't I Think of That?" Teams that don't have an adaptive mentality are often stumped as to why they hadn't thought of cutting-edge solutions to new issues and problems.

NAPSTER DISASTER

Shawn Fanning had his eyes set on attending Pittsburgh's Carnegie Mellon University. But his application was rejected, so instead he went to Boston's Northeastern University, sporting the closely shaved haircut that became his signature look—a "Marine-doubling-as-Metallica-fan." It would be on Northeastern's campus that Napster—the technology that would delight college students, anger record labels and artists, and change the music industry forever—was born.

Napster appeared publicly on the first of June in 1999. The program, once downloaded, tapped into users' hard drives to access their music. After logging on to the internet, users could search for songs that existed in other users' hard drives and download them on their own devices through a peer-to-peer (P2P) file transfer. In other words, after one participant purchased and loaded the MP3 files on their computer, logged into Napster's central server, and designated their music directory as "shared," it was available for all Napster users to download. It was like a potluck dinner and all-you-can-eat buffet combined, where every person brought music to the site and then sat down to an endless feast of free music.

But there was a problem. Although Napster spared users the cost of purchasing CDs, the actual music wasn't free—it was pirated, in violation of copyright law.

Napster didn't last long, but while it was in full force, it sapped millions from the music industry—and the industry fought back. Individual artists, concerned that they wouldn't be fairly compensated for their work, sued the start-up. The Recording Industry Association of America (RIAA) eventually brought Napster to court for copyright infringement and won. Napster had to change its model to include filtering technologies to impede the exchange of illegal MP3 files. By the end of April 2001, the number of songs available to each registered user declined from 220 to 37.

By July 2001, Napster was forced to shut down its network and disappoint registered users—which stood at seventy million at the business's peak. The company declared bankruptcy in 2002.

Though ultimately unsuccessful, Napster created a new standard and expectation for music consumption. The role of the consumer changed: no longer chained to expensive sixteen-dollar albums, consumers discovered the satisfaction in being able to select and listen to whatever song they wanted for free or at a very low cost. And they liked it.

Record labels, however, were initially unwilling to change their models of music production and distribution—and therefore did not adapt to the industry's changing landscape. Instead, they assumed that once Napster shut down, business would resume as usual. Albhy Galuten, the senior vice president of Universal Music Group from 1995 to 2003, said that record companies "perhaps were a little smug and confident" about their own business in light of Napster's collapse, and failed to consider how "consumer adoption, the youthful lack of respect for copyright, and the anonymity" would make digital distribution "unstoppable as a model."

Put bluntly, record companies had a good thing going and didn't want to change that. Embracing digital music would undercut lucrative CD sales, and executives didn't relish negotiating new record deals with artists to account for digital music. In the end, they believed that the pain in paperwork wasn't worth the prize—the heyday of CDs could be extended.

In his book *Appetite for Self-Destruction: The Spectacular Crash of the Record Industry in the Digital Age*, Steve Knopper argues that if record labels had joined forces with Napster in February 2001 and enticed customers to purchase ten songs every month for a dollar each, the partnership would have brought in more than $1.5 billion a year.

They'd also have access to the start-up's then 26.4 million users, its flexible pricing model that catered to listeners' preferences, and its successful methods to communicate with customers, saving overhead on supplies like trucks, crates, and music stores typically associated with album sales.

But neither Napster nor the record industry wanted to join forces— illustrating the disconnected nature of the old systems and new innovations. While Fosbury had experimented and adopted an entirely new approach to high jumping, the nineties music industry was unwilling to do the same.

For example, Sony, both an entertainment and a consumer electronics company, was afraid that its listeners were pirating music. Before the iPod and the ascendance of Apple, Sony developed the MiniDisc for users to store numerous full-length albums—knowing very well consumer appetite for storing and playing music. But "frozen by its fear of piracy," Sony failed to innovate in the market and create an appealing product for users to select and store individual songs on a device.

TALE OF TWO CITIES

∎

Pittsburgh, Pennsylvania, once the center of American steel, sits atop a rich seam of nearly sulfur- and slate-free coal. By 1910, the city was producing twenty-five million tons of steel—60 percent of the nation's total output. But the loud clangs of America's steel mills began to quiet in the 1970s as foreign competition, decreased demand, and shifts in manufacturing battered the industry.

Pittsburgh, however, achieved a renaissance, and now it is recognized as a center for research, technological innovation, and education. The city boasts a strong "eds and meds" economy with the University of Pittsburgh, University of Pittsburgh Medical Center (UPMC), and Carnegie Mellon close by, and it has renovated its riverfront to attract tourists. Investors have also sought to make Pittsburgh an epicenter for start-ups. No single hero brought about this large-scale adaptation—the city simply underwent a series of small changes.

Flint, Michigan, suffered a similar kind of collapse. Once called "Vehicle City," the birthplace of General Motors faced economic devastation as the automotive industry slowly shrank. But Flint did not achieve Pittsburgh's transformation. Today it is more commonly remembered for the 2014–19 crisis involving tap water contaminated with lead and a resultant Legionnaires' disease outbreak than for its industrial heyday.

Admittedly, Flint did not have Pittsburgh's resources—neither the sums of philanthropic money nor the universities. Its city leaders wanted to create downtown attractions (which would come at the expense of Black neighborhoods), and there was talk of a freeway and modern factories to stimulate the economy, but these efforts failed, and over time, the city became even poorer, and more racially and politically divided. Often good intentions and even thoughtful planning are not enough—adaptation is complicated business.

Pittsburgh and Flint, like Fosbury, sailed backward over the metaphorical high jump—leaping into uncharted territory as the ground shifted beneath their feet—but only Pittsburgh successfully adapted to clear the bar.

If the conundrum resembled a three-legged race, where hardware and the new demands of entertainment latched two legs together and stumbled into the future, Apple entered the contest with a niche market that would rise above these contradictions—providing the hardware (iPod) as well as the platform (iTunes) where users could purchase and store their music. To prevent the piracy that Sony had so vehemently avoided, iTunes made deals with record labels. This move headlocked Sony into allowing Apple to take over the digital music market.

Albhy Galuten from Universal Music Group explains that record labels had two choices: "Either you don't do a deal with Steve [Jobs], in which case people continue to just email the MP3s to their friends, or you do a business with [Jobs] and he has a store, and then you can sell things." Most major record labels chose the latter—and Apple stormed forward, claiming the digital market that Sony and other more traditional record labels had failed to obtain.

Ever since, the music industry has continued to adapt, eventually moving away from downloading models toward streaming services, such as Spotify, Pandora, YouTube Music, and Tidal. These companies follow a model similar to Napster's: they allow users to cherry-pick the individual songs they want to listen to rather than require them to commit to purchasing an entire album. Additionally, these services, with the exception of Tidal, scratch the free-music itch by offering basic plans at no cost. Users can upgrade for a reasonable price.

Artists have also had to adapt to this new reality of music production and distribution that reduced the amount of royalties they once received with more traditional record, cassette, and CD sales. Taylor Swift famously criticized Apple Music for not paying royalties during its three-month free trial period, and others have aired similar grievances—continually requiring the streaming services to adapt and consider their royalty payout models.

At the same time, musicians, especially those who are up-and-coming and who do not have the platform and reach of celebrities like Taylor Swift, must continually seek out new ways to reach potential listeners and generate income streams from their music. As a result, they (at least pre-COVID-19) spend more time on the road touring and making their money from concert sales. When the pandemic made those options infeasible, artists released new surprise albums and employed new mediums to make music (and money) outside the existing infrastructure.

Adaptation is ongoing and iterative within an industry, as well as across enterprises—as organizations have to jump new bars, with new shoes, and at new heights, to achieve the shifting definition of success. Fear of change is only natural—adaptability requires the ability, willingness, and, I'd argue, courage to dare to become something different.

THE iPHONE KILLER

What do rubber boots, paper, televisions, and mobile phones all have in common? Nokia Corporation, a multinational telecommunications, information technology, and consumer electronics company based in Finland, has had a hand in producing all of these products on a massive scale. Started as a paper mill in 1865, Nokia adapted into a telecom business in the 1990s.

The Nokia 9110 Communicator is a cell phone dinosaur, but at the time, it was one of the hottest items. When the phone was closed, it was your typical dialing phone, but when opened, it had a computer screen and a full QWERTY keyboard—and access to the internet. The device was a revolutionary and intriguing technological feat.

Throughout the 1990s, Nokia climbed the ladder to become one of the world's premier telecom businesses and notably the top manufacturer of mobile phones in the latter half of the decade—a position the company would hold for more than ten years. The phones look like walking clichés

The Nokia 9110 Communicator was once the sharpest mobile device on the market.

now—nearly indestructible, clunky pieces of archaic mobile power—but they were in vogue in their day.

Nokia strode forward into the new millennium, devoting time and energy into research and development. Their efforts paid off even as new competitors entered the space: in 2007, the company held on to 50 percent of the market share for mobile phones. In 2009, they put their Nokia 5800 on the market, turning heads with what press called the "iPhone Killer" that was coming after Apple's touchscreen products. Nokia eventually joined forces with the software company Symbian, and the resulting market dominance became a source of Finnish national pride as users around the world carried their devices in purses and in pockets.

By now it's a familiar story: hubris and inaction soon took over, and Nokia rested on its laurels as Apple, Android, and Microsoft crept into the market. Apple made a splash in January 2007—but Nokia maintained a strong lead, shipping 115 million devices in the first quarter of 2008 as Apple trailed behind with 1.7 million. At this point, Samsung, another competitor, had only a 15 percent share of the market. Why worry, when the competition was so far behind?

There were many reasons to fret. While Android, Microsoft, and Apple prioritized software and built their hardware to accommodate their operating system, Nokia relied on outsourced Symbian software that differed between devices.

Its phones' systems were clunkier and harder to use. But more important, the purchasing psyche had changed. Nokia once prided itself on producing indestructible phones with tireless battery life; the alternatives on the market, especially the iPhone, were quicker to die and easier to crack and break. It turned out that new customers didn't care that they now had to plug their devices in overnight, nor were they concerned about damaging their phones. The phone had *changed* consumer preferences—not the other way around.

It was a shift Nokia hadn't been prepared for, and its declining numbers showed it. The year 2009 was particularly bad: in a mere twelve months, the company hemorrhaged 70 percent of its market value. By April 2012, Apple's market cap had grown sixty times greater than Nokia's. The bread and butter of its business—its devices and services revenue—

fell 40 percent that year. The company tried to make other smartphones but to no avail.

Nokia was forced to do the unthinkable: offer its highly prized devices and services business, which historically provided 90 percent of its revenue stream, to Microsoft, who at the time was attempting to develop its own mobile brand. The money from the sale would help keep Nokia afloat. The company had changed seemingly overnight.

Failure, however, need not be permanent—even in a ruthless technological era where progress waits for no one. Although Nokia no longer dominates in the mobile device market, the company is now firmly in the network infrastructure space. As Nokia chair Risto Siilasmaa relays, "Anytime anybody in the world sends a bit into the Internet, be that email, or video, or music, it will go through some Nokia equipment or Nokia software somewhere along the way. That's almost guaranteed."

How did Nokia manage to accomplish such a large-scale shift? Through what Siilasmaa calls Nokia's "distant cousin," also known as the firm's "corporate orphan": the Nokia Siemens Networks (NSN).

Historically, NSN was an independent company that Nokia and Siemens jointly owned—because the two companies' respective investments in 3G and 4G technologies were too pricey for either to shoulder by itself. NSN focused on telecommunications infrastructure and was long regarded as a "money-losing sinkhole" as Nokia set its eyes on its more lucrative devices and services division. The market was dominated by Chinese companies, and Nokia long struggled to expand, or sell, what it saw as a runt of a business.

But that changed in 2013, when Siemens sold its stake in NSN to Nokia. Thanks to an increased investment in mobile network infrastructure, as well as company reorganization, for the first time, NSN was making money. To reflect the company's autonomy from Siemens, NSN was now called Nokia Solutions and Networks. At one point in 2013, the success of Nokia Solutions and Networks helped keep the flailing devices and services unit afloat as its sale with Microsoft was being finalized.

As Siilasmaa recalls, the "ignored distant cousin . . . had begun to metamorphose into perhaps not quite yet the heir apparent but certainly something that looked increasingly and intriguingly attractive." The small shifts of change turned into a full-scale evolution.

Like the clunky phones of the 1990s, the old Nokia soon became obsolete. Less than 1 percent of the company's one hundred thousand employees today worked in what was once the old Nokia. Nokia has also made a series of acquisitions in the past few years, most notably the telecommunications equipment company Alcatel-Lucent, which increased Nokia's customer base, expanded the breadth of its assets, and even enabled Nokia to tap into Bell Labs—which had produced cutting-edge developments from which Nokia could benefit. Today Nokia is focused on offering the only end-to-end 5G network portfolio available on a global basis.

Though exhausted from the trials and tribulations of selling its beloved identity to Microsoft, Nokia leaned hard and turned the ship anyway—with the wind finally at its back. In the end, its failures, although painful, offered the opportunity to turn its weaknesses into strengths in order to survive, and thrive, amid a changing landscape. In the same way, we can remain open to the possibility of transformation—though the shift feels trying, the effects are promising.

Efficiency Reconsidered

In 2003, when I took over the Special Operations Task Force, the organization had been purpose-built around efficiency. It was a rational approach to maximize the output from resources—to make the most X with the least Y. For years, this system served us well. As long as what was required of us was relatively consistent and predictable, structures and processes could be tweaked and retweaked to be as efficient as possible. However, whenever the unexpected emerged, this reliance on efficiency became challenging. A machine designed and finely tuned to cut grass can't suddenly perform as a sewing machine. And even a good user's manual won't turn a trained technician into a competent bricklayer.

So, when both our foe and the operating environment in Iraq evolved, we discovered we were fundamentally unprepared. Faced with the options to adapt or fail, there was no real choice. Transforming our operating model and culture into a collaborative Team of Teams with more robust communication networks became an imperative.

To adapt, the Special Operations Task Force had to overcome an almost reflexive resistance to change in order to reshape roles and responsibilities to cope with the problem set we were presented. We could not allow ourselves to be like the 1990s record labels. We could not ignore the effects of a disruptive enemy and expect old methods to compete in new environments. Like Nokia, we had to accept a new reality and change.

In the end, we all must find the willingness to fundamentally adapt our responses to risk in our changing environments if we are to compete and survive.

Efficiency alone is not enough to guarantee success and survival. Our teams require the willingness and ability to change to the conditions that are ever shifting beneath our feet. Organizations must identify interdependencies and address contradictions before competitors can circumvent them. Additionally, they need to be aware of the second-order ripple effects of change and be unafraid of integrating the old with the new.

Adaptability is rarely ever comfortable and often requires us to find new ways to jump to clear higher and higher bars—but it is an absolute necessity.

YOUR TURN

Is your organization positioned to adapt to changing conditions?

Does a preoccupation with efficiency inhibit your ability to adapt?

What other factors inhibit your ability to adapt to changing conditions?

THE BOTTOM LINE

Every threat is different—so too must be our responses. Constantly changing threats demand continuous adaptation.

CHAPTER TWELVE

Leadership

THE INDISPENSABLE FACTOR

*I pledge you, I pledge myself, to a new
deal for the American people.*

—FRANKLIN DELANO ROOSEVELT,
ON ACCEPTING THE DEMOCRATIC
PARTY NOMINATION FOR
PRESIDENT, JULY 2, 1932

> *Leadership, more than any other factor, can
> make the system function or fail.*

BUILDING A ROAD TO RUIN

The most painful part of my preferred running route in Alexandria, Virginia, is a steep hill on Braddock Road, named after the British major general Edward Braddock. At an intersection at the bottom of the rise, a small rusted cannon sits atop a modest pedestal of stones that once cobbled the city's streets. The gun, one of Braddock's originals, was placed there in May 1915, presumably with some ceremony by the Colonial Dames of America, to mark the route used by the expedition that carries the general's name. The cannon remains there to this day, most passersby unaware of its origin.

At the onset of the French and Indian War in the spring of 1755, Braddock's forces used the road, then a rough dirt track, in a campaign to capture Fort Duquesne, a French position located at the confluence of the Monongahela and Allegheny Rivers in what is now the city of Pittsburgh. The effort was part of an ongoing mission to prevent the French from expanding into the Ohio River Valley. Two hundred fifty French regulars and Canadian militia, supported by Native American warriors from several different tribes, would defend the fort located on ground that would later become the center of American steel production.

The 650-foot uphill stretch in Alexandria, at the very outset of the march, was not the most difficult leg of Braddock's 250-mile journey to Fort Duquesne. Reaching it would require Braddock to move his force of 2,100 soldiers, including two professional infantry regiments of British soldiers, militia from several of the colonies, and a massive wagon train of artillery, ammunition, and other supplies, well into the frontier. Ultimately, the force would have to travel through 120 miles of difficult, heavily wooded terrain and cross the Allegheny Mountains before Braddock could engage the enemy.

Nothing about the expedition was easy. Although a seasoned military officer of Britain's highly regarded regiment of Coldstream Guards, Braddock had to focus on coalescing his diverse force into an effective team and wrestle with the complexities of logistics in the American wilderness. To ensure a trafficable supply line for the duration of the operation, Braddock had a small army of axmen hack out a crude but usable road, an effort that slowed their movement. To complicate matters, Braddock also found himself with an inadequate supply of pack and draft horses, and an unreliable band of colonial contractors who often failed to secure foodstuffs and other supplies.

The commander of such an undertaking might be forgiven for concentrating on these vexing logistical challenges rather than focusing on the repeated warnings from veterans about frontier warfare against the native tribes. Militia leaders—including twenty-three-year-old George Washington, a lieutenant colonel in the Virginia militia and already a veteran with a bitter defeat imprinted on his memory—warned Braddock that combat in challenging terrain against irregular enemies was both different and dangerous. Even the Duke of Cumberland, in faraway Britain, relayed the king's concerns to General Braddock about operations on such unfamiliar terrain against the French and their Native American allies.

However, Braddock, considering the superiority of his forces over the French, as well as the professionalism of his two British regiments, did not expect winning the actual battle to be the biggest challenge. He reasoned his forces were well equipped for the fight.

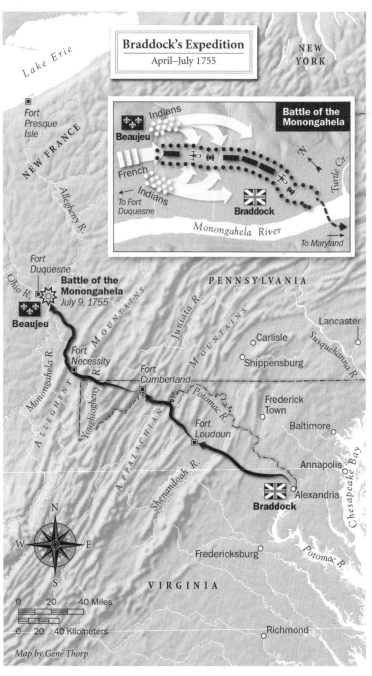

Braddock's troops made the long 120-mile trip to
Fort Duquesne through the Allegheny Mountains.

On July 9, 1755, as his army approached Fort Duquesne, it appeared at first that Braddock's assessment was correct, and on the French side confidence wavered. But Native American warriors, initially concerned about confronting an enemy of this strength, were won over when the French commander appeared before them bare-chested and in tribal war garb, inspiring them to battle. They sallied out to engage the British in the forest before they could reach the more open ground around the fort.

Although hoping to ambush the approaching redcoats, the French and their tribal allies were unable to get into position early enough, and the fight quickly became a confused "meeting engagement." The well-trained British regulars initially formed ranks and loosed devastating volleys of musket fire against their foe. But almost immediately the warriors and their French compatriots maneuvered to the flanks, instinctively using the thick foliage and broken terrain. Unable to catch more than glimpses of their elusive foe, Braddock's forces soon collapsed into panicked retreat that ultimately left the British and their militia battered in a bloody rout.

Major General Braddock himself was wounded while trying to rally his soldiers and died four days later; his body was buried, and the column marched over the site to prevent his remains from being located and desecrated. Perhaps ironically, when replying to Benjamin Franklin's letter that warned of the dangers of attack, General Braddock had referred to the Native Americans as "savages," writing: "These savages may, indeed, be a formidable enemy to your raw American militia, but upon the King's regular and disciplined troops, sir, it is impossible they should make any impression."

Whenever I walk part of Braddock Road or stand on the site of Fort Duquesne, not very far from where the Pittsburgh Steelers play football on the refurbished banks of the rivers, I become fascinated, although not surprised, that the battle resulted as it did. The British had numerical and armament superiority, and the French and Indians had not been fast enough to set and spring a clever ambush for the initial attack. But in a confused melee, Braddock's army simply fell apart as the battle progressed. The loss by the 44th and 48th Regiments, two British regular army units, was unexpected. In the end, their failure appears to have come down to leadership.

What does that really mean? How can one man's poor leadership be the ultimate reason for defeat of an entire army?

To be sure, Braddock's strategy was flawed from the start. His plan to besiege Fort Duquesne with heavy artillery burdened his already slow-moving column, eventually causing him to divide his force. Braddock wasn't, as some might suggest, cowardly, stupid, or incompetent—he'd proven his abilities and expertise during his career. Nor was his army lacking in talent, including professional British officers schooled and experienced in war, and a complement of capable colonists, including George Washington, as well as a young wagon driver named Daniel Boone. Even during his fateful defeat, Braddock displayed stoic courage. Arguably, Major General Edward Braddock was "just what the doctor ordered" in having the skills and expertise to forge a force and defeat the French.

But the fact remains, the sixty-year-old Braddock, despite his training and experience—and in some ways perhaps because of it—was unable to

Though the British were superior to the French and Indian forces,
the Battle of the Monongahela, as it is formally known,
was an embarrassing defeat.
(BY ROBERT GRIFFING; PUBLISHED BY PARAMOUNT PICTURES INC.)

leverage the advantages he possessed over his enemy. He refused to heed repeated warnings that combat against the French and their native allies in this wilderness differed dramatically from traditional European military habits. When confronted with a complex challenge in an unfamiliar environment, he was incapable of providing the kind of leadership required for the force to adapt to the situation.

Washington biographer Douglas Southall Freeman sums it up well:

> Braddock, of course, was entirely ignorant of the type of combat that prevailed in America. What was worse, he was not a man to learn. He lacked all originality of mind and exemplified the system that produced and schooled him, a system traditional, methodical, and inflexible. A man of his training was not apt to fail to do everything the regulations and the accepted tactics prescribed. It was still less likely he would do anything more.

SYMPTOMS OF WEAK LEADERSHIP

An Unclear Mission. The organization does not understand what it's trying to do. This is all too common.

Lack of a Strategy—or Failure to Follow It. There is a lack of alignment across the team on "how" the mission is to be accomplished. Often strategies brief well but are either unrealistic or simply ignored.

Poor Communication. The parts of the organization that must be coordinated and synchronized don't talk to one another.

Inability to Seek Information and Adapt. Teammates fail to raise their head and look around the horizon to adapt to conditions as they are and will be.

Poor Morale and Cohesion. Team members lack a sense of belonging and commitment to the organization—and to one another.

The System Doesn't Function. The leader fails to make the overall system work—to pull together and function. This is difficult to measure directly, but it is the ultimate test.

It is generally accepted that Braddock's Defeat was due to a leadership failure, but what exactly does that entail?

THE INDISPENSABLE FACTOR

Leadership determines how well the entire Risk Immune System interacts to function. Where leadership effectively stimulates and coordinates the other Risk Control Factors, the Risk Immune System is strong and resilient. Where it falls short, even strengths in one or more areas may prove unable to prevent failure.

In Braddock's case, his ineffective leadership impeded his command's ability to assess and respond to an unknown foe—creating a vulnerability that put the command, and the lives of his men, at great risk. Major components of Braddock's column, by design and tradition, had a clear structure, a narrative of professionalism, an inclination for action, and a technological advantage over their enemy. Against a familiar foe, such as European forces in English territory, they would have likely fared well. In the unsettling environment of the American wilderness, however, Braddock's biased attitude, failure to leverage diversity of thought, and reluctance to adapt led to fatal *systemic* vulnerabilities in his force—causing a humiliating defeat.

In short, Edward Braddock's real leadership failure was his inability to keep his army's Risk Immune System from functioning effectively.

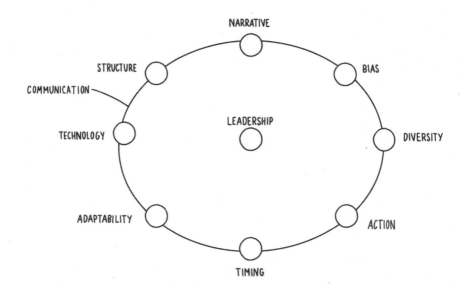

We tend to look for leaders to provide something few ever really could—salvation from the things that threaten us. But the more constructive analysis would be to acknowledge that the real requirement in the people who lead us is not status but actual *leadership*, or the ability to effectively oversee the multidimensional Risk Control Factors—to turn the dials, so to speak—to enable the Risk Immune System to operate successfully.

"THIS NATION ASKS FOR ACTION, AND ACTION NOW"

In early March 1933, the president-elect of the United States was a fifty-one-year-old stamp-collecting Harvard graduate who had been left partially paralyzed from the waist down by polio. Franklin Delano Roosevelt, or FDR, as he was known, had served as assistant secretary of the Navy during World War I and later as governor of New York. But in the minds of many, he was an unlikely figure who lacked the gravitas of most of the thirty-one commanders in chief who had preceded him.

When FDR entered the Oval Office, the task ahead was indeed daunting. The stock market crash of October 1929 had matured into the Great Depression, an economic calamity that was spreading across the globe. America's gross domestic product had fallen 30 percent since 1929, ten thousand banks had failed, and more than 24 percent of workers were unemployed. Worse, a frustrated malaise had settled over the nation as initial actions taken to address the situation, largely conservative fiscal and tariff moves, had had little effect. Like dominoes falling one after another, the pillars of American economic prosperity, confidence, and social cohesion toppled to the ground. The United States, once an energetic economic juggernaut, had stalled. For many, the very premise of the republic's greatness, a nation formed "of the people, by the people, for the people," came into question.

Perceptively, Roosevelt, although a scion of America's elite, understood that his nation's population was vulnerable to a loss of belief in the political and economic system. Democracy is an exercise in compromise, and capitalism requires faith that talent and hard work will be rewarded.

In March 1933, America's faith and commitment to both concepts were wavering. It was not a great leap to see autocracy and fascism spread from Europe and Asia to the United States to infect George Washington's "great experiment, for promoting human happiness." Confidence and resiliency, Roosevelt concluded, must be restored to a society growing increasingly brittle and prone to crack.

Put differently, America's Risk Immune System, battered and struggling, needed to be tended to and rebuilt.

When Franklin D. Roosevelt accepted the Democratic nomination, he told the American public of his plans for a "new deal" to draw the nation out of its economic malaise. Reflexively empathetic to the hopes and fears of the nation, Roosevelt believed that as the president he would need to define his role as chief executive from manager to cheerleader, unlike his predecessor Herbert Hoover, who had a more restrained approach.

The newly sworn-in president's inaugural address set the tone. On a cold, gray day on March 4, 1933, Roosevelt laid the course for his twelve years in office and offered an extraordinary glimpse into what soldiers would describe as a leader "shaping the battlefield" for the fight ahead. Beyond his memorable declaration, "the only thing we have to fear is fear itself—nameless, unreasoning, unjustified terror which paralyzes needed efforts to convert retreat into advance," Roosevelt communicated a compelling narrative of where the country needed to go, and he set values-based guideposts for the route we would take.

Beginning with an energetic hundred-day burst of activity, Roosevelt largely executed the strategy he'd outlined that first day in office, and he did so in the face of often vociferous opposition from various individuals and interest groups.

On Sunday, March 5, 1933, President Roosevelt declared a "Bank Holiday" to close—and stabilize—banks for four days. When Americans waited that Thursday with bated breath for the banks to reopen, he extended the bank closure for another three days. Tensions rose.

The following Sunday, citizens across the country crowded around their radios to listen to the first of Franklin Roosevelt's fireside chats. Worried parents, many with curious children sitting on the floor around them, leaned close to hear what the new president had to say. Then FDR's strong, soothing voice reached out to the nation:

> My friends, I want to talk for a few minutes with the people of the United States about banking—to talk with the comparatively few who understand the mechanics of banking but more particularly with the overwhelming majority of you who use banks for the making of deposits and the drawing of checks.

Immediately, by addressing the nation's citizens as friends and acknowledging their financial anxieties in language anyone could understand, the new president began to put an entire nation at ease. Roosevelt didn't minimize the magnitude of the challenge, but he signaled absolute commitment to solving it. He explained that the government would inves-

President Franklin D. Roosevelt addressing the nation
and allaying their concerns during one of his "Fireside Chats."
(PHOTO BY UNDERWOOD ARCHIVES/GETTY IMAGES)

tigate banks, closing some, opening ones that were "sufficiently solvent," and assisting those that could be viable.

During those fifteen minutes on the radio, Roosevelt assured Americans that "it is safer to keep your money in a reopened bank than it is to keep it under a mattress," and when the banks were open again for business on March 13, people slowly began to redeposit their savings—a small act of faith in the future. Within the next two weeks, more than half of the funds Americans had removed nationwide had been returned.

The stock market also responded. On the New York Stock Exchange's first full day of trading after the closure on March 15, it boasted the single largest percentage price increase ever recorded. With money moving back into the banks—and the public's confidence rising slowly like stacks of coins and bills—Roosevelt turned to systemic banking issues that had necessitated such closures in the first place. In June 1933, Roosevelt signed the Banking Act of 1933 that separated commercial banks from investment banks and created the Federal Deposit Insurance Corporation (FDIC) to protect the savings of everyday Americans. The creation of the Securities and Exchange Commission (SEC) would follow the next year.

To help set and implement the program, Roosevelt leveraged a notably diverse group of advisers. They included veterans of the "Brain Trust," a group initially composed of Columbia University professors who worked with Roosevelt during his presidential campaign to brainstorm solutions to the social and economic issues of the day. He would intentionally force advisers who had different views to work together. The friction would make productive fire as they experimented their way through the New Deal.

To be sure, Franklin D. Roosevelt was not a perfect leader without personal flaws; neither was he immune from missteps. In 1937, after having won reelection in a crushing landslide over Republican Alf Landon, Roosevelt, frustrated with repeated opposition to New Deal initiatives from the conservative Supreme Court, proposed a plan to overcome resistance by increasing the size of the court with handpicked justices. In retrospect, this was a bad idea that reflected a combination of frustration and arrogance.

Overall, however, President Roosevelt had a master political leader's Fingerspitzengefühl, or *fingertip feel*, for assessing opportunity or risk, and a knack for deftly tailoring his message and actions to the audience or conditions at hand. Inclined to rapid action, he leveraged a remarkably diverse range of talent from the Brain Trust and his mass of advisers to advance or retreat in the right moment. And he used the technology of the day—the radio—to speak directly into the homes and hearts of the American people. As a result, Roosevelt's opponents found him both frightening and exasperating—the wheelchair-bound chief executive was maddeningly difficult to pin down or stop.

Against the odds, FDR's leadership established a robust and resilient Risk Immune System.

WHAT LEADERS DO

For most of my lifetime, I've studied, watched, and emulated leaders I admire. I'm not alone: my father, who graduated from West Point right at the end of World War II, described to me how, in the wake of General George Patton's armored thrust across Europe in the final year of the conflict, a number of Patton imitators appeared in the Army. Some reflected only flashes of the famous tanker's flamboyant persona, but others, as my father described, adopted ivory-handled pistols and coarse language in a pitiful attempt to be someone they weren't.

But when I graduated from West Point thirty-one years after my father (ironically, Major General George Smith Patton, Patton's also flamboyant son, handed me my diploma), I still didn't quite know what kind of leader I wanted to be—besides, perhaps obviously, *a good one.*

Now I think the more fundamental question is, *What do good leaders do?*

In the preceding chapters, we described a multidimensional Risk Immune System. The ability of that system to mobilize and energize a combination of Risk Control Factors through effective leadership determines how well organizations respond to the endless cavalcade of threats that arise. For example, think of a nuclear power plant technician manipulating a dashboard of dials to produce power while avoiding an explosion or a meltdown—in a sense, that's what a leader does.

THE PERFECT COVID-19 LEADER?

Of course, no one has done everything right. But judging by the range of qualities and behaviors we've seen—what might *very very good* look like for the next crisis?

Communication skills will be paramount. Prime Minister Jacinda Ardern of New Zealand addressed the fears of citizens by doing Facebook Live briefs (like FDR's Fireside Chats)—sharing the reality of the virus, explaining rationale for decisions, and instilling hope.

Adaptability has differentiated leaders. Some have pivoted their employees to working from home, changing how teams operate and their businesses function—leveraging technology in new ways. Taiwan, under Tsai Ing-wen, employed the best technology available: the Public Warning System and tracking systems to locate and isolate potentially infected citizens.

Crises demand action. Some Asian leaders, leveraging SARS pandemic experience, such as Hong Kong's Carrie Lam and South Korea's Moon Jae-in, acted quickly and aggressively to keep infections low. Governor Gavin Newsom moved swiftly to shut down California, but saw that success largely undone when the state reopened early.

Leaders are made, not born. So it is not unhelpful to identify and seek out the qualities and behaviors needed for the inevitable "next time."

This chapter provides two contrasting illustrations of leadership. On one hand, Major General Edward Braddock, schooled in the craft of European warfare, stuck to what he knew, even when the gauges were all screaming for dials to be adjusted and tactics to be modified. The devastating result was Braddock's Defeat, the general's infamous loss in the French and Indian War. On the other hand, the wily and, to some, "slippery" President Franklin D. Roosevelt made a habit, almost a fetish, of continually manipulating the tools at his disposal—policy, advisers, and communication—in an effort to bring the US financial system to full capacity.

To be clear, the best leaders are not instinctively Machiavellian puppet masters, and leading by personal example remains essential and effective, but at the end of the day, leaders don't actually do very much themselves—they help individuals and organizations perform. And they do this by acknowledging that every situation is different—and context is everything.

Generals who flawlessly fought the last war typically lose the one they're actually in—because conditions have changed and they haven't. In the same way, leaders get frustrated when something that resonates brilliantly with one group—like the young, for example—falls flat with another, like those of middle age. Skilled leaders develop the ability and willingness to sense the context of a given situation and respond accordingly.

So how does a good leader apply *the indispensable factor* of leadership? Leaders must determine the context of the situation, assess what's needed, and drive adjustments for each Risk Control Factor.

Communication, the essential enabler of the Risk Immune System, doesn't happen spontaneously. As we saw in Chapter 3, natural reluctance, even outright resistance, to sharing information must be overcome through demanding leadership and personal example. Leaders must also constantly monitor potential intentional and unintentional misinformation. At the end of the day, the leader must *know*, not just hope, that communication is flowing. Get that wrong and your ship won't hit any icebergs—because you're dead in the water.

Narrative, or the story we tell about ourselves, is powerful, and it begins with leaders. But if an organization espouses values or objectives that aren't reflected in its own words and behaviors, a critical "Say-Do" gap emerges. Nothing produces cynicism faster or undercuts credibility within an organization like the disconnect between narrative and reality. Leaders must ensure and personify the validity of the narrative.

Structure, or how we organize ourselves to function, goes a long way to determine how all of the Risk Control Factors interact. Leaders are critical in designing the organization's structure, while also acknowledging that a flow chart never fully reflects how an organization actually works. Running an organization is like maintaining an aging gasoline engine: leaders must constantly monitor, tweak, and coax the structure to be a strength, not a hindrance.

Technology, the increasingly omnipresent component and determinant of how well an organization operates, cannot be a "fire and forget" solution that is implemented and then endured. As the Soviets learned through Lieutenant Colonel Petrov's unlikely disobedience, technology can have unanticipated consequences. It falls to leaders to be constantly aware of how technology can be incorporated, calibrated, and leveraged to best support the needs of an organization.

Diversity, often confused solely with gender or racial representation, actually reflects an organization's commitment to ensure a spectrum of expertise and perspectives, and in a larger sense, a desire to access a broader range of talent, leaving no one who can contribute on the bench. Without deliberate effort from leadership, most teams will select members who look, think, speak, and behave like they do or come from a similar background. Leaders must consciously build the team that's most effective, and that rarely means the one that is most homogeneous.

Bias, the conscious and unconscious assumptions that influence what we believe, are often as comfortable as building a team of like-minded people—and just as dangerous. Leaders have the power to leverage biases, and the responsibility to leave them behind. In 1964, President Lyndon Johnson, a product of Texas and a member of the traditionally segregationist southern component of the Democratic Party, chose to lead the nation in a different direction that resulted in the Civil Rights Act. Leaders must acknowledge the biases that exist and steer their organizations to a better course.

Action, our willingness and ability to overcome the inertia that inhibits an organization from *doing,* is essential to survival. The video rental giant Blockbuster learned this lesson the hard way: its failure to act when the time was right led to its demise. In the same way, although the signals may not always be clear, it falls to leaders to posture the organization to see and respond to them—and to push to overcome reluctance to action.

Timing means acting when the moment is right. Although organizations often know they must act, overcoming inertia or knowing when to wait for the best opportunity requires good leadership. As the failed relief efforts during Hurricane Katrina show us, it is easy to delay doing what must be done, and leaders must be able to control the trigger—decisions like that are rarely made by committee.

Adaptability, or the willingness and ability to change when needed, comes naturally to chameleons but not to organizations. Adapting often means leaving behind the old and embracing something new long before the necessity is evident—and that's where leaders must have both the foresight and the courage to drive change.

Leadership is central to calibrating our Risk Immune System—a complicated, multidimensional construct—for optimal performance. Leadership is not a mechanical process governed by rigid rules—but rather an art as much as a science.

Leaders are necessary to make the entire system work.

FEEDING THE DOG

For most of my military career, and still to this day, my mentor is an Army officer with a thick southern accent—evidence of his Alabama upbringing. From the beginning, Major John Vines, later a lieutenant general who commanded both the storied 82nd Airborne Division and XVIII Airborne Corps—each in combat—provided me with professional advice and homespun wisdom of stunning value.

One of his favorite sayings was about assigning clear responsibility: "If three people are responsible for feeding the dog—the dog is going to starve."

If you're not sure who's responsible, it's time to figure it out. If you're a leader, and unless you can confirm others have the responsibility—you probably need to assume you do.

Is leadership facilitating or inhibiting the Detect—Assess—Respond—Learn process?

How does leadership help the Risk Control Factors function individually and in concert?

From your leadership perspective, what factors need the most work to ensure your Risk Immune System is performing?

Do members of your organization identify with and feel committed to the organization—and to each other? How can this unity be promoted?

The Risk Immune System is an organic process but it does not function automatically. Leadership is essential to orchestrate the interactions and synergy of the Risk Control Factors.

Part Three

STRENGTHENING THE SYSTEM

DOING WHAT WORKS

The Special Operations Task Force of previous wars had been smaller and composed of a homogeneous collection of professionals. Some wore the high-and-tight haircut of Rangers, some sported shaggy manes and impressive mustaches. But all moved with the physical presence of athletes and the confidence of men who'd done this before.

Now, as one operator told me, the force was a bit of a "shit show." The room where we met was a former Iraqi aircraft bunker. It was the size of an auditorium and required innovative use of hanging foam to deaden the noise of scores of conversations and frequent PA system announcements. Some of the old hands complained that this setup was something alright, but it wasn't Special Operations.

But although the Special Operations Task Force had a new look and feel, it was still a lethal force combating Abu Musab al-Zarqawi's al-Qaeda in Iraq.

That day, as we had been for two and a half years, but particularly over the past three weeks, the force was honing in on the Jordanian-born terrorist himself. Watching the Special Operations Task Force focus was a sight to behold. From a small area near the western wall of the bunker, members of a national agency were providing telephone and computer communication intercepts. As a small team sent frequent HUMINT, or human intelligence, reporting updates, a bank of tables holding consoles carried downlinks of full-motion video from unmanned drones watching over multiple targeted areas.

Twenty or so operators in the middle of the room planned, replanned, adjusted, and coordinated potential operations as we sought to posture ourselves for the moment when definitive intelligence of Zarqawi's location could be confirmed.

Various technologies supported the hunt and communication was constant. In the past, the team would have looked like clones of actors in old-fashioned action movies, but now it was shockingly diverse. Old guys, young women, doctors, lawyers, logisticians—they all leaned in. Outwardly they may not have looked intimidating, but by early that evening, because of them, the iconic terrorist Zarqawi was dead.

This Special Operations Task Force had successfully completed many critical missions before, and would do it again. Developing the capacity to function as a team had been a long, hard-earned skill that took some time to master—but in the end, that is what wins.

CHAPTER THIRTEEN

Game Time

*Boston's freeway system is insane. It was clearly designed by a
person who had spent his childhood crashing toy trains.*

— BILL BRYSON, *The Lost Continent*

> **Against the greatest threats, winning is
> most often the product of teamwork.**

Going Underground

At first glance, the concept was simple: move critical traffic arteries in
downtown Boston from surface highways and unsightly elevated thor-
oughfares into spacious tunnels, which would provide enough capacity to
unlock the city's daily traffic gridlock and return valuable land to other,
more people-friendly uses. What could be hard about that?

As it turned out, almost everything.

From its earliest proposal in 1982, everything about the project that
ultimately became known as the "Big Dig" was massive. The plan to build
161 lane miles of roadways, half of which would be underground (and
some underwater), through a busy city without interrupting the teeming
activities of the metropolis was not only huge but also audacious. The
project also aimed to connect key roadways, extend the I-90 Massachusetts Turnpike, rework critical interchanges, and build new bridges over
the Charles River.

The "gee whiz" statistics support this: 541,000 truckloads of earth
moved and 3.8 million cubic yards of concrete placed. But perhaps more

stunning was the use of then cutting-edge technologies and techniques to build gargantuan tunnel sections with the countless utilities and other equipment necessary for them to be safe and efficient. And this was no "green field" construction environment. Tunnels had to thread their way under a city already crossed by America's oldest subway system and other "below ground" realities of a long-existing urban area.

But it got done, and when completed in 2006, twenty-four years after planning commenced, and sixteen years after construction began, its impact was unquestionable. Traffic flow improved and Boston's historic downtown reclaimed land, and an ambience, that had long been lost.

Just as it's better to eat sausage than to watch it being made, finishing the project wasn't always pretty. The Big Dig suffered challenges and failures on a massive scale. Completion was eight years behind plan, and the original cost, estimated at $2.6 billion, swelled to $14.8 billion. The public was bombarded with stories of improperly mixed concrete and a ceiling collapse that killed a motorist who was using the new roadway. Corruption—some charged—was endemic, and haphazard planning was inadequate to meet unexpected problems with weak soil, underground utilities, archaeological discoveries, and the like—all of which slowed progress and increased costs.

Arguably, the problems encountered by the most technically difficult highway construction project in the nation's history should have been better anticipated. And in the aftermath, Andrew Natsios, CEO of the Massachusetts Turnpike Authority who oversaw the Big Dig project, thoughtfully observed:

> The political controversy surrounding this Boston's Big Dig could have the effect of throwing cold water on any plans for farsighted infrastructure development around the country.

This and similar experiences often breed a feeling that we're in an age when, although badly needed, government can't accomplish big things anymore. That's not always the case, but in confronting daunting challenges—government doesn't work automatically—it takes effort. And in early 2020 just such a challenge was once again on Boston's doorstep.

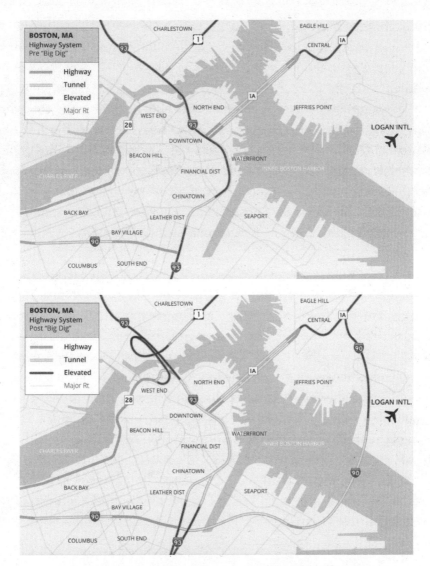

As these before and after maps show, Boston's Big Dig project aimed to better connect the city—freeing up roads and minimizing traffic.

THE BATTLE BEGINS

Every city considers itself unique, but Boston can make a pretty convincing case. Known for its enthusiastic sports fans, recognized for the twenty-nine college institutions that enjoy academic admiration, and remembered for its rich history that stems from the 1630 settlement of the

Massachusetts Bay Colony, it is a city particularly rooted in the cause of American independence. Having lived there in the mid-1990s, my wife and I feel a special connection to every aspect of it—except the winter weather.

Massachusetts's major metropolis watched intently as its southern neighbor (and frequent competitor), New York City, took the first on-slaught of COVID-19. While New York City's hospitals filled, Boston re-viewed its readiness for a pandemic. Relevant plans existed, but most had been prepared with little expectation of actual execution, and gaps and seams invariably emerged. Those had to be closed—and then some.

As they readied, Bostonians were unaware that COVID-19 was already within the "city walls."

Unlike a more conventional enemy, COVID-19 approaches quietly, with little fanfare, announcing its presence only days after its arrival. For Boston, the full assault commenced on February 26, 2020, as 175 execu-tives of the biotechnology firm Biogen gathered from around the world and checked into the Boston Marriott Long Wharf Hotel for a confer-ence. Unbeknownst to the participants, this was to be a "super-spreading event." The gathering—examined through scientific study of the genetic sequences of the COVID-19 virus transmitted—likely led to the infec-tion of twenty thousand people in four surrounding counties in the state by May.

With a foothold established, the dominoes fell rapidly. On March 8, the city recorded nine total cases. On the tenth, the Commonwealth declared a state of emergency. The Boston Public Health Commission followed suit with a public health emergency on March 15. On March 17, Saint Patrick's Day, schools shut their doors. On March 20, Massa-chusetts passed a grim milestone with its first recorded death from the coronavirus.

Girded for War

Soldiers often remark in frustration, "We have to fight the war we have, not the war we wish we had." Books and movies make earlier wars feel more heroic, more straightforward, and less complex than the one you're in. I suspect that's always been the case.

Governing can be a lot like that. Leading is typically a full-contact sport in which success demands leveraging a wide range of organizations and personalities against an ever-changing set of challenges to the well-being of the people. At the city level, governing departs sharply from the theoretical and enters into the realm of the practical. Transportation systems must run, hospitals must serve patients, schools must educate, and these and a host of other often-forgotten services must operate—every single day.

The business of government has a rich history in Boston, a city of roughly 695,000 with a greater metropolitan population of nearly 5,000,000. It is behind the colorful stories and proud traditions that business gets done. The obvious arms of municipal authority—the city's fire, police, and sanitation departments—function alongside less-often discussed public health, housing, and services arms, and together they keep the capital city of the state of Massachusetts the living, thriving organism that it is. Juggling the countless requirements to make Boston a city in which all of its interests are balanced—from financiers to tourists, from teachers to the homeless—and striving to meet these needs with both effectiveness and compassion are always difficult. In early 2020 it was about to get much more so.

As COVID-19 approached, Mayor Marty Walsh, the fifty-three-year-old son of Irish immigrants who had settled in the working-class neighborhood of Dorchester, watched intently. In his sixth year as mayor, Walsh, a former labor union president and state representative, understood how his city operated—and he had managed a massive crisis before.

Five years earlier, in the winter of 2015, more than nine feet of snow pummeled the city. Bostonians are no strangers to snow: when it comes down in giant heaps, people simply plow and shovel it out of the way and move on. So that winter the city braced itself for its first blizzard of the season, recording just over two feet of snow through January 26 and 27. But with barely any respite, another storm came the following week, adding sixteen inches to the growing piles. And the following week yet another blizzard arrived, adding twenty-two more inches of snow. Bostonians were swaddled by snow for *ten weeks* straight—the heaviest downfall in Boston's snowy history.

What began as a typical winter season quickly turned into a citywide emergency. With new piles of snow arriving week after week, city services couldn't clear it out of the way. Recognizing this, Mayor Walsh, early in his first term, prioritized making the roads workable and safe, reaching out to other northeastern state governments to secure heavy equipment to move and melt the massive piles of snow. He organized the plowing and storing of the snow into "snow farms" around the city where the downfall could be piled and safely melt. When the governor issued a travel ban to protect citizens' safety, Mayor Walsh instituted a parking ban in the city. He canceled school early on so that parents could find other arrangements in time.

Snowstorms came weekend after weekend. Cars already buried under
snow were further covered as the accumulation piled up.
(AP PHOTO/ELISE AMENDOLA, FILE)

Walsh internalized a key leadership lesson—to decide and act early. These measures would pay off later when infected droplets, not snowflakes, would cover the city. As COVID-19 emerged, the mayor knew that the dynamics of a pandemic would be similar to that of the "Snowmageddon" of 2015, where he'd juggle normalcy with crisis and have to take quick action, be adaptive, and be honest with the public.

But how serious a threat was the novel coronavirus?

Like many others, Marty Walsh was not overly concerned at first. He remembered the containment of SARS and doubted that COVID-19 would make it to the United States as any appreciable threat. His feeling continued through the first weeks of the new year, but it was challenged when a student newly arrived from Wuhan, China, brought the first case to Boston. The student was isolated, and the mayor hoped that this diagnosis would be the last.

The first few days of March proved him wrong, as more cases sprung up as red dots on the city's map. By this point, the mayor had switched his perspective and acknowledged a virus of this type *would* be in Boston— the question now was how many people it would infect.

The answer began with a handshake—or, more accurately, the lack of one.

With questions about the virus in the back of his mind, but the city's economy front and center, on the morning of Wednesday, March 4, 2020, Mayor Walsh—along with Kathryn Burton, soon to be sworn in as his chief of staff—met with Eric Rosengren, president of the Federal Reserve Bank of Boston. Mayor Walsh, now on the third year of his second term as mayor, was eager to hear Rosengren's long-term views of the economy. The conversation took a different course, however.

It began as soon as they entered the room. In a departure from his normal practice, Rosengren would not shake Mayor Walsh's hand, a rejection of traditional physical pleasantries. And the discussion that followed was radically different from what the mayor had expected. Rather than cover projections for the city's economic growth, Rosengren devoted thirty-five minutes to what he assessed to be the most pressing issue—the looming threat of COVID-19. The city would have to shut down its economy and schools, he warned, and he then delivered a gut punch: Boston could not host its traditional marathon on the third Monday of April.

It was one of the most intense meetings Mayor Walsh had ever attended. If Rosengren's grim prognosis was accurate, the city would have to screech to a halt and take previously unthinkable steps to contain the pandemic—and do it right away.

Seeking a more scientific opinion, Walsh met with Dr. Jeffrey Leiden, the executive chairman of Vertex Pharmaceuticals, to confirm or deny what Rosengren had predicted. Dr. Leiden shared a similar assessment, and his medical concerns complemented Rosengren's economic forecast. Not long after, Brian Golden, one of the mayor's key advisers and an Army reservist, provided another data point: a major Army exercise had been canceled due to worries about COVID-19.

These three perspectives, piled on top of one another like the snow on the streets in 2015, convinced Mayor Walsh that COVID-19 would be a far more serious threat to his city than he'd previously realized. Direct, aggressive action was required, and the mayor mobilized his team.

But nothing about governance is simple, and in the face of a pandemic it is hellishly complicated. From the start, the mayor and his team recognized that the challenge they faced wasn't simply surviving the tsunami of health-care and financial impacts of COVID-19, which would hit the most physically and financially vulnerable the hardest. From experience, they knew that the city's normal operations also had to continue unabated even as they were reacting to this new crisis in real time. Operations like the education system had to continue under vastly different conditions. Remote learning and other adaptations—perhaps merely discussed in theory in the past—had to suddenly become a reality.

To further complicate the problem, there had been no lead-up. Instead of being able to study the virus for months, reorganize functions, and formulate a deeply researched defensive strategy, the virus was already upon them. Necessary changes had to happen now. And rather than gathering the leaders and stakeholders in city hall to hash out the details, almost everything had to be done virtually—in many cases, by people who required the help of their teenage kids to coax home videoconferencing systems into working.

Simply put, Mayor Walsh and his team had to govern faster and more collaboratively than ever before—and do it under the challenges of COVID-19.

"LET'S KICK SOME ASS TODAY"

Kathryn Burton hadn't expected to start her job in the middle of a global pandemic. Burton, born in Canada but experienced in Massachusetts government, began her role as Mayor Walsh's chief of staff on March 9, 2020. She'd jumped into the whirlwind of a new position in a city government about to undergo some dramatic changes. Just over two weeks later, she was tasked to lead Boston's daily Crisis Response Forum meeting.

Walsh and Burton recognized that for the city to work its way through the pandemic, they had to radically communicate on a new level. And at the outset they found themselves struggling with conflicting data and sources of truth, and lacking one confirmed information-sharing platform.

The solution they arrived at proved instrumental in the city's ultimate success.

Both Walsh and Burton knew they'd have to strengthen the lifeblood of their governing system and connect all relevant stakeholders (such as governmental departments, hospitals, essential nonprofits) throughout the city onto a singular communication forum—from which the COVID-19 responses would grow. Here, the city could deal with issues large and small and solve problems in real time, driving unified operations for the city of Boston during the pandemic.

On March 25, 2020, the Crisis Response Forum daily video teleconference call, or the CRF, was born. The CRF started promptly at 8:00 A.M. each morning and lasted an hour. The few employees working from the Mayor's Office would brief the rest of the team from their floor in Boston City Hall, while the other stakeholders called in from kitchens, living rooms, and home offices.

Burton led the session—which reminded me of the Operations & Intelligence video teleconference that had been so critical to my Special Operations Task Force in Iraq—and she drove a disciplined agenda. The briefer would appear on screen when it was their turn to communicate updates about the past and upcoming twenty-four hours and report on needs for resources. As the participants listened to the briefs, they connected and collaborated in real time with other stakeholders, cut deals, and coordinated with other team members.

At the end of each CRF, Burton would present a list of tasks for each group that *had* to be completed by the next CRF—the mayor's team relentlessly tracked those action items. Walsh typically congratulated the team on progress reported in meetings, but he was stern and exacting when it came to what must still be done. He would routinely remind the team about the most important aspect of their mission, often invoking his widowed mother as an example of those the city must keep in mind as policies were set and work got done. Unless given a special extension, priority teams had to rapidly check their action items off their list, acting swiftly and effectively to ensure that they kept up with the virus's blistering pace.

The shift to remote daily meetings was neither painless nor friction-free for the mayor's team. For those who had long worked in government, the virtual meetings radically changed how they functioned. The mayor had to create a clear narrative about priorities and hold the city accountable to an unyielding schedule of actions and expectations. With steady pressure, he guided his staff to resist the inertia of conducting "business as usual"— trading in bureaucratic churn for fast, declarative action in response to a virus that wouldn't wait. He'd end his CRFs with a five-word phrase of encouragement: "Let's kick some ass today."

No Longer Business as Usual

As a politician and a former labor union leader, Marty Walsh is stereotypically effective at connecting people—not only across agencies but among elected officials and the general public as well. His extensive experience gave him an astute knack for getting the right minds in the room to have the right conversations, even if they didn't always get along.

To combat COVID-19, Mayor Walsh formed eight priority groups to tackle the eight primary strategies that would drive the city's crisis response efforts—which ranged from coordinating the public health response, to supporting Boston's schoolchildren and their families, to soliciting and distributing PPE. This arrangement forced teams to be diverse—in some priority groups, people who typically didn't work together were assembled to actively engage on a shared problem. These groups would meet to prepare their briefs, and in doing so, they would identify gaps in one another's plans, provide solutions to tough problems, and connect their teams to resources. Regardless of whether or not these groups had worked together before, they'd have to come together to provide a unified message during the day's CRF.

Though not without hiccups, this arrangement paid off in a big way. Programs that hadn't worked together before—like two job training and educational programs that served slightly different populations—now exchanged resources and shared meeting spaces. The Food Crisis Working Groups made connections about available resources, using idle school buses (and still-employed bus drivers) to drive around the city and deliver food to children in need.

Connections like these happened over and over again, to the steady drumbeat of each morning's CRF. As the beat of the drum got faster and faster, the responses to COVID-19 issues picked up the pace. Out of these daily meetings came plans consequential to combating the virus: to stage ambulances in such a manner so that patients could get in and out of the vehicles more quickly, and to erect a thousand-bed field hospital, Boston Hope, in only a few days' time. Ultimately, the CRF made way for the Coordinated Leadership Forum, as the Commonwealth's efforts transitioned from response to recovery. Although convened less frequently, these meetings helped the city continually defend against the virus at a predictable cadence.

"Doing My Part"

Should Boston's successful response to COVID-19 be attributed to the leadership of Mayor Marty Walsh, to the city employees' hard work, or to the residents themselves? The answer is actually all three—they were all part of a connected system.

Mayor Walsh, as the leader of Boston, had to make the right decisions at the right time—his fast and aggressive mandates to shut down the city saved lives. He didn't shirk potentially unpopular decisions—like his early cancellations of schools to ensure families had time to coordinate during the 2015 snowstorms—a quality that served him well as the leader of a city fraught with COVID-19.

When asked about his role, however, Walsh rejected the idea that Boston's successful response to the pandemic was "his win."

Whenever someone credits success to Marty Walsh, his response is always the same. "Then Kathryn Burton is Marty Walsh. And Marty Martinez is Marty Walsh. And Emily Shea. And Sheila Dillon," he says, naming his chief of staff, the chief of health and human services, the commissioner of the Age Strong Commission, and the chief of housing and director of neighborhood development. Their efforts and those of many others, Marty Walsh stressed, were the real sinew of success.

The mayor's humility is endearing, and it is partly correct. Members of Boston's extended team got the job done by overcoming hurdles that in less difficult times limited progress on more mundane matters. But in the crisis, largely due to his leadership, they engaged and collaborated as never before. The team performed well because Walsh provided the leadership needed.

Only the mayor himself could make the difficult decisions to shut down the St. Patrick's Day Parade and the Boston Marathon, but he alone couldn't safely build the city back up. He could oversee the CRF, but Kathryn Burton (and all the briefers who were trading information) had to actively participate in order to connect the city in its response. The mayor could keep the grocery stores open and help coordinate the delivery of Chromebooks for virtual learning to students all over Boston, but the brave grocers and teachers had to do their part to keep residents' stomachs full and to keep the children learning.

In his thick Boston accent, Walsh matter-of-factly describes his leadership: "I was just doing my part." Just as all the citizens of Boston were doing every day, he reported to his job.

RISK IMMUNE SYSTEM

Ultimately, Boston's response to COVID-19 illustrates how a successful Risk Immune System is supposed to function. The city rapidly detected the threat of COVID-19, assessed its vulnerabilities to the risk, and responded in kind. The city's robust communication system—driven by daily Crisis Response Forums—as well as the mayor's tireless leadership enabled the team to alter its course quickly and adapt to the threat at hand with a clear, assertive bias for action to successfully lead Boston through the most formidable pandemic the city has ever known.

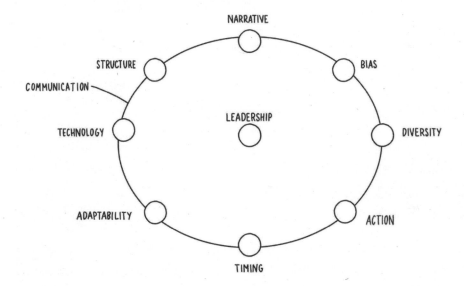

To be sure, Mayor Walsh and his team made missteps that required constant adjustment. But they had their hands on all the right dials, calibrating the Risk Control Factors to operate a connected system. And as time passes, Boston's response to COVID-19 will be remembered as a deep source of pride, not because the city boasted a stable of geniuses who devised a secret weapon to combat the virus, but because it was the product of a group of leaders who understood that they had to change how they operated in this unique environment to ensure their focus was always on what was needed to best protect the city. Facing a similar threat and equipped with similar resources, some governments and organizations performed impressively, but many more did not. Boston rose to the occasion.

Well done.

> **THE BOTTOM LINE**
>
> **Boston succeeded in its fight against COVID-19 because the city consciously focused on making its whole Risk Immune System work.**

CHAPTER FOURTEEN

Building the Capacity

All things are ready if our minds be so.

—KING HENRY V,
IMMEDIATELY BEFORE THE BATTLE
OF AGINCOURT FROM
SHAKESPEARE'S *Henry V*

| *Most battles are won before the contest*
begins—by those who are most prepared. |

LIVING ON THE FAULT LINE

It was 5:12 A.M. on a Wednesday morning in 1906 when the citizens of San Francisco were awakened by a catastrophic noise. The city's historic earthquake, estimated to have been the equivalent of 7.9 on the later-developed Richter scale, set off a devastating train of events—but it also began a process of rebuilding and learning that has been important to this day.

The immediate effects of the quake were disastrous: buildings were damaged and destroyed and many people were killed. But the fires, which began soon after due to ruptured gas lines, were even more lethal. Exacerbated by the use of dynamite to bring down damaged structures, the flames were difficult to control on account of countless quake-severed water pipes. Adding to this challenge was a lack of leadership, as the city's fire chief engineer had been fatally injured in the initial earthquake. In the end, more than 80 percent of the city was destroyed, up to three thousand lives were lost, and half of the population was left homeless.

The fires that followed the San Francisco earthquake
of 1906 were equally, if not more, destructive.

Despite the tragedy wrought, relief and reconstruction efforts rapidly gained momentum, and by 1915, San Francisco had been largely rebuilt and regained the vibrancy for which it had been recognized.

In 1906, the risk of earthquakes was known, but the understanding of their causes was still in its infancy. Advancements in geophysics and instrumentation to predict future earthquakes didn't yet exist, and there was insufficient understanding of how these episodes actually affected the earth, so engineers were unable to adapt construction methods and materials to mitigate their impact. The bitter collision of the progress of civilization and nature's awesome power added both to the pain resulting from the earthquake and to the ultimate value of the experience over time.

Like many risks, the 1906 earthquake was not in man's power to accurately predict. Scientists of the time believed an earthquake *caused* faults to form (when the opposite is actually true) and so had no way of predicting unexpected tremors. But after the earthquake, scientists got to work, establishing the State Earthquake Investigation Commission—the

nation's first ever "integrated government-commissioned scientific investigation" into these disasters.

Committed to solving the riddle of why the earth would periodically
tear itself apart, they hiked the full distance of the rupture to see up close
the extent of the fault's slip, examining the local soil and rock, as well as
the building materials in the affected areas. Scientists created and conducted triangulation surveys that assessed how the angles between fixed
"monuments" changed over time. This ultimately led to the development
of the "theory of elastic rebound" that explains how plates slowly shift and
distort, increasing pressure along a fault, until they slip in an earthquake
to return to their "undistorted state."

The commission's findings were captured in what's known as the Lawson report—named after the head of the State Earthquake Investigation
Commission, the geologist Andrew C. Lawson—and have enabled scientists to better understand the San Andreas Fault system and how the world
has continued to shift since 1906. The research has helped forecast when
faults will slip and the strength of the impending earthquakes. It has also
guided building codes and regional zoning decisions, and assisted in the
conception of appropriate insurance policies for future disasters. Tireless
analysis has empowered San Francisco, and cities around the world, to be
prepared for future earthquakes—even if the time, location, and exact
nature of such events cannot be predicted.

We all live in the shadow of one risk or another. But we cannot allow ourselves to be fatalists. It is a mistake to argue that because we can confidently
predict neither the timing nor the precise nature of emerging threats that we
should act as though the horsehair holding the sword above Damocles's head
will either break or it won't—and simply await our fate. This is not only unnecessarily passive but also a false choice. For even if we do not know when
(or if) the horsehair will break, there is always much we can do to prepare.

DETECT—ASSESS—RESPOND—LEARN

More than anything, the historic San Francisco earthquake of 1906 shows
us that individuals and organizations can indeed prepare for a wide range
of potential risks. We begin by diagnosing the problem and assessing our

own Risk Immune Systems and then look to strengthen the system—as one interconnected whole. A healthy Risk Immune System successfully executes four imperatives: **Detect, Assess, Respond**, and **Learn**.

When functioning optimally, our Risk Immune System will rapidly **Detect** any emerging threat, **Assess** our potential vulnerability and determine how it must be dealt with, **Respond** as effectively as possible, and **Learn** from the process for future use as required. Together, they constitute the process that a healthy Risk Immune System uses to operate effectively, creating resiliency.

Strengthening the Risk Immune System is analogous to training the human body. While we must make each of the Risk Control Factors as strong as possible on its own, we must also acknowledge that most activities require us to exercise a combination of Risk Control Factors. This process naturally looks and feels like teamwork, and in most networks or systems that is often the most difficult part.

But let's do a quick reality check before we go further.

I long ago accepted the fact that even if I matched Michael Jordan's competitive drive, I could never equal his mastery of basketball. Our potential for the sport was simply too unequal. But even if I couldn't reach Jordan's skill level, with hard work and practice I could become adequate on the court. In the same way, we can all tap into our range of talents and resources to stay competitive, and even thrive.

So while it is certainly true that to some extent, like Darwin's dark conclusion, *we are what we are, and there's not much we can do about it*, there is also much that we can do to make ourselves more fit, more able to compete and survive. We must not be like Damocles, too often fearful and frozen when it comes to taking action. Rather, we must take control, placing our hands on the dials of our Risk Immune System.

There are steps we can take, and, like all important journeys, this one starts at the beginning.

TYING SHOES AND MAKING BEDS

In May 2014, Admiral Bill McRaven, the commander of all US Special Operations Forces, gave a commencement speech at his alma mater, the

University of Texas, with a single, powerful message: *every day, make your bed*. The self-discipline of unfailingly executing simple acts, he argued, has an outsize impact on an individual's overall performance and character. Rarely are critical lessons communicated with such elegant simplicity.

Similarly, when talented young basketball players reported to the University of California, Los Angeles, to play for another US Navy veteran, the legendary coach John Wooden, he famously began practice by teaching them how to tie their shoes. Wooden believed in a singular pursuit of excellence, and throughout the winningest career in coaching history, he practiced the tenet that excellence is always built upon the basics. His message was straightforward: "It's the little details that are vital. Little things make big things happen."

When taking command of the 2nd Ranger Battalion, the unit that fifty years earlier had, under intense enemy fire, climbed the cliffs of Pointe du Hoc for the D-Day invasion of Normandy, I realized that it was impossible to know where—or against whom—Rangers would next fight. So I met with the leaders of the unit, and together we decided to establish a training regimen of just four basic tasks—building a foundation of Physical Conditioning (to include long foot marches under heavy loads), Marksmanship, Medical Skills (to provide immediate first aid), and Small Unit Drills. We called these the Big Four.

When I moved up to command the entire regiment, my regimental sergeant major and I implemented the Big Four across training and focused relentlessly on mastery of the building blocks of combat effectiveness.

Ensuring that every single member of an organization is proficient in the basic skills necessary to perform their role is essential to maintaining a healthy Risk Immune System. But even before mastering basic skills, grounding both individuals and organizations with answers to the most basic questions that relate to narrative is essential:

What are our values?
What exactly do we do—and why do we do it?
What is expected of each of us?

The Big Four provided a clear set of expectations for soldiers in what the unit prioritized.

Once each member of an organization has the skills *and* values necessary to overcome risk, it takes collaboration, cooperation, and that intangible magic that we ultimately call teamwork to take it to the next level. And great teams work together—hard.

WORKING OUT

Forging an elite military counterterrorist unit, a sports team, or any other organization follows a remarkably similar model. Team members are indoctrinated in the narrative that reflects the culture of the organization, trained to the needed level of proficiency in a series of individual tasks, and then brought together to perform increasingly complex tasks that demand teamwork to effectively respond to continuously changing situations. Although individual talent and task competence are important, winning and losing on the playing field or battlefield often hinge on how well the team interacts. Example after example can be related about the higher-priced, more accomplished set of players or soldiers that was taken down by a more cohesive set of lesser talents.

Training, or strengthening, your Risk Immune System is no different. Developing the system's core strengths begins with assessing the health and functioning of your Risk Immune System, which then allows you to strengthen individual Risk Control Factors, as well as the interaction of the factors within the system.

Too often we force our Risk Immune Systems to develop their collective capability when risk is at our door—in other words, when we are actually responding to emerging threats. The price of this "on-the-job training" can be expensive. Costly failures in actual operations, where you are facing and reacting to risk in real time, dwarf the investment required to train and develop the system beforehand.

Thankfully, various solutions have proven effective in building this kind of capacity. There is no single "perfect" solution or activity that will develop every part of your system, but a combination of them, like a hockey team running different drills on the ice, can simultaneously reinforce individual skills and collective collaboration.

In the following pages, we introduce eleven specific Solutions. All of them can, and should, be modified to the specific needs of your organization. The Solutions are:

1. *Assumptions Check*
2. *Risk Review*
3. *Risk Alignment Check*
4. *Gap Analysis*
5. *Snap Assessment*
6. *Communications Check*
7. *Tabletop Exercise*
8. *War Game (or Functional Exercise)*
9. *Red Teaming*
10. *Pre-Mortem*
11. *After-Action Review*

But first things first. Before we charge off conducting exercises and drills, let's figure out what's needed most. Begin with an effective diagnosis as outlined in the next chapter.

THE BOTTOM LINE

Readiness for risk is less a function of accurately predicting specific threats and more about building resiliency into the organization through a healthy Risk Immune System.

CHAPTER FIFTEEN

Assessing the System

*At the outset of the fight against al-Qaeda in Iraq we fixated
on understanding our enemy—but it quickly became
apparent we needed to first understand ourselves.*

—LIEUTENANT GENERAL SIR GRAEME
LAMB, FORMER COMMANDER,
UK SPECIAL FORCES

*The surgeons I like best diagnose carefully—
before they start cutting.*

READY TO FIGHT

That morning began early, even though the day before went late. In fact, the lieutenants, the youngest officers in the battalion, had only driven back to their quarters to shower and don freshly starched uniforms before returning to the unit area where the barracks were a bustle of activity.

It was day 1 of our annual IG (Inspector General) inspection, a week-long examination of the organization's health—theoretically our "fitness to fight." And it was high stress. A poor showing was likely fatal to the battalion commander's career. We all felt the associated pressure.

In theory, the five-day diagnostic, which involved inspections of our weapons, radios, vehicles, uniforms, barracks, and every other aspect of the 1st Battalion, 504th Parachute Infantry Regiment (1/504 PIR), would confirm the combat readiness, as well as the health and welfare of the 1970s paratroopers I served with. The standards of the inspectors, on even the most minute details, were famously demanding, but we'd done little besides preparing for more than a month. Six hundred paratroopers, led by professional soldiers, ought to be able to clean and maintain equipment—some of which, like small squad stoves, we never used.

I remember that day, and the preceding weeks, clearly. Our vehicles were showroom clean (even the tires shined), and a special detail had re-cleaned and reassembled every gas mask in the company to ensure individual paratroopers wouldn't do it incorrectly. I remember one inspector offered to get a cup of coffee while one of my fellow officers "found" (meaning quickly produce and backdate) a missing training record (which he'd refused to do), and I can still see images of troopers displaying field equipment they'd purchased just for the inspection (because cleaning their normal field gear was onerously difficult).

Curiously, what I don't remember is whether we passed the inspection.

I presume that we did, but like every other member of the 1/504 PIR, I had no illusion that we were truly ready for war. Overall, our maintenance sucked, our marksmanship was abysmal, and leadership was wanting. In later decades, after the US Army had gone through an impressive resurgence of professionalism, I would describe my first unit to incredulous younger soldiers. I'm sure they assumed that I was exaggerating, but I was not.

Since the dawn of warfare, armies have attempted to gauge their readiness for battle. Analysts tallied the number of soldiers, horses (and later trucks), cannon, and other equipment, and observed formations and field exercises to determine the discipline and competence of the force. Naturally, large, ramrod-straight men with handlebar mustaches moving with uniform precision were impressive, but experienced strategists understood that those qualities only went so far.

To be sure, in warfare, quantity matters. At the Alamo, the pluck and heroism of the roughly 180 defenders couldn't prevent 4,000 Mexican soldiers from overwhelming them. And because experience has shown that force ratios above a certain level reliably produce an outcome, planners are taught that attackers usually require at least a 3:1 advantage in numbers over defenders to succeed. There are always exceptional cases, but as a rule of thumb, rough quantitative measurement is an important metric.

Of course, those measurements must be accurate. Counting tanks that don't run, guns that won't shoot, or untrained soldiers is a dangerous habit. To maintain an illusion of power, militaries often knowingly "gut," or remove, units of soldiers (as the US Army has done several times in our history), while maintaining the overall number of commands. In other cases, as with my unit in 1977, an artifice of readiness was maintained through statistics and inspections that failed to assess actual warfighting capacity. These assessments weren't intentionally misleading, but they were insidiously dangerous.

While quantitative metrics, when correctly measured, can provide one component of an accurate assessment of an organization (certainly a lack of adequate resources, including personnel, is a flashing warning light), the qualitative "yin" to the quantitative "yang" is essential to complete an effective appraisal.

In the case of armies, that qualitative estimation is often elusive and ephemeral. Soldiers' effectiveness begins with training, but experience, morale, unit cohesion, commitment to a cause, and countless other factors intertwine to produce an intangible—but very real—component to the force's combat power. Although all of the paratroopers in our battalion were volunteers for airborne duty, and the majority were well-intentioned young Americans, most lacked the necessary training and discipline. For example, during the annual IG inspection, one paratrooper was caught smoking marijuana midmorning—as the inspection was being conducted.

And the unit's efficacy is heavily, though not entirely, dependent on leadership. Although most armies strive to forge these qualities into reliable strengths, the reality is that the conditions in which the force will fight—which are notoriously difficult to predict beforehand—and the unexpected threats that emerge can become dominant factors in determining the outcome.

MAINTAINING COHESION IN THE FIGHT

In the spring of 1940, with the German Wehrmacht fresh from victory in Poland and poised to attack westward to France, soldiers, politicians, pundits, and populations sought to assess the likely outcome. Although operationally impressive, the Nazis' eastern assault had been against the Poles—and both historically and quantitatively, France's military was a more formidable force.

But Germany's campaign lasted just six weeks, slicing across France with stunning, seemingly unstoppable, speed until France capitulated. The French Army that had mobilized in the fall of 1939 and girded for battle found itself dazed, demoralized, and defeated.

What can we learn from France's searing experience?

If we're not careful, it's easy to learn the wrong things. The image of unstoppable Wehrmacht armored units and Stuka dive bombers pummeling French forces after a daring thrust through the "impenetrable" Ardennes Forest distorts the reality. During the preceding decade, France had constructed the massive Maginot Line to anchor her defense against German invasion (and it largely did), and French tanks, which when combined with their British allies outnumbered Hitler's, boasted more powerful guns and better armor than the German machines. In reality, although the German blitzkrieg campaign was well executed, factors of leadership and France's inability to maintain a cohesive effort did as much to determine the outcome.

While it is prudent to examine potential threats, we *must* look at ourselves, diagnosing the weaknesses and vulnerabilities that are in our control to affect. In May 1940, France possessed all of the necessary components, on both a strategic and an operational level, but couldn't get the pieces to work together. It's a familiar story—time and time again leaders and organizations look outward, instead of assessing how their own internal vulnerabilities determine the strength of their Risk Immune Systems.

But can we *really* do that? Can we really know how the team will play, or how the army will fight, before the contest actually begins? Or are the conditions of competition too unique, too dependent on context, to allow us to accurately predict performance?

The answer is both reassuring and disappointingly tentative. We can, in fact, measure how well our organization's Risk Immune System functions—and those insights can illuminate ways to strengthen it. But the process requires a deft combination of quantitative and qualitative analysis, leavened with the judgment of thoughtful people. Still, this analysis provides the most effective road map for an organization, preparing it for the widest possible spectrum of threats.

MEASURE TWICE—CUT ONCE

The task of assessing a Risk Immune System appears, at first glance, to be a daunting one. Risk Immune Systems are, after all, living, changing structures that ebb and flow as threats arise and weaknesses are tested. But I'd argue that, in concept at least, assessment is relatively simple. It consists of three parts: a quantitative assessment, a qualitative assessment, and a mature judgment of whether things are working as they should be. The three components are complementary—we can only approach accuracy by painting a holistic picture.

Let's start with "mature judgment." What, you might ask, is that? Well, it's exactly what the term implies. Most experienced military leaders can visit a unit in the field or in their barracks and make a relatively accurate assessment of the morale and discipline of the soldiers within minutes. How soldiers wear their equipment, carry their weapons, dig fighting positions,

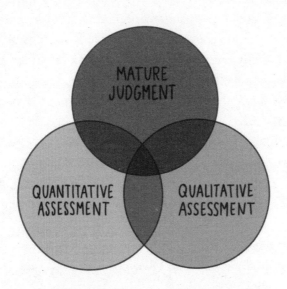

and respond to sergeants speaks volumes to the practiced eye. And an articulate commander with good posture and straight teeth can't convince a seasoned soldier that their unit is better than it actually is.

It comes from knowing what really matters. I remember the initial impressions of some outsiders to the most elite elements of my Special Operations Task Force in Iraq. Beards, casual demeanor, and unusual attire can be off-putting, but veteran leaders noticed immediately that equipment was not only configured to fight but also maintained religiously.

If you want to assess how well a car is maintained, you listen to the engine, take it for a drive, and pump the brakes. In the same way, to assess how well your organization functions, observe your team in action (even if it is just a drill or business war-gaming). If something doesn't work as designed—you can't win games, make a profit, or build products—you don't need any other insights to know that *something* is wrong.

To put it in simple terms, if things don't smell or feel right—trust your instincts. Dig further.

But even if nothing screams mismanagement, it's often necessary and invariably valuable to go further and take a deep dive. Most organizations can conduct both a quantitative and qualitative assessment in a straightforward manner—simply by asking a series of questions. The answers can be illuminating. Here's how using a research-based approach to create quantitative and qualitative assessments can help fill in the picture.

In this case, we are assessing the narrative Risk Control Factor. Leaders should ask themselves the following question and then poll the organization to develop a clear understanding:

Are our culture and actions in alignment with our narrative—and are they consistent across the organization?

Posed qualitatively, the question can evoke open-ended answers from teams and peers that often provide thoughtful insights.

To get a quantitative view, simply change the punctuation to turn this question into two statements for teams and peers to evaluate:

Our culture and actions are in alignment with our narrative.
(1 = Strongly Disagree, 2 = Disagree, 3 = Indifferent, 4 = Agree, 5 = Strongly Agree.)

Our culture and actions are consistent across the organization.
(1 = Strongly Disagree, 2 = Disagree, 3 = Indifferent, 4 = Agree,
5 = Strongly Agree.)

Leaders can repeat this process over and over—combining their qualitative curiosities with a set survey for their teams—whenever they want a snapshot of their Risk Immune System. Taken together, these qualitative and quantitative responses are a formidable combination: the quantitative responses illustrate the problem, while the qualitative answers give data context and meaning.

Despite the value each Risk Control Factor brings to an organization on its own, the real health of the Risk Immune System is determined by its interaction with other factors. I like to think of this as like baseball: the ability of one player to hit it out of the park belies how the entire team will perform as a unit. To make an accurate assessment of how well your organization is functioning, you must explore how the Risk Control Factors operate as a single system. Capture the essential aspect of how the Risk Control Factors interact by asking qualitative questions: How do your biases affect which technology systems you will and won't try? How does your expedited product timeline influence how quickly your team will adapt to customer feedback? How does your team communicate a change in the company's branding narrative?

Based on the nature of your business, your organization will focus more on some Risk Control Factors than others. For example, a fast-food restaurant will focus on timing, while communication and adaptability will be more important for a highway safety authority. But resist the temptation to assess only factors that feel relevant—as Boeing did during the crashes of the 737 MAX.

Pairing your quantitative and qualitative responses will give you a robust understanding of the strength of your organization's Risk Immune System.

FINE-TUNING THE SYSTEM

The greatest risk to us is us. Our own weaknesses and vulnerabilities stand in our way to best respond to and counter threats. That's the bad news.

The good news is this: we have the power to diagnose our own Risk Immune Systems, and to strengthen them accordingly. As you leaf through this book, your own hands are at the dials—you can assess your Risk Immune System, identify weaknesses, and solve for them. Risk is not a menacing specter that we stand before, shaking and powerless; rather, it is an opportunity for us to practice self-reflection and improve ourselves. And diagnosing the problem isn't as harrowing, challenging, or time-consuming as one might expect.

CRASH AND BURN

On October 29, 2018, Lion Air Flight 610 crashed less than thirteen minutes after takeoff—plunging into the Java Sea. Months later, on March 10, 2019, Ethiopian Airlines Flight 302 crashed only six minutes after takeoff. Both planes were Boeing 737 MAX 8 aircraft.

Post-crash analysis placed great focus on the newly installed automated control system of the 737 MAX—when it malfunctioned, the planes were forced into irrecoverable nosedives. Subsequent examination found that the pilots *could* have responded effectively if they had been trained and familiar with all aspects of the new automated system. But the updated control system had largely been left out of their training (and even removed from the flying manual).

While both crashes began with equipment-related situations, the threat was lethal only because the pilots' lack of training left them vulnerable.

Just as the body needs annual examinations, Risk Immune Systems require frequent assessments. When conditions change—for example, competitors enter the market, new teammates arrive with different skill sets, perspectives, and expectations—you need to examine your Risk Immune System. Most organizations do not have the resources to conduct constant training exercises, so these periodic "big picture" assessments are invaluable snapshots of how the system functions day to day, not just in terms of a particular threat.

Rather than see the Risk Immune System as an end to achieve, challenge yourself to see it as an organic, ever-changing process. Adjust as necessary.

As with everything in life, I believe iteration is key. Assess your Risk Immune System once, and then assess it again. Try new quantitative and qualitative metrics. Use novel formats to question your team and always keep track of their reactions and responses. Over time, you'll get better—and your assessments will become more accurate. Like the human immune system, your Risk Immune System will grow strong as it interacts with new threats. Through it all, be vigilant about diagnosing weaknesses when you see them.

The next chapter aims to be a user's guide to create a healthy and robust Risk Immune System by targeting and strengthening any weaknesses revealed by your assessment.

THE BOTTOM LINE

Effectively strengthening the Risk Immune System first requires understanding where it is strong and where it is weak.

CHAPTER SIXTEEN

Symptoms to Solutions

MAPPING WAYS TO STRENGTHEN
YOUR RISK IMMUNE SYSTEM

SYMPTOMS *(Problems You Observe)*	RELEVANT RISK CONTROL FACTORS	SOLUTIONS TO DIAL UP YOUR RISK IMMUNE SYSTEM *(Exercises That Strengthen the System)*
"TWO LEFT FEET" Your teams produce uncoordinated responses to risk. **EXAMPLES:** *Miscommunication at the Battle of Balaclava dooms the Light Brigade.* *US mischaracterization of COVID-19 hinders an effective response.* *Overstock's board of directors fails to rein in an unstable CEO.*	Communication, Structure, Action & Timing	**RISK ALIGNMENT CHECKS** Prompt your organization to consider how different functions are assessing risk. Correcting risk misalignment can lead to a more coordinated response. **GAP ANALYSES** Prompt your team to identify interdependencies and redundancies in its processes and plans—so the team has a singular and even response to risk. **COMMUNICATIONS CHECKS** Allow your organization to examine its processes for sharing information—potentially plugging communication gaps and giving all parties the same operating picture from which to respond to risks. **RED TEAM EXERCISES** Encourage a nonbiased third party to identify weaknesses in responses to risk, flagging where your organization's structure and communication flows breed a mismatched response.

SYMPTOMS *(Problems You Observe)*	RELEVANT RISK CONTROL FACTORS	SOLUTIONS TO DIAL UP YOUR RISK IMMUNE SYSTEM *(Exercises That Strengthen the System)*
"BURYING RESPONSIBILITY" Responsibility for risk oversight is unclear or buried within your organization. **EXAMPLE:** *Lehman Brothers unintentionally undermines the effectiveness of the chief risk officer—ensuring ineffective risk management.*	Structure & Bias	**GAP ANALYSES** Enable your organization to critically assess where the responsibility for tasks lies in your organization—to expose where risk functions could be buried and rendered ineffective. **TABLETOP EXERCISES** Prevent the burying of risk management functions within a team by encouraging your organization (through scenario-based discussions) to identify responsibility and accountability for risks. **WAR GAMES** To pressure-test your organization's plan, bring buried risk functions to the surface and press your organization to counteract risk in a real-time simulation format.

SYMPTOMS *(Problems You Observe)*	RELEVANT RISK CONTROL FACTORS	SOLUTIONS TO DIAL UP YOUR RISK IMMUNE SYSTEM *(Exercises That Strengthen the System)*
"TECH CREATES A PROBLEM" Automated processes that offer speed and efficiency prove to be a two-edged sword, with unintended and sometimes unrecognized consequences—i.e., new risks. EXAMPLE: *Lieutenant Colonel Petrov prevents nuclear war between the Soviet Union and the United States by overriding technical warnings.*	Technology, Communication & Bias	**ASSUMPTIONS CHECKS** Examine how your organization is interacting with technology, and how its usage can create unrecognized vulnerabilities. **SNAP ASSESSMENTS** Use technological platforms in a productive way, to allow your organization to develop a clear picture of threats immediately. These assessments can, in the same breath, illuminate the weakness of such information-gathering platforms. **COMMUNICATIONS CHECKS** Challenge your organization to take a closer look at how its technological systems are sharing important information about risks in real time.

SYMPTOMS *(Problems You Observe)*	RELEVANT RISK CONTROL FACTORS	SOLUTIONS TO DIAL UP YOUR RISK IMMUNE SYSTEM *(Exercises That Strengthen the System)*
"TOO LITTLE OR TOO LATE" Your organization either fails to respond to a threat or acts too late to be effective. **EXAMPLES:** *Officials delay critical decisions in the face of Hurricane Katrina at great cost.* *Special Operations Forces continue to employ counterproductive tactics in Afghanistan.*	Timing, Action & Communication	**SNAP ASSESSMENTS** Give teams a clear picture of the impending threats in real time so that your organization can rapidly adjust its own responses to the risk at hand. **COMMUNICATIONS CHECKS** Acknowledging that the problem with responding to risk often comes from a failure of information arriving fast enough to be effective, these checks examine how information flows through your organization. **WAR GAMES** Compel teams to react to risk in a simulation format, testing how your organization **Detects**, **Assesses**, and **Responds** to risk in a stressful environment. **PRE-MORTEMS** These exercises happen before an event occurs, identifying how a potential response to risk will function in practice so that your organization can make adjustments early.

SYMPTOMS (Problems You Observe)	RELEVANT RISK CONTROL FACTORS	SOLUTIONS TO DIAL UP YOUR RISK IMMUNE SYSTEM (Exercises That Strengthen the System)
"DENIAL" Your organization refuses to see, admit, or respond to a threat—creating serious vulnerability. **EXAMPLES:** *Blockbuster fails to successfully respond to changing market conditions.* *Google ignores disconnects between the firm's culture-defining narrative and contracted business.* *The music industry embraces the status quo at a time when technology is driving fundamental change.*	Communication, Bias, Action, Diversity & Leadership	**RISK REVIEWS** Encourage your organization to get ahead of the curve by periodically taking a closer look at external threats, as well as its own internal vulnerabilities. **ASSUMPTIONS CHECKS** Prompt teams to examine their belief systems that determine whether a hazard is a risk or not.
"AGGRAVATING THE PROBLEM" Actions taken to mitigate risk actually make the problem worse. **EXAMPLE:** *Lehman Brothers renders the chief risk officer powerless, preventing her from intervening in risky decision-making.*	Action, Timing & Adaptability	**ASSUMPTIONS CHECKS** Press your organization to look at its plans for responding to risk, exploring the assumptions that lead it to believe a plan will work. **TABLETOP EXERCISES** Enable teams to have discussions about what actions they will take, what logistical processes they'd employ, what resources they'd like to use to produce a productive (and not damaging) response to risk. **WAR GAMES** Prompt your organization to put its plans into practice, forcing it to act against its opponent, and determine whether its planned solution rightly addresses the problem. **RED TEAM EXERCISES** Bring in a third-party participant to identify if actions will backfire and make a risky situation more hazardous.

SYMPTOMS *(Problems You Observe)*	RELEVANT RISK CONTROL FACTORS	SOLUTIONS TO DIAL UP YOUR RISK IMMUNE SYSTEM *(Exercises That Strengthen the System)*
"IT'S EXTERNAL, NOT INTERNAL" Your organization's tendency to believe that external factors will have the greatest adverse effects prompts it to fail to address its own vulnerabilities. EXAMPLE: *The US government fails to examine its own vulnerabilities revealed in the Crimson Contagion exercise when responding to COVID-19, making an already dangerous virus more deadly for Americans.*	Bias & Leadership	**RISK REVIEWS** Take a broad look at all potential risks to your organization—from external threats to internal vulnerabilities. **ASSUMPTIONS CHECKS** Ask your organization to more deeply consider what it classifies as a risk: external threats, its own vulnerabilities, or a combination of both. **RED TEAM EXERCISES** Deeply consider all the ways a plan might fail, taking stock of both internal and external hazards.
"EFFICIENT RESPONSE BACKFIRES" Your organization's tried and true efficiency-centered model cannot change fast enough to respond to increasingly complex risks. EXAMPLES: *Flint, Michigan, was a city purpose-built around automotive efficiency, yet it failed to adapt (as Pittsburgh had) when manufacturing was outsourced.* *Record companies in the 1990s relied heavily on their older ways of production, failing to update their business plans and processes to compete in the burgeoning digital age.*	Adaptability, Action, Timing & Structure	**SNAP ASSESSMENTS** Assist your organization in rapidly identifying how the environment has shifted for a more agile, adaptable response to the risk at hand—and help it react accordingly. **WAR GAMES** Randomly introduce new scenarios in a simulation, prompting your organization to adapt to changing conditions in real time. **RED TEAM EXERCISES** Be suspicious of old solutions to new complex problems, and leverage a third party to flag how the slow churn of efficiency often stands in the way of more adaptable responses to risk.

SYMPTOMS *(Problems You Observe)*	RELEVANT RISK CONTROL FACTORS	SOLUTIONS TO DIAL UP YOUR RISK IMMUNE SYSTEM *(Exercises That Strengthen the System)*
"DO AS I SAY, NOT AS I DO" Your organization offers contradictory counsel when the leader's narrative bumps heads with the work teammates are completing on the ground. **EXAMPLE:** *"Don't be evil," Google's mission statement, directly clashed with the contracts it was signing and the business it was pursuing.*	Narrative, Communication & Leadership	**RISK ALIGNMENT CHECKS** Prompt your organization to analyze how a team—from a leader to a lower-level employee—is assessing risk. Identify any mismatches in how the team is describing, or interacting, with the hazard at hand. **TABLETOP EXERCISES** Enable leaders to have a scenario-based conversation about risk with their teams so they all walk away with a clear picture of what the leaders and their constituents plan to do in response to risk.
"THE DOMINOES KEEP FALLING" By failing to consider the second- and third-order effects of its actions, your organization invites more risk. **EXAMPLE:** *The Ferrari Formula 1 team in the 1998 Hungarian Grand Prix knew that a radical three-pit-stop race would have advantageous long-term effects against better seeded competitors.*	Communication, Structure, Technology & Timing	**RISK REVIEWS** Challenge your organization to consider all the threats facing its teams—on a repeated basis. **TABLETOP EXERCISES** Encourage teams to map out a response to risk (including the associated effects) well in advance. **WAR GAMES** Create simulations that can test developed plans (and their second- and third-order effects) in real time.

SYMPTOMS (Problems You Observe)	RELEVANT RISK CONTROL FACTORS	SOLUTIONS TO DIAL UP YOUR RISK IMMUNE SYSTEM (Exercises That Strengthen the System)
"LIVE AND DON'T LEARN" The tendency for your teams to continue to make the same mistakes, applying the same solutions to ongoing problems. **EXAMPLES:** *The Crimson Contagion exercise offered a series of recommendations for the US government to best prepare for the inevitable next pandemic—ones that went unheeded.* *The Joint Chiefs of Staff continually recommended aggressive approaches to President Kennedy—even after the failed Bay of Pigs mission.*	Action, Bias, Adaptability, Diversity & Leadership	**ASSUMPTIONS CHECKS** Enable your organization to challenge the assumptions and beliefs that guide how it can **Detect**, **Assess**, and **Respond** to risk so that teams can bring fresh perspectives to risk for a more effective response. **AFTER-ACTION REVIEWS** Assist your organization in aligning around an effort: analyze what went well, what could have gone better, and what elements to sustain and improve for the next time your team encounters risk.

CHAPTER SEVENTEEN

Solutions

THINGS WE CAN DO

The more you sweat in peace, the less you bleed in war.

—GENERAL H. NORMAN
SCHWARZKOPF JR.,
FORMER COMMANDER
OF THE UNITED STATES
CENTRAL COMMAND

*Doing nothing is an option—
often a stupid one.*

SOLUTION #1

ASSUMPTIONS CHECK

American visitors to London will quickly notice warnings painted on crosswalks reminding them that traffic flows in a direction opposite to what they are accustomed. Despite these cautions, pedestrians often find themselves looking the wrong way for oncoming vehicles—sometimes with tragic consequences.

Unconsciously, we often assume things to be a certain way, before being reminded they are not. When we looked at President John F. Kennedy's frustrating experience around the failed Bay of Pigs invasion of Cuba in 1961, we saw a plan constructed on a series of assumptions about the relative weakness of Fidel Castro's military and the readiness of the Cuban people to rise up in opposition to him. It was neither the first, nor the last, time an operation was launched based on a series of invalid assumptions.

*London offers friendly reminders for visitors who
may be unfamiliar with its flow of traffic.*
(CLAUDIO DIVIZIA / SHUTTERSTOCK)

Assumptions are not inherently bad; they are, in fact, essential to developing almost any plan. In the absence of perfect information, planners must make certain assumptions to allow their preparations to go forward. For example, one might need to assume the availability of certain resources, such as money or transportation, or the presence of a yet-unproven market for a new product.

But organizations also need to know how much of this understanding is built on a foundation of fact, and how much of their reality is built on faulty assumptions. Often, assumptions are unconsciously made during planning, as stakeholders assume that what has happened in the past will continue. Our biases can inform our assumptions, affecting the way we see the world and make sense of uncertainty. All assumptions must be questioned and, when possible, confirmed as facts.

During the planning process, it is critical to first identify all relevant assumptions being used and then move to test their validity. The very nature of assumptions is that they cannot be proven to be correct, so the objective of these tests should be to assess the reasonableness and importance of assumptions. Essentially, stakeholders must reflect what they expect (not hope) will happen—and understand the impact if their assumptions prove untrue.

A good assumption, if identified, would remain in place until a fact is known. Once an assumption is revealed to be a bad one, organizations may be required to change plans in their entirety.

An Assumptions Check is an effective way to begin a planning process. Consider the following example:

SITUATION

A popular Virginia-based airline (FlyVA) has hubs in Washington, DC, Newark, Denver, Phoenix, and Charlotte. It had an extraordinary performance the year before, boasting one of the highest percentages of on-time departures in the business, initiating transatlantic service to London, and partnering with new food and other vendors to enhance the customer experience.

But last year is in the past, and as the management team refines its long-term strategy and budget for the upcoming year, members recognize the need to identify and test any assumptions underpinning the plan they are developing.

GOAL

To identify all relevant assumptions baked into the business plan, whether intentionally or unintentionally, then test their validity. The team will discard or adjust any invalid or unnecessary assumptions and refine the airline's plan accordingly.

STRUCTURE OF THE EXERCISE

To ensure an unbiased process, the airline has intentionally selected a neutral moderator to conduct the session, a person generally familiar with the airline business who has no ties to (and hopefully no biases about) FlyVA.

To participate in the assumptions check exercise, management has assembled key leadership from across the normal functions of the business, as well as other employees of the airline from the cockpit to baggage claim, to avoid having blind spots in the process. Because some assumptions will lead to extended discussions, two hours have been allotted for the exercise.

EXERCISE

In preparation for the exercise, participants have received the latest version of the draft budget (business plan) for the upcoming year, and the moderator begins the exercise by asking the CEO, supported by the chief operating officer and chief financial officer, to rapidly review the plan. Nothing new is tabled, but it is essential to establish a common understanding of the plan.

The moderator then leads the groups in compiling a list of the assumptions the plan is based on.

For businesses like an airline, there are a number of categories of strategic assumptions that are typically appropriate. FlyVA has identified:

- **Overall Environment:** Global and national economic environment in which FlyVA operates (e.g., GNP, tax policies, trade barriers)

  In this case, FlyVA sets assumptions on macroeconomic growth rates, inflation, and fuel prices for the coming year.

- **Market Dynamics:** Government actions, speculation, and other factors that impact the industry market beyond normal supply and demand for FlyVA's product.

  FlyVA considers assumptions on COVID-19-related travel restrictions, air traffic control changes, and antitrust actions toward the airline industry.

- **Customer Needs and Demands:** Desires or expectations that drive what the customer will or will not buy.

  FlyVA considers whether customers will fly on full aircraft (post-COVID-19 considerations), and monitors customer feedback on specific factors like frequency of flights from certain locations, onboard entertainment expectations, and fees for checked bags.

- **Action of Other Stakeholders:** Vendors (including aircraft manufacturers), airport management, and other players all impact execution of FlyVA's business.

  FlyVA considers the viability of needed vendors and aircraft maintenance times (given COVID-19's impacts on their workforces, and other supporting efforts).

- **Finances:** The availability and cost of money are essential to a capital-intensive business like FlyVA.

  FlyVA sets a range of expected costs of borrowing and determines potential cash requirements in a downturn.

- **Workforce:** The availability and cost of talent, to include required training, labor relations, and other considerations.

  FlyVA considers employment costs (primarily wages and health care), training, availability of needed talent (primarily pilots and skilled mechanics).

- **Internal Management:** The airline's ability and processes to operate itself.

  While FlyVA has a set of established business processes, it reviews the viability of those processes to identify any that must be significantly overhauled, and whether the airline has the experienced talent in place to execute them. Because IT is so integral to almost every process in the airline, FlyVA specifically reviews the strength of its systems to execute existing and projected processes.

- **Strength and Weakness of Assets:** The value and vulnerabilities in the airline's airport access (gates), maintenance facilities, aircraft (both owned and leased), and other assets.

  Because an airline's strength is more than just airplanes and crews, FlyVA considers the value and viability of all its facilities and equipment.

Once the list of assumptions is complete (and the list above is not intended to be complete), the moderator leads the team through "pressure-testing" each one. Take the assumption about finances and borrowing, for example: FlyVA made assumptions about the range of costs of borrowing money so it can determine cash requirements in a potential downturn. A moderator can pressure-test this assumption by looking at past ranges—making adjustments to account for inflation, to ensure that the business can even survive on the money that would be available in that set range. At this point, the participants may be faced with the reality that the assumptions aren't correct (perhaps the range wouldn't carry FlyVA through a downturn), and accordingly will need to find different solutions within the airline. This process can be completed for the rest of the assumptions throughout the exercise.

Most assumptions are not judged as "correct" or "incorrect," because an assumption about almost any factor can be proven incorrect in an instant. What is critical is to judge whether the assumption is *reasonable* based on available knowledge and then to understand the implications if the assumption proves invalid (as some invariably will).

The most dangerous assumptions are those we make unconsciously, particularly when our biases influence our judgment. The most common is for individuals, and even sophisticated organizations, to assume that things will continue in a certain way, or in an established direction, because that's what our experience has been thus far. It's helpful to remember that things stay the way they are—until they don't.

This exercise was advantageous for FlyVA, and any organization can use it in its planning process. Before the Thanksgiving buying season, a small grocer can run an Assumptions Check on securing, delivering, and selling inventory. A business reopening after COVID-19 may find value in conducting an Assumptions Check as it develops its strategy going forward.

> **BRINGING IT ALL TOGETHER**
>
> An Assumptions Check will specifically strengthen my narrative, bias, and action Risk Control Factors by focusing on what messages I send, testing my preconceived notions, and enabling me to act appropriately.

SOLUTION #2

RISK REVIEW

At heart, health-care practitioners are risk professionals—they identify health hazards that currently, or could, affect their patients. When you stride into a doctor's office for an annual physical—an often awkward, yet necessary, interaction—your physician takes a snapshot of how your body is functioning. Blood tests, height and weight, and a battery of other "system checks" allow your "body mechanic" to analyze your condition and compare the results with your health history. These periodic examinations enable physicians to make critical assessments, prescribe or adjust medications, and recommend other actions as required.

To be most effective, risk should be measured consistently and over time. Knowing the context of your body's performance through the years significantly improves your doctor's ability to effectively assess the meaning of periodic health checks. In other words, knowing what your normal is helps identify what isn't.

We should think about risk, as the product of external threats and internal vulnerabilities, in the same way. It's essential for organizations to routinely assess both hazards and weaknesses to develop the clearest picture of all the risks they face. Snapshot assessments have value, but it is within the context of the broader picture that individuals and organizations can determine what normal, "healthy" operation is, and when to react to changes that can signal rising risk.

The Google we encountered in Chapter 4 may well have benefited from a very thoughtful Risk Review. While the carefully crafted narrative the company had shaped since its founding—"Don't be evil"—was not inherently or automatically a problem, it did reinforce employee attitudes and expectations around certain kinds of work, and their right to oppose it. So, when management decided to partner with the Department of Defense in Project Maven, a significant number of employees who valued the right to communicate their feelings openly put Google's management into a difficult conundrum. A rigorous Risk Review might have identified the tension between emerging business ventures and the firm's narrative and culture as a potential risk to the company's cohesion, as it ultimately proved to be.

Risk Reviews should be conducted regularly within an organization. A detailed annual process with quarterly reviews and updates is usually about right, but when circumstances change significantly, as with COVID-19 or other major events, it is wise to conduct a thorough review of what constitutes risks to the organization more often.

Let's see how our airline does it.

SITUATION

Coming off a strong year, FlyVA still recognized the turbulent, almost fickle, nature of the airline industry, so it took the annual risk review very seriously. So seriously, in fact, that the CEO herself took on the role of chief risk officer and led the process.

GOAL

To identify the risks facing the airline—meaning both the threats and the vulnerabilities surrounding the organization. This review includes risks the organization perhaps hadn't considered and begins to think about ways to avoid or mitigate them. The results of the process will be reflected in the annual Form 10-K filed for the Securities and Exchange Commission and be available to the general public.

STRUCTURE OF THE EXERCISE

Because FlyVA is still a relatively young airline, it begins the process by reviewing risks often reflected in its 10-K filings, evaluating historical records of risks that have emerged to challenge airlines and soliciting input from all parts of the business, to include critical business partners that provide maintenance support, catering, and other key functions.

As the list is created, FlyVA identifies five aspects of each risk:

Source of the Risk: where the risk comes from
Probability: the likelihood the risk will emerge and have to be dealt with
Consequences: the costs or other ramifications if the risk materializes
Indicators: how the risk's emergence can be detected .
Mitigation: what the airline can do to avoid or reduce any consequences

EXERCISE

As the exercise is conducted, FlyVA's CEO and chief risk officer begins by displaying the list of risks assembled from previous years and inputs from across the organization. Each risk is assessed for validity and considers both external threats and internal vulnerabilities. It's critical to view the list as a flexible, living document. Rarely will risks appear exactly as expected but instead emerge in mutated form, or combined with one or more other risks.

Although our airline has assembled a significant list, we will look at just three of the more noteworthy:

RISK: Rising jet fuel costs increase expenses and pressure profits per flight.

Source: Finance

Probability: Medium. Jet fuel prices are an airline's most volatile expense. Although recent fuel prices have been favorably low for airlines, oil prices are notoriously volatile and sensitive to geopolitical and global economic factors. While fuel prices impact all airlines in the long haul, the use of fuel-efficient aircraft types and fuel hedging programs can give one or more competitors a short-term advantage.

Consequences: Any rise in fuel costs can immediately impact FlyVA's profitability.

Indicators: International and political circumstances, instability and conflict in the Middle East, tensions between the United States and oil-producing states, refinery outages, and weather and environmental concerns can all affect jet fuel prices.

Mitigation(s): FlyVA can consider increasing ticket prices, reducing flight schedules to those with relatively high passenger loads, and hedging fuel purchases to avoid subsequent additional rises.

RISK: FlyVA faces labor disruptions.

Source: Human Resources

Probability: High. FlyVA has positive relationships with its labor unions, but like other airlines, it is subject to labor union campaigns designed to pressure the entire industry.

Consequences: Campaigns by labor unions could threaten FlyVA's reputation, and although less likely, prolonged labor strikes would curtail or severely limit the airline's ability to operate until an agreement is reached—with serious adverse economic effects.

Indicators: Labor union strategy announced or indicated (by efforts at other airlines) and/or employee feedback indicating dissatisfaction.

Mitigation(s): FlyVA can work closely with its labor unions to ensure its workers are satisfied with wages, benefits, working hours and conditions, etc.

RISK: FlyVA's IT systems experience a major disruption.

Source: IT Department

Probability: High. FlyVA depends on a combination of its own IT network, as well as a variety of third-party vendors, to operate its kiosks, apps, in-flight wi-fi, etc. Networks may experience malfunctions due to natural disasters, computer viruses, and even hackers.

Consequences: Serious disruptions in customer service, potential delays, and flight cancellations can occur if FlyVA's systems experience disruption. FlyVA may also experience increased costs, compromise client-sensitive data, and lose its own data and revenue. Operational impacts can be huge—reputational impacts can be even greater.

Indicators: FlyVA's IT organization, tasked to monitor its networks for all causes of disruption, should be able to detect hazards immediately.

Mitigation(s): FlyVA has put in place mechanisms to protect data and transfer operations, but the rapid growth of FlyVA systems and their vulnerability require constant vigilance and increased focus on resilience.

The danger of Risk Reviews is that they become a mechanical process that is done with little real thought. I've had experiences with organizations that list their risks, almost any of which could destroy them, but essentially discount them with either "That'll never happen" or "We're screwed if it does, so why worry about it?"

Risk Reviews are not intended to be paranoia-creating exercises, but they should be seriously executed, and the results must not be filed away without action. Instead, organizations should follow up the exercise with real resourcing decisions (e.g., expensive but important cybersecurity expenditures) and an attitude that communicates "If this happens, there will be a day after, and what will we wish we had done, and what will we then have to do?"

BRINGING IT ALL TOGETHER

A Risk Review will make me focus on the timing, adaptability, and action Risk Control Factors: helping my team understand when hazards may arrive, how to be willing and able to change when they do, and how to then successfully execute against our plan.

SOLUTION #3

RISK ALIGNMENT CHECK

Misalignment can be painful. On the morning of July 2, 1863, at the Battle of Gettysburg, Major General Dan Sickles, a politician turned Union soldier already infamous for fatally shooting his wife's lover (and subsequently using the first successful temporary insanity defense), added to his controversial reputation. Sickles cemented his place in history by repositioning his III Corps from their assigned location at the southern end of the Union's "Fishhook" shaped defense to ground he judged better—the Peach Orchard.

Historians have ever since argued over the impact of Sickles's decision to depart from the orders he'd been issued, instructions from the overall Army commander, Major General George Meade. Those orders were crafted to establish an unbroken defensive line designed to retain the high ground of Cemetery Ridge. When Sickles moved his corps forward almost a mile to the higher ground of the Peach Orchard, he clearly got

Major General Dan Sickles sitting with Major General Samuel Heintzelman,
previous commander of the Army of Potomac's III Corps.

better terrain for his men, but the salient created ultimately disrupted the
cohesion of Meade's position and almost resulted in the line being broken
on Gettysburg's violent second day.

On one hand, Sickles, who lost a leg during the battle and—according
to legend—was evacuated from the field smoking a cigar and cheering on
his troops, made a rational and ultimately correct decision to choose better ground to defend. Seen through the lens of a single unit commander,
it made sense to find the very best place to fight. But armies are more than
a single unit, and the Union Army's defense of Cemetery Ridge depended
on unbroken cohesion, even if some units had to occupy less advantageous terrain—a somewhat different perspective.

Risk alignment is crucial for all organizations—it's not enough to acknowledge that different parties within an organization will have separate
views on the probability and consequences of risk. The Risk Alignment
Check enables leaders to have a full view of the varied perspectives so that
they can rightfully assess risks.

While different parts of a broad team will typically view both the probability and the consequences of a risk differently, it is critical that all are

aware of the varied perspective. Absent that common understanding, one part of the team can be less vigilant or concerned about the emergence of a risk because they lack an appreciation for how it can impact another part—or the entire organization.

The Risk Alignment Check would have been helpful for Overstock to assess the capabilities of its CEO, Patrick Byrne. As we discussed in Chapter 8, when Byrne voiced "deep state" conspiracy theories, the board of directors likely found them odd, but less important than the value of his business acumen. The underwriters of the company's insurance policy, however, saw it differently, and viewed the CEO's bizarre behavior as a risk to the company.

Let's see how FlyVA might conduct a Risk Alignment Check.

SITUATION

FlyVA recognizes that although all parts of the business are aiming toward a singular goal of the airline's success, there are differing perspectives that need to be accounted for.

GOAL

To identify where the disconnects in assessment of potential risks are, to stimulate cross-communication, and to refine plans for the most effective mitigation.

STRUCTURE OF THE EXERCISE

Team members are given a potential risk and asked to plot the intercept of probability and consequences on a simple X/Y axis graph. The exact place where organizations plot the risk doesn't have to be precise; rather, the goal is to develop an improved understanding about how teams are thinking about each hazard.

EXERCISE

The airline begins the exercise with a historically inevitable risk: an economic recession. Predictably, the teams judge the probability as nearly certain (demonstrated on the Y-axis). However, assessments of the consequences of a recession, shown on the X-axis, vary widely.

Fully aware of how GDP directly drives consumer demand for air travel, the finance team makes an assessment that an economic recession will have a devastating impact on FlyVA and depress revenue. At the same time, like many airlines, FlyVA has a high proportion of debt compared to capital. And many of the airline's expenses are fixed (leases of aircraft and airport property, debt, pension funding obligations, etc.). For the team that has to make the finances work, a recession is a frightening prospect.

The human resources team is also concerned, knowing that its employees will value job security during a recession, even as the airline's profits decrease. Decisions to freeze hiring, raises, promotions, or professional development expenditures are attractive to the finance team, but frightening to those responsible for talent management.

Interestingly, the public relations team regards a recession as both a risk and an opportunity. FlyVA will need to reduce marketing expenditures, but the airline's lower-cost pricing strategy offers a chance to make a more affordable value proposition to customers when travel budgets are tight.

The IT team is unfazed by the prospect of a recession (though it has to tighten its belt on some of the pricier technical implementations). The engineering team similarly doesn't see the impact of the recession risk to be as catastrophic—its objective is to make planes function as safely as possible, whether they are flying through a recession or during financially stable times.

At the conclusion of this phase of the exercise, FlyVA's teams are developing an increased appreciation for how different things look from vantage points across the firm.

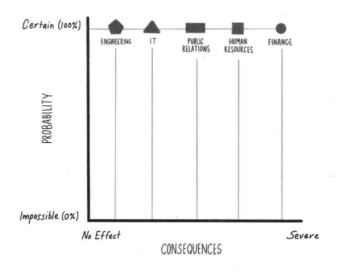

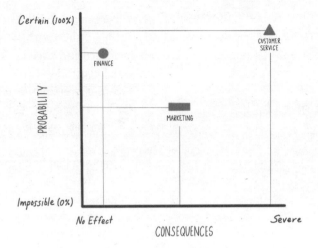

Risks where both the probability and consequences are less certain become more complicated. One of these that FlyVA identified was an option to reduce costs by using a less expensive, and arguably lower quality, food vendor.

The finance team reasons that even a slight decrease in quality (airline passengers have low expectations for in-flight food anyway) will save significant cost and is unlikely to materially affect ticket sales.

Not surprisingly, the customer service team holds a radically different view. Believing that customers develop long-term feelings about an airline through different aspects of the flying experience, often taking things like safety for granted, it believes that any possibility of a social media firestorm about soggy sandwiches, lumpy morning oats, or near-stale granola bars poses a truly existential risk for an airline desperately trying to build long-term brand loyalty.

The marketing team comes down somewhere between finance and customer service. It has tried to advertise new, more expensive, and tastier food services in the past but found that passengers, though they'd gripe about bad food, did not generally base their airline choice on food selection.

None of these differing assessments of risk are necessarily wrong—in fact all could be partly correct. But what's really important is that decisions must be made with as full an appreciation as possible of the various risks involved.

Whether you're an airline like FlyVA, a public volunteer library, or a fast-casual franchise, your organization is necessarily a team of many—each person or working group necessarily brings a different perspective about risk. Aligning those is crucial to best compete and survive.

BRINGING IT ALL TOGETHER

The Risk Alignment Check will target my narrative and diversity Risk Control Factors—studying how my understanding of risk aligns with that of others, and ensuring that diverse perspectives are taken into account when assessing risk.

SOLUTION #4

GAP ANALYSIS

We're all familiar with the game of volleyball. Whether you're a skilled athlete in the sport or have played it in gym class or on a sunny beach during a hot August day, we know the typical expectations to "bump, set, and spike" the ball over the net. One of the most frustrating aspects of volleyball is when nobody calls the ball—the ball soars over and your team watches, frozen, as it bounces on the ground between players who could have successfully tried to hit it back. The other team receives the point, and your team hangs its head, victim to having a gap in the court that could have easily been closed to preserve your point—and your dignity.

Gaps also cause problems off the court time and time again. From Major General Dutch Keiser's out-of-position 2nd Infantry Division in Chapter 5 to Braddock's Defeat in Chapter 12, we know that gaps in our defenses can be fatal to our forces. But this concept applies to business as easily as it does to military formations or volleyball: when information fails to pass from point A to point B, when resources aren't relayed to another in time, or when our bias for inaction creates gaping holes in our plans.

A Gap Analysis—a short assessment that identifies the holes between an organization's current actions and their desired end—can be crucial in improving our plans. Let's see how FlyVA used a Gap Analysis.

SITUATION

FlyVA is disappointed with its airplane "turnaround times," or the length of time it takes between an airplane's landing and its subsequent departure. FlyVA's current turnaround time is fifty minutes. The airline wants to decrease this number to thirty-five minutes, an aggressive, and accordingly expensive, endeavor.

GOAL

To assess openings and gaps in the current fifty-minute turnaround process, which will help the airline identify ways to maximize its efficiency. The aim is to cut turnaround time by fifteen minutes through increasing manpower, introducing more redundancies into the system, connecting employees, and initiating new processes.

STRUCTURE OF THE EXERCISE

A moderator will be responsible for running the exercise, soliciting documentation of processes, and gathering representative employees to talk through the airline's current turnaround process.

EXERCISE

The moderator will first discuss all turnaround procedures, from the plane parking at the gate, to deplaning passengers, cleaning the cabin, delivering food, making mechanical repairs, conducting safety checks, and reboarding new passengers.

The moderator will then identify the crew members responsible for each step of the process and identify any lags, unclear steps, and handoffs that unnecessarily slow down the procedures. They will also isolate areas of opportunity: new processes and new connections that can be leveraged to speed up the process as it exists.

Through the gap analysis exercise, FlyVA manages to figure out that its slower turnaround time is largely because of manpower: it simply does not have enough people to clean the planes, do the safety checks, and unload and reload baggage in less than fifty minutes. The airline then identifies the number of people that *would* keep up with the demand. The exercise concludes with recommendations for the number of extra airplane cleaners, on-call mechanics, and gate agents FlyVA should keep on standby to facilitate a faster boarding and deplaning process.

Gap Analyses, in total, can both explain *why* a process is not working and predict what is required to close the gaps in order to meet a more ambitious target. School administrations could use this exercise to identify the most efficient bus routes, and it would also help hospitals to better triage patients. In fact, a Gap Analysis would benefit any company that wants to identify inefficiencies in its current process, or needs help brainstorming a new one.

BRINGING IT ALL TOGETHER

A Gap Analysis targets the structure and timing Risk Control Factors, ensuring that my team is assembled in such a way that we respond quickly and successfully to threats we encounter.

SOLUTION #5

SNAP ASSESSMENT

Let's go back to the Battle of Gettysburg and Major General Dan Sickles. On July 2, 1863, Major General George Meade rode to find Sickles and his troops far forward of the planned line. With Confederate forces approaching, Meade realized instantly that unanticipated actions would be needed to save the line—and the army.

Had modern communications existed, Meade likely would have reached out to the commanders of his seven infantry and one cavalry corps—roughly ninety-five thousand officers and soldiers—and instantly apprised them of the situation. He would have sought their inputs on the impact and potential ways to mitigate the risks, and after rapid consideration, the army commander would have directed action. This is essentially what he did. But even on a relatively compact battlefield filled with cannon smoke, Meade's signal flags and couriers took time to relay the message.

Today, amid the accelerated speed and increased complexity of the "battlefields" upon which all organizations operate, the importance of leveraging the communications tools available to us is indisputable, but it requires some thought and process. Particularly in times of crisis, the ability for everyone to connect with one another in real time carries almost as much risk as it does promise. Therefore, organizations must be intentional to be effective—and that takes practice.

Snap Assessments are technology-enabled, short-term, limited-scope processes that can be employed to offer immediate feedback on a potential hazard. Snap Assessments are a helpful solution if a crisis develops quickly and organizations need split-second insight from team members with close proximity to the problem. Like any important process, Snap Assessments should be exercised so that they are effective when needed.

Let's look at how FlyVA leverages a Snap Assessment.

SITUATION

Arizona's Department of Transportation informs FlyVA that its Phoenix hub may shut down later that evening to allow for repairs of recently damaged electrical power equipment—and that the outage could require closure of the airport for up to seventy-two hours. FlyVA quickly surveys the organization to identify the impact of the closure and determine the best way to respond.

GOAL

To quickly inform stakeholders of the hub's closing, identify the impact and ramifications of this hazard, and focus FlyVA's abilities to mitigate the damages.

STRUCTURE OF THE EXERCISE

A snap assessment occurs in two phases: an information-gathering and assignment phase, as well as a mitigation phase. The first phase simply requires contextual information and a limited-scope question that will produce valuable results (e.g., "What will happen if the Phoenix hub closes?"), a deadline (e.g., "Please let me know your thoughts by 3:00 p.m. today"), and a target audience (e.g., "I need responses from legal, sales, marketing, and operations team leads"). Snap assessments need to ask questions that will produce valuable results—offering information that organizations can willingly use.

After receiving the responses, the organization gathers the team together (typically via video teleconference) to assess the results. Leaders assign individuals to address particular issues: one employee might retrieve all incoming flight records to help redirect passengers; another might meet with IT to program an explanation of the seventy-two-hour delay on the airline's app.

Once the assigned personnel complete their designated tasks, the group meets again later in the day to discuss solutions, identify interdependencies, and coordinate necessary actions. Their repeated touchpoints enable them to react to the environment in real time and adjust as necessary.

EXERCISE

FlyVA has developed an app for mobile devices that facilitates very rapid response from any location to make snap assessments of risk in the moment. The airline leverages desktop video teleconference software to provide on-demand collaboration capability as the situation demands. For small issues, FlyVA finds the app with its quick written responses to be sufficient. For larger threats, like an airport closure, FlyVA uses both the app and video meetings.

Snap Assessments can be helpful for any organization that needs to take a quick pulse on an situation: for example, a hotel catering business responding to reports of a contained kitchen fire or a performing arts center reacting to a power outage. All organizations can benefit from having a forum to be able to react and respond to the situation at hand—especially in times of crisis.

BRINGING IT ALL TOGETHER

Snap Assessments will focus on the communication, timing, and adaptability Risk Control Factors: helping us spread the message of a threat, respond at the right time, and shift our own processes as conditions change.

SOLUTION #6

COMMUNICATIONS CHECK

In the tragic aftermath of the 9/11 attacks, experts realized that messages had not been successfully transmitted among the New York City Fire Department (FDNY), the dispatchers, and the 9-1-1 operators. Though the FDNY ordered that both World Trade Center towers be evacuated at

8:57 A.M. that day, the 9-1-1 operators and dispatchers never received this message—with horrifying consequences.

As we discussed in Chapter 3, the 9/11 Commission created after the attacks also concluded that, in advance of that day, a tremendous amount of relevant intelligence existed across the US government. This information had not been communicated across the various departments and agencies in a manner that would allow them to form a coherent picture of the impending threat. Essentially, we "knew" about the upcoming attack, but we didn't realize that we knew it.

As we've learned, a functioning Risk Immune System requires that information flow through an organization, reach the appropriate people and teams within the necessary time frame, and be understood by the intended recipients. Communication is always more difficult in practice than on a whiteboard, but without the process functioning, failure is likely.

Checking the health of an organization's communication processes is a simple undertaking, but it should be done regularly, even if the need is

A New York City Fire Department firefighter dispatched to Ground Zero.
(PHOTO BY JOSE JIMENEZ/PRIMERA HORA/GETTY IMAGES)

not apparent. Like a person whose lifestyle has facilitated the buildup of plaque in their arteries, yet ignores signs and delays checkups until a heart attack or other event provides a belated wakeup call, far too many of us fail to check our communication systems.

FlyVA understands that the success of the company depends on healthy communication, so on a regular basis it tests its systems using a scenario-driven process called a Communications Check.

SITUATION

To guarantee that the airline can respond quickly to unforeseen risk, FlyVA conducts regular communications checks. The airline uses a scenario where a passenger becomes violently ill aboard a flight after eating the served food. It is unclear whether the passenger's body simply rejected the food, or if there is a larger health concern for the other passengers on board.

GOAL

To ensure that the necessary messages are communicated efficiently and effectively during this crisis, and to assess if information goes through an organization operationally and culturally. The communications check aims to identify if the message was not only distributed and received but also understood by the recipient.

STRUCTURE OF THE EXERCISE

These communications checks have two tiers: the first is a raw assessment on the communications infrastructure (is information physically flowing from point to point?), which can be conducted by an IT professional. The second tier is an actual simulation—during which organizations will determine if information is flowing in a timely, accurate, and effective manner.

EXERCISE

In the first step of the exercise, IT does a system check to see if information moves as it is supposed to across designated platforms (radios working correctly, etc.). This is a routine part of any airline's operations, but it should be prioritized for any organization that is examining its communications processes.

The second step is more nuanced. In the simulation, from the moment the sick passenger presses a "Call Attendant" button, information begins to flow. The system is designed to prioritize any medical needs to protect the health of the passenger, but soon after, operations, legal, public relations, and other parts of the FlyVA team are notified so that they can be prepared to act or respond as appropriate.

During this communications check simulation, participants must also assess nonobvious contacts who will need to be informed in the case of an emergency. Does FlyVA's board of directors need to be notified? What about the parents of any unaccompanied minors who are entrusting the airline with the successful and safe transport of their child? Communications checks challenge participants to consider the full scope of personnel who must recognize a risk to orchestrate the most effective response to it.

The simulation concludes with a debriefing during which the facilitators first ask the employees how they *thought* the exercise went. How did they communicate? What communication channels were more helpful than others in transmitting messages? Did the information go to the right person in a timely manner? Were there any dropped balls—messages not relayed quickly enough, or the intent of messages corrupted?

The facilitators will then cross-reference these results with the takeaways from the IT department (who will be observing the communication traffic to ensure all messages are being delivered as intended), tracking which platforms the employees used the most frequently, which ones they over- or underleveraged, and how that affected the response.

Finally, the teams make recommendations about how to best communicate during the event, offering an exhaustive list of best practices and lessons learned to ensure that information flows seamlessly throughout the organization. Though the events will be unpredictable and unexpected, a robust communications process will enable FlyVA to react favorably to risks it encounters.

Just as a patient's pulse and blood pressure can signal their health, an organization's communication methods can indicate the viability of the Risk Immune System. As the lifeblood of the system, communication should be a priority for teams—to ensure that the right information is getting to the right person at the right time. Any organization that has to pass information, from an assembly line at a meat processing plant to a law firm working through a case, can benefit from a Communications Check.

SOLUTION #7

TABLETOP EXERCISE

In 2019, the US government conducted a series of exercises called Crimson Contagion as a response to the influenza pandemic in 2009 (which many people hardly know occurred), and the more familiar Ebola and Zika outbreaks, which spanned from 2013 to 2016. Crimson Contagion presented two tabletop exercises, a seminar, and then a functional exercise (or a "war game") and was designed to scrutinize issues of policy decisions, structure, information sharing, and resourcing with the goal of better positioning the nation for the next pandemic. The findings presciently identified weaknesses and shortcomings that would become all too evident in early 2020.

CRIMSON CONTAGION SERIES: AN OVERVIEW

The Crimson Contagion series used a stair-step approach in which the two tabletop exercises (conducted in January and April 2019, respectively) familiarized and "educated" the community of participants about current plans, policies, and capabilities. The seminar in May 2019 allowed all involved to discuss how the federal government would provide capabilities and resources to enable local and state responses to a pandemic.

Finally, the war game, a four-day functional exercise, followed—where the community physically responded to a simulated pandemic scenario, going beyond simply talking about the problem and mitigation techniques. The final war game emphasized a "whole-of-community" response that included representatives from 12 states, 19 federal agencies and departments, 74 health departments, 87 hospitals, 15 tribal nations and pueblos, and more than 100 "healthcare and public health private sector partners." Our next solution discusses war games in further detail.

Although follow-up action on issues uncovered or clarified during Crimson Contagion was largely not executed, the intent and construct of the overall series offer a solid framework for organizations seeking to strengthen their Risk Immune Systems.

Unlike the Communications Check, which allows teams to analyze how information is successfully transported from the messenger to the receiver, Tabletop Exercises help groups map out and plan logistical processes and resource requirements for both personnel and work materials, as well as establish responsibility and accountability in all stages of a reaction to potential hazards.

With this in mind, we now turn to FlyVA, which conducted a Tabletop Exercise in the face of a major snowstorm.

SITUATION

Meteorologists have predicted more frequent storms, stronger winds, and higher precipitation levels than usual for this upcoming winter season. Acknowledging these cautions, FlyVA's executive team prompts the organization to conduct a tabletop exercise to develop the most effective plan possible to deal with these inevitable blizzards. Snowstorms are nothing new, but each constitutes a unique challenge that is difficult to assess accurately until it develops fully—at which point reaction time is severely limited.

GOAL

To educate FlyVA on the issue of a winter storm, establish relationships with appropriate contacts, confirm contact information for necessary parties, and align on expectations. Additionally, tabletop exercises aim to investigate logistical and communication processes, as well as resource requirements, during a winter storm response—isolating what team members are both responsible for and accountable for during a crisis. As the location and impact of each storm is unique, organizations discuss their plans (which are general in nature), with the understanding that many specifics will be worked out as the situation develops.

STRUCTURE OF THE EXERCISE

Knowing that January and February are heavy snow months in the United States, FlyVA conducts the tabletop exercise the May before the winter season—which gives the airline adequate time to build out the exercise, address findings, and implement useful changes. The exercise brings together the community of pilots, flight attendants, air traffic control operators, gate agents, airline subcontractors, the Federal Aviation Administration (FAA), and other stakeholders to share information and perspectives.

The tabletop exercise is structured as a scenario-driven conversation that moves chronologically through the emergence and impact of a powerful snowstorm. Moderators drive the discussion along the scenario timeline using a set of pre-identified points of discussion that have historically proven critical to winter storm response.

Background and scenario reading materials have been sent to participants in advance of the tabletop exercise (not a requirement for all tabletops, but useful if organizations would like to prepare). Four hours have been allotted for the exercise, and coordinators have arranged an auditorium configured with seating for each of FlyVA's teams, outfitted with a screen that will project slides to guide the discussion.

Through these discussions, teams identify gaps, or actions that their colleagues assume others are doing (often wrongfully so). When possible, participants identify and agree upon solutions in the room. If further approval is needed, the issues are recorded as "Decisions Required" and briefed at the conclusion of the tabletop exercise. There is a note taker present during a tabletop exercise who captures the major issues and concerns for follow-up action.

Although structured by the scenario and led by moderators, conversations during a tabletop exercise should be as free flowing as possible. Moderators allow the group to examine all facets of the winter storm response, bringing stakeholders together in a conversation to identify how they'd respond to risk.

EXERCISE

After reviewing ground rules, moderators use a series of slides to establish the scenario—a storm detected near Nova Scotia. Moderators then lead participants through a discussion of how information about the storm's movement and intensity should be interpreted and shared throughout the organization. Team members discuss the timelines for key decisions and major logistical requirements, as well as the communication processes necessary to best respond to risk.

One of the issues participants quickly identify is that throughout the course of the storm, it is easy for flight crews to get out of position. The storm-related flight delays prevent pilots and attendants from arriving at their next destination on time to staff aircraft. Crews stuck in hotels hundreds of miles away from their assigned airport unnecessarily slow down already backed-up planes.

Acknowledging the legal requirement for pilots and crew members to rest between flying shifts, the dispatchers will work with the pilots to consider new flight plans. The crew scheduling team discusses the logistical process of tracking down employees' locations and reassigning pilots and crews to new flights. It will also work to book rooms for relocated pilots and passengers, referencing existing relationships with the airport hotel to block several dozen rooms in case of a major storm.

With this discussion on the table, the moderator injects a new change into the operating environment: there has been a major accident right outside the airport, so relocated pilots cannot leave the airport for the hotel until hours later than expected. This mishap delays the legal amount of rest they must have to safely operate a plane—so there are no pilots cleared to operate rescheduled flights. Now what? Will FlyVA need to fly new pilots in from other locations? Further delay or even postpone the existing flights?

The team doesn't have to solve this issue right away, but it can discuss proposed courses of action as it moves through this scenario to identify what sorts of materials would be required, what logistics would need to be ironed out, etc. By transparently discussing these issues in advance of the crisis, the team can collaborate more effectively and successfully to relocate pilots and crews in the event of a major storm.

The Tabletop Exercise is useful for any industry that wants to take a hard look at processes without committing to a resource-intensive simulation. Throughout this exercise, moderators work to overcome the effects of groupthink and hierarchy by giving participants an equal ability to express their insights. Afterward, the moderator should deliver the main takeaways and recommendations to the organization. Identified issues, necessary decisions, and logistical requirements can all be ironed out and addressed after the event has concluded as the organization slowly develops a plan to respond to risk.

SOLUTION #8

WAR GAME (OR FUNCTIONAL EXERCISE)

The board game Risk is focused on a singular goal: to build an army and conquer enemy land. War Games similarly aim to conquer risk but require significant resources for the participants to play.

The less formal Tabletop Exercise brings together stakeholders to build familiarity with a problem and explore potential solutions. A War Game (as it's called in the military), or Functional Exercise (the more common term in civilian sectors), pressure-tests the plan that has been developed and trains teams to execute. Because the process is highly detailed and the objectives are ambitious, War Games are conducted less frequently than Tabletop Exercises, and they are effective only if the requisite resources are committed. But they can be the difference between success and failure if done correctly.

A number of times during my career, I found myself in a war game: the defense of South Korea and the invasion of southern Iran when I was a captain, and later we tested plans for the overthrow of Noriega's regime in Panama and the invasion of Iraq. Initially using dice, and later complicated computer algorithms, to determine the outcome of engagements with the enemy, the exercise would involve executing a detailed plan against an enemy and be played by colleagues detailed for that purpose.

Some of our players were assigned to act as the enemy. Although they were generally instructed to operate as our foes would, clever opponents periodically subjected friendly forces to setbacks, some of which were stunningly embarrassing but invaluable to uncovering weaknesses in our plans or processes.

*Military war games often use a physical map for
participants to simulate where they would actually act in real time.*

For Crimson Contagion, the four-day war game served as the cap-
stone to the planning process. In the exercise, a community physically
responded to a simulated pandemic scenario, going beyond simply talking
about the problem and mitigation techniques. Although the virus itself
was the "enemy," the actions and interactions required to deal with it
served as an effective opportunity to refine plans and build capacity. Had
the entire series been followed up by correction of identified weaknesses,
the COVID-19 experience in America would likely have been far different.

Although best known in military circles, War Games can be excep-
tionally valuable in business. The opponent can be a competitor in the
marketplace or an unpredictable event an organization must respond to,
such as a pandemic, a natural disaster, or an accident.

There are three main elements of War Games: action, reaction, and
counteraction. After an opponent moves, players must react and fire back—
simulating competition as they would in the real world. The game has a
push and pull at its heart and can become intense as organizations develop
a living and breathing response to a simulated enemy. War Games are only

as helpful as the intent behind them, however: as organizations design these "force-on-force" scenarios, they must thoughtfully consider what they want their players to learn from the simulation.

Now let's look at how FlyVA conducts a fully resourced War Game to determine the potential impact of a snowstorm that would significantly disrupt service.

SITUATION

In order to test a worst-case scenario, the exercise organizers have proposed a disruptive snow event that strikes during the heart of the Christmas holiday season. Several hubs are temporarily closed due to weather, and flights across the entire Northeast United States are impacted.

GOAL

To evaluate FlyVA's plans to best respond to a winter storm risk and identify necessary changes. A secondary objective is to build the competence and confidence of the FlyVA team to respond to a significant snow event.

STRUCTURE OF THE EXERCISE

War games should be conducted in the environment where employees would operate in the event of a crisis (including physical locations). One group will play the part of the organization, modeling how competitors and customers will react to changes in the environment, and another will play the enemy. Throughout the course of the war game, the exercise controllers will inject new developments and the participants must respond to them. As actions are simulated, the controllers provide feedback (as in real life, not all actions go off as planned or desired), and the players respond to the new reality.

EXERCISE

FlyVA sets up the war game to take place in selected cockpits, in control towers, at gates, and in airport operations centers—in other words, the physical locations where FlyVA's employees work during normal operations. Because daily flights cannot be halted for the exercise, the simulation comes with logistical complications. Exercise messages are carefully fenced off from actual operations and all begin with EXERCISE TRAFFIC. While the primary "enemy" during the war game is the storm itself, a group of employees also plan to model the actions of competitors and customers. Business partners and vendors are invited to participate and provide insights.

After conducting a tabletop exercise in May, FlyVA decides to conduct a war game in late July—early enough to allow the airline to take corrective actions before the winter season. They "host" the exercise from their primary operations center located at headquarters, not far from Dulles Airport in Northern Virginia, but there are participants from all of FlyVA's hubs working in "exercise cells," kept separate from ongoing daily operations to avoid any confusion.

The war game kicks off with players conducting normal holiday season operations. Game controllers inject several typical occurrences (maintenance issues and employees calling in sick) before passing along a series of weather reports that show the rapid approach of a storm system threatening to have broad impacts across the Northeast.

Players continue the simulated execution of normal operations, but FlyVA leadership also activates a pre-designated response cell that begins monitoring and disseminating detailed weather forecasts, reviewing established processes for adjusting flights, and preparing to execute the complicated recovery plan that will need to be implemented almost as soon as the storm has passed.

The scenario unfolds. Exercise controllers continue to inject new developments that the participants must respond to. As the war game concludes, FlyVA's leadership feels deflated. Carefully constructed plans proved inflexible, and the airline's IT backbone didn't have the capacity to make huge shifts in reservations, flight schedules, crew assignments, and other requirements quickly enough to facilitate recovery. Embarrassingly, the airline found itself unable to return to robust operations for several days after the weather had improved.

The war game, however, was a success. Armed with new experience and insights, the idea of a monster snowstorm was no longer the bogeyman that terrified the team. The road ahead would bring a series of challenges, some very intimidating, but none that couldn't be tackled with more planning, some targeted investments, additional training, and a bit more practice. Any business can simulate its equivalent of the winter snowstorm—seeing its plans and responses in action for future improvement.

Though resource-intensive, War Games are an extremely effective way to track how your organization reacts to risk in real time. Whether you're staging a large event with many moving pieces that can't fail or rehearsing an important performance that needs to be perfect, a War Game will sharpen your team's ability to respond and adapt to the environment as conditions inevitably shift.

BRINGING IT ALL TOGETHER

War Games bolster all Risk Control Factors, testing our whole Risk Immune System as we react to a scenario in real time.

SOLUTION #9

RED TEAMING

Marine General Paul Van Riper was just trying to do his job: successfully play the enemy (in this case Saddam Hussein's Iraqi military). It was the Millennium Challenge 2002, a massive exercise with more than 13,500 service members to identify challenges American military forces would face, and Van Riper was tasked to lead the opposition. Knowing that the American powers had a "strategy of preemption," Van Riper's team beat them to the punch, launching an attack that, had it been real, would have killed twenty thousand American soldiers. Ironically, Van Riper was criticized for his efforts and told that since he wasn't following protocol, his attack was delegitimized. Predictably, American forces ultimately won the war game.

Millennium 2002 was an almost classic example of effective red teaming. In having Iraqi forces execute a preemptive attack that American planners had confidently assumed away—with devastating results—Van Riper awakened everyone to the reality that things could go very differently than expected.

CENTER OF GRAVITY

Dick Fosbury's famous Fosbury Flop was unique in that it allowed the jumper to keep their center of gravity *below* the high-jump bar, even as their feet flew above it. Your center of gravity is important in how you travel (in a literal sense, giving you control over your movement) and equally as important in how you fight.

The Prussian general Carl von Clausewitz's military strategy book *On War* stresses that fighting groups attack one another's centers of gravity. He argues that war is a "collision between two centers of gravity," or between the places in which they find their power and dominance.

In Red Team exercises, opposition forces aim to identify and then attack an organization's center of gravity to win. These exercises can then inform an organization of its vulnerabilities when facing risk.

The entire concept of Red Teaming is based on an assumption that organizations are typically ineffective at assessing themselves, leaving them vulnerable to huge blind spots that wily red teamers can exploit. This exercise can serve as a healthy reminder of our own infallibility and is invaluable in uncovering unseen vulnerabilities and risks.

In Red Team exercises, opposition forces are not unlike vaccinations: they introduce foreign substances into the body that flock to weaknesses. Vaccinations, like Red Team exercises, aim to strengthen the body's response to future risks.

For this reason, Red Team exercises work best when external players are brought in and take an outsider's look at the ways in which an organization can fail. These players should be distant *enough* from the day-to-day operations that they aren't biased, but close enough to know the context.

To be the most helpful, the Red Team exercise needs to be anchored around a singular topic so that those leading the exercise have a very clear understanding of what they aim to Red Team, or what is most essential for their analysis.

Let's see how FlyVA uses Red Team exercises.

SITUATION

FlyVA conducts a red team exercise to see how well equipped it is to deal with a public relations scandal.

To identify all vulnerabilities that would prevent the airline from best **Detecting**, **Assessing**, and **Responding** to a public relations risk, and to ultimately put efforts in place to mitigate damages.

STRUCTURE OF THE EXERCISE

Red team exercises first require teams to consider their centers of gravity (see page 275), thinking through all the aspects of the organization that could potentially be vulnerable. If an "enemy" were to attack their organization (realistically, if a competitor or a customer incited a scandal to adversely affect their business), what would be the source of the downfall?

Once the organization has identified its centers of gravity, it should recruit a third party to help assess the plan—with the centers of gravity in mind. Where is the organization most vulnerable? What blind spots should it be aware of?

Whatever configuration this exercise takes—from long-form workshops to shorter, sometimes even anonymous, exercises—red team exercises aim to find all the holes in an organization's plan before it even has the chance to properly deflate.

Because it's not possible to red team an entire Risk Immune System with a single exercise, the process should instead be an iterative series of exercises directed at different parts of the organization. Responding to identified vulnerabilities in each effort gives the best view of the overall health of the system itself.

EXERCISE

FlyVA identifies several centers of gravity when considering how their public relations team would handle a scandal: their recognized commitment to safety, their promise of comfort, their guarantee of trustworthy booking sites, and the well-being of all of the passengers and their belongings while in the airplane cabins.

After identifying all centers of gravity, FlyVA can then work with an external actor to pinpoint *all* the ways these centers of gravity could collapse in on themselves in the midst of a scandal. In this case, FlyVA runs a long-form workshop, seeking contributions from team members and stakeholders alike, to find all the weaknesses and vulnerabilities in a plan before it even has the chance to crumble.

Red Team exercises come in many shapes and forms (refer to Micah Zen-ko's *Red Team: How to Succeed by Thinking Like the Enemy* to learn more). The main idea is that you can't grade your own homework—you can't see all the flaws in your own plans and logic, which necessarily invites more risk into your organization. These exercises, aided by a third-party facilitator, will make a world of difference in minimizing your vulnerabilities when facing threats.

BRINGING IT ALL TOGETHER

Red Team exercises focus on the bias, adaptability, and action Risk Control Factors, challenging assumptions and focusing on our organization's center of gravity so we can act decisively and adapt when we need to.

SOLUTION #10

PRE-MORTEM

Operation Eagle Claw, the botched 1980 attempt to rescue Americans held hostage in Iran, failed catastrophically. It's clear now that this operation was a compound risk by any measure: a series of interdependent steps that combined to create significant risk to mission success. While a careful review in advance of Operation Eagle Claw would likely *not* have changed the mission, it might have led to modifications to the plan or a failure to receive presidential approval.

Operation Eagle Claw could have benefited from a Pre-Mortem, an exercise that requires organizations to test actions before they are executed and identify every possible reason for failure in advance (*pre-mortem* translates to "before death"). Though bleak, this exercise aims to prevent tragedies by applying a skeptical eye to every step in the process to put measures in place to mitigate risk. While we acknowledge that testing the validity of actions before they are executed is speculative, a well-managed Pre-Mortem can help eliminate problems with a reaction to risk before they even emerge.

A Pre-Mortem is markedly different from a Risk Review. While the latter allows for a broad examination of risks within an organization, the

The carnage of the failed Operation Eagle Claw mission.
(AP PHOTO)

former is used to test a specific plan for execution. Pre-Mortem exercises are best executed early enough to make the detailed planning and rehearsals pay off, although not too late that there is no time for adjustment of the plan. The Pre-Mortem also requires much more judgment and intuition than the Risk Review, where facilitators ask participants to go through a specific operation or event, and then share what their gut says is likely to prove problematic.

Pre-Mortems are valuable because they can elicit concerns people have that are sometimes difficult to publicly raise during preparation. Before an event occurs, the Pre-Mortem prompts the question: "What are you worried about?" In some instances, having responses provided anonymously produces candor difficult in many organizations. Teammates are hesitant to be viewed as naysayers, so the Pre-Mortem constructs a situation where it's not only okay, but expected, for participants to voice their deepest concerns.

As we saw in Operation Eagle Claw, participants often have the best sense of where the vulnerabilities lie in the plan; in the same breath, they can also become emotionally wedded to them or blind to their weaknesses. A Pre-Mortem with a good moderator can be very helpful in pulling those apprehensions from the team to best identify any and all potential risks at hand.

Let's examine how FlyVA conducts a Pre-Mortem exercise.

SITUATION

FlyVA has conducted tabletop and war game exercises in advance of a snowstorm, so the airline is feeling comfortable about its approach when a storm inevitably hits. While the aforementioned exercises take place in May and late July, the pre-mortem takes place during the third week of January, immediately before an expected storm arrives.

GOAL

To identify all the ways FlyVA's winter storm responses may fail in advance, prepare mitigation efforts, and adjust responses accordingly. Pre-Mortems also aim to check parts of the plan that are assumed will work, but more closely consider the impacts as the risk approaches.

STRUCTURE OF THE EXERCISE

A pre-mortem would be a focus group–like session in which a variety of stakeholders speculate about what could potentially go wrong with the storm response. The owner of FlyVA gathers the group and asks, "What are you worried about now that the storm is approaching?" The participants offer dozens of concerns, such as having no pilots or crews and broken de-icing machines. The group pays particular attention to the risk of the maintenance crews or the third-party local mechanics FlyVA relies on to identify and fix issues not showing up in the snowstorm. If there are no maintenance crews, the planes cannot be fixed to successfully transport customers when the weather clears.

EXERCISE

This pre-mortem exercise is most effective when it gathers a variety of stakeholders, so FlyVA ensures that pilots, gate agents, even members of the FAA, who understand the protocol of recruiting these third-party vendors, are present.

During the pre-mortem, participants list all outstanding risks to the airline, drilling down on the risk of relying on third-party local maintenance workers. Participants list a litany of outstanding concerns: Will the local maintenance professionals even be able to get to the airport in the event of a major storm? What if they are unable or unwilling to assist with the necessary repairs? What sorts of backup arrangements does the airline have in place, in the event the local maintenance team doesn't show? Does the airport have any plows or safety equipment to help transport these workers safely to the aircraft?

FlyVA can address all of these concerns to the best of its ability, given the short time frame until the actual storm hits. It considers transportation plans to ensure that the mechanics are positioned safely to assist when it becomes necessary, and they establish structures to incentivize the workers to make repairs during these precarious times.

As the exercise continues, the conversation moves beyond emergency maintenance to consider all facets of the winter storm response as the plan coagulates in the final moments before the snow starts to fall—giving stakeholders time to make last-minute, yet critical, changes.

Pre-Mortems show us that it is never too late to consider the risks to our organization. Before the curtain opens, before the firing gun starts the race, the team is given time to be pessimists and guess how the plan will fail. These solutions are particularly helpful for teams whose conditions are volatile until the very last minute.

BRINGING IT ALL TOGETHER

The Pre-Mortem exercise focuses on the timing and action Risk Control Factors, helping us change our plans to be most effective before it's too late.

SOLUTION #11

AFTER-ACTION REVIEW

In the military, as soon as a fight is over, units run a hot wash—a quick and raw assessment of what just happened while the experience is still fresh in their minds. Hot washes aim to quickly identify issues that must be addressed immediately and can't await a more thorough review.

After-Action Reviews are more calculated and careful assessments of a past event. Participants gather once the dust settles, the curtain closes, the

After-action reviews are common practice in the military.
They help to align participants on what can be improved for the next operation.

off-site concludes, a few days or weeks after the event, rather than a hot wash's few minutes or hours, to identify what went well and what didn't.

In the same way, organizations use After-Action Reviews to determine what exactly happened in a given scenario, all the while isolating what could or should have been done differently. These reviews are often tense. While most people assume that what happened during an event is clear to everyone, there are often competing understandings of an operating environment. Each participant has a different view of history—the "action" under review may have been a serious failure that implicates a variety of team members and may even threaten their employment, so there is a tendency to blunt the findings.

But this exercise also provides great value. Through frank discussions, teams can identify which behaviors and practices to sustain and which to improve. Additionally, teammates can create commitments to actions and assign owners to each.

There might be resistance to conducting an After-Action Review after a successful effort. Some may argue that success means that a plan is good and execution effective. But that's often not the case. In combat, victory doesn't mean you got it right any more than defeat means that you did it wrong—there are just too many factors involved. And sometimes there may be pernicious incentives to skip After-Action Reviews, or to neutralize the message that comes out of them. A serious After-Action Review, therefore, will require continued emphasis from organizational leadership.

A successful After-Action Review is one that leads to not only a common understanding among a group but also calls to action. Errors are not career enders, nor do onetime successes anoint any team member for posterity. Organizations with a self-assessment culture can move forward quickly after past events, correcting action and adjusting their behavior for more favorable future outcomes.

After-Action Reviews can be conducted after simulations like a Table-top Exercise or a War Game to give participants an opportunity to analyze what went well and what didn't. It's more useful, however, when After-Action Reviews take place after the actual event itself. This way, the review offers applicable insight into the direct response.

To more clearly understand their usefulness in practice, let's consider FlyVA's post–winter storm After-Action Review.

SITUATION

A winter storm *actually* hits in late February (after the tabletop, war games, and pre-mortem exercises were complete), and it was as bad as FlyVA had feared: eight inches of snow across the northeastern seaboard, the Newark hub closed, and flights throughout New York, Pennsylvania, and Massachusetts severely delayed. FlyVA's board of directors has requested an exhaustive after-action review to address the response to the risk.

GOAL

To provide the organization with a clear understanding of the event, as well as ways to improve future responses to similar hazards.

STRUCTURE OF THE EXERCISE

A well-run after-action review is carefully structured and requires a neutral stakeholder to serve as a moderator (no matter how well-meaning an internal moderator might be, their personal involvement may skew the results of the exercise). Having a senior leader like an operations director or a respected outsider moderate may lead to quelling or controlling real arguments that break out during the process that could distract from the exercise. In our example, an operations director from Phoenix, who was not immediately responsible for the Newark hub's storm response, may be well suited for the role.

The moderator takes notes during the exercise and serves as an arbiter of fact if competing versions of history emerge. Therefore, the moderator must know what happened, be an effective communicator in a group dynamic, and be able to speak truth to power when necessary. The moderator also ensures that the organization doesn't fall down rabbit holes to stall the progress of the conversation.

A moderator needs to first specify the action being reviewed—the purpose is not to assess the entire organization but a discrete action that the organization undertook in the past—and ensure that the conversation sticks to the issue identified.

With a problem statement established, the moderator needs to use a discernible timeline of events to encourage participants to describe what happened, why it happened, what went well, and what did not go well, guiding them to identify which areas can be maintained and which areas need to be improved.

Finally, the moderator assigns an owner to each follow-up action item to create large-scale change for the next risk of this type.

EXERCISE

FlyVA's after-action review begins with a fifteen- to twenty-minute chronological history of the storm response, from the airport's initial warnings, to the series of flight cancellations and rebookings, to when flights resumed as normal once the storm had passed. Each of the departments within FlyVA offers its own version of the event, explaining how its particular branch **Detected**, **Assessed**, and **Responded** to risk. This discussion would focus on the timeline from the airport's first knowledge of the storm, to the series of flight cancellations and rebookings, and all the way to when flights resumed as normal after the storm had passed.

Once everyone has a shared understanding of the situation, the moderator leads the group to examine and assess each stage of the response, department by department. The gate agent team, for example, assesses their members' actions before the storm hit, naming what they did well and what procedures they'd sustain, what they did poorly, and how they could improve the next time a storm hit. The gate agent team then assigns a team member to own each addressed area of improvement—ensuring that one member of the team can be held accountable for implementing the identified changes.

This solution continues for all stages of response: when the storm begins to hit, when the storm is in full force, when the airline has to rebook customers, and when the airline resumes its normal operations. In every stage (for every part of the organization) facilitators have to push participants to be critical of their actions in the spirit of improving their response to the next inevitable winter storm.

The after-action review concludes with a summary of the findings that covers all the lessons learned during the exercise, preparing the organization for future challenges.

All organizations can benefit from After-Action Reviews. The best lessons are the ones captured after the event—but not too long after. Once the team has had the opportunity to reflect on what went well and what didn't, After-Action Reviews are critical to cement the lessons learned, no matter whether the event was a roaring success or a tragic failure.

BRINGING IT ALL TOGETHER

After-Action Reviews strengthen the action and leadership Risk Control Factors, encouraging the leader to help the organization identify how it can sustain and improve its behaviors and processes.

The Myth of Helplessness

The more we value things outside
our control, the less control we have.

—EPICTETUS,
GRECO-ROMAN PHILOSOPHER

There is a story, likely apocryphal, that relates how King Canute the Great, an eleventh-century ruler of Denmark, England, and Norway, grew weary of his sycophantic entourage proclaiming his omnipotence. By all accounts, Canute was a realistically modest man and decided to settle the issue once and for all.

Taking his advisers to the ocean shore, he had his throne placed on the sand in front of a rising tide. As the water inexorably rose, Canute loudly ordered it to stop—to retreat before it wet his royal feet.

Predictably, as it had for as long as anyone could remember, the tide rose anyway, and Canute's robes and slippers were soon soaked. The king's flatterers were also quieted. There were forces that no one, not even the king, could do anything about.

The rising waters brought by Hurricane Katrina, the inexorable advance of disruptive technology, the despair of Depression-era unemployment, and Santa Anna's army surrounding the Alamo all invite a kind of stoic fatalism: the temptation to assent to that which is outside our authority. And often we suffer, go bankrupt, even die, accepting the inevitability of threats we can neither prevent nor avoid.

We tell Canute-like stories, name buildings, and sometimes even erect statues to those who bravely "go down with the ship."

Coco Chanel would have recoiled in disgust: "*My life didn't please me, so I created my life.*"

Dealt a weak hand by the loss of her mother and desertion by her father at a young age, the twentieth-century fashion icon and business leader remained anything but passive. She was all about controlling what she could. Coco assessed the environment, identified her opportunities, and acted—literally until the day she died.

Yet the mythology of helplessness persists. Faced with clear indications of a pending terrorist attack or the reality of a deadly pandemic, we're unable to imagine how the threat might materialize, or we will not overcome the inertia of inaction to respond effectively to it. The scourges of AIDS, COVID-19, and climate change, among others, are judged to be acts of God or nature that fail to mobilize us for action.

But inaction, *including a failure to prepare for action*, is little more than a dodge. As we've shown in the preceding chapters, there is far more that lies within our control than outside it. The steps we can take in advance of threats to build and strengthen our Risk Immune Systems, coupled with the actions we can take to facilitate that system's effective function, are often the difference between success and failure, victory and defeat, or even life and death.

Effectively dealing with risk is not relying on a novice gambler's luck and the next turn of a card, nor is it covering your ears as you walk through a minefield in the hopes that if you don't hear the boom then it won't eviscerate you. Dealing with risk is the active practice of controlling every single factor within your reach. It begins with making your bed each morning and tying your shoes correctly—and working constantly to stretch your ability to reach ever higher. Seeking control is not a practice for the paranoid—it is the logical objective of anyone for whom the outcome is important.

When we understand the Risk Immune System that our organizations should nurture, we are steps down the road to success.

DOROTHY:

Oh, will you help me? Can you help me?

GLINDA (THE GOOD WITCH OF THE NORTH):

You don't need to be helped any longer. You've always had the power to go back to Kansas.

—FROM *The Wizard of Oz,* 1939

Acknowledgments

WE WROTE THIS BOOK DURING the COVID-19 pandemic. It would not have been possible without the time, help, and commitment of our colleagues, friends, and family who diligently supported our writing process from a socially safe distance.

Many thanks to Eric Robinson for his tremendous efforts in the early shaping of our thinking and drafting of initial chapters. Henry Gent helped our team clarify our message and worked diligently on our first iterations of the Prologue and Chapter 3. Micah Zenko's guidance on how to structure our book, and his assistance with Part 3, was crucial. Jen Keister, Cleo Haynal, Sabriyya Pate, Chike Aguh, and David Livingston were incredibly helpful in developing Part 3.

Other McChrystal Group teammates helped us make our book practical to its users. Tim Lynch, Todd Sanders, and Rachel Meyer were diligent and patient in giving us details about Boston as we drafted Chapter 13. Tom Maffey, Ted Delicath, Billy Don Farris, Mary Carroll, Sebastian Little, and Martha Deeds gave us vital information about war games, tabletop exercises, and fusion cells. Victor Bilgen, Morgan Silvers, and McChrystal Group Team Science helped us bring Chapter 15 to life. We thank Ellen Chapin and Cleo Haynal for their painstaking attention to detail as we fact-checked our manuscript and are grateful for Lina Than's drawing talents for many of the images scattered throughout the book.

McChrystal Group writing alumni—Sam Ayres, Teddy Collins, Jay Mangone, and Phil Kaplan—were generous in helping us to navigate the ins and outs of project management. Thank you to Rudy Valentine, who would prepare a breakout room for us to collaborate even as our office was closed, and Cherylanne Anderson for fitting in giant chunks of time for us in the calendar to collaborate.

We relied on many experts to make our story accurate: Dr. Kristina Talbert-Slagle helped us with our immune system discussion; Kosh Sadat reviewed our discussion of night raids; Keith Nightingale provided us with precious information about Operation Eagle Claw; Drew Erdmann and Philip Zelikow provided invaluable counsel on the Cuban Missile Crisis, and Richard Shultz provided guidance on Project Maven. Secretary Marty Walsh and Kathryn Burton were generous with their time and energy as we told their COVID-19 story. Gene Thorp created state-of-the-art maps for our book to make our images come to life. Thank you to Holly Butrico for the "Fosbury Flop" addition to the book, and John Storrie for providing airline guidance for Part 3.

Our thanks to a group of accomplished leaders who graciously conducted conversations about risk: Tom Greco, Dr. Jeffrey Stern, Klaus Diem, Dannette Smith, Mike Hayes, Jaime Bland, Rob Karofsky, Andrew Bhak and his team, Henrik Andersen and Eduardo Medina Sanchez, Fred Seigel, John Roese, Anthony Noto, Kurt Ekert, Dr. Joseph Steele, Mitch Snyder, Sam Deshpande, and Rick Caruso. We also thank our reviewers: Charlie Goodyear, Liam Collins, Igor Tulchinsky, Skip "Ace" Rawson, and David Moldawer. Our book would not have been possible without the tireless efforts of our editor, Noah Schwartzberg, as well as Adrian Zackheim, Nina Rodriguez-Marty, and Kimberly Meilun. We continue to enjoy our partnership with Penguin Portfolio through the years.

Finally, we thank our families: Annie, Sam, Stacey, Emmylou, Elsie, and Daisy McChrystal, and Paul, Laura, Erin, Holly Butrico, and Hunter Conti, who frequently visited when we were writing from home. While much of the work and writing would have been done at the office, we brought the books, pages, and hours spent over computers to home—this book is as much yours as ours.

Notes

Prologue: Crimson Contagion

ix **The fifty-two-year-old traveler:** David E. Sanger et al., "Before Virus Outbreak, a Cascade of Warnings Went Unheeded," *The New York Times*, March 22, 2020, https://nytimes.com/2020/03/19/us/politics/trump-coronavirus-outbreak.html.

ix **virus spread quickly through human-to-human contact:** *Crimson Contagion 2019 Functional Exercise Draft After-Action Report*, Coordinating Draft, U.S. Department of Health and Human Services, Office of the Assistant Secretary for Preparedness and Response, October 2019, 8, https://int.nyt.com/data/documenthelper/6824-2019-10-key-findings-and-after/05bd797500ea55be0724/optimized/full.pdf#page=.

ix **hospitals across the country were overrun:** Ailsa Chang, "What Last Year's Government Simulation Predicted about Today's Pandemic," *All Things Considered*, National Public Radio, March 20, 2020, https://npr.org/2020/03/20/819186528/what-last-years-government-simulation-predicted-about-todays-pandemic.

ix **patients experiencing fevers, chills:** *Crimson Contagion 2019 Functional Exercise Draft After-Action Report*, 8.

ix **America's medical supply chain failed:** *Crimson Contagion 2019 Functional Exercise Draft After-Action Report*, 39; Sanger et al., "Before Virus Outbreak."

ix **An ill-defined leadership structure:** *Crimson Contagion 2019 Functional Exercise Draft After-Action Report*, 1–3.

ix **to infect 110 million Americans:** Sanger et al., "Before Virus Outbreak"; *Crimson Contagion 2019 Functional Exercise Draft After-Action Report*, 9.

x   **mortality rate roughly five times greater:** The mortality rate of the Chinese respiratory virus was 0.533 percent. The predictions of the mortality rate of the flu in 2018–19 were 0.096 percent, roughly five times worse. "Estimated Influenza Illnesses, Medical Visits, Hospitalizations, and Deaths in the United States—2018–2019 Influenza Season," Centers for Disease Control, accessed November 19, 2020, https://cdc.gov/flu/about/burden/2018-2019.html.

x   **In fact, the outbreak starting:** The description reflects the exercise as it was reported in its draft report, and we've added some detail (mostly the note about frontline workers) to depict how the simulation likely felt in practice.

x   **our nation was woefully underprepared:** Sanger et al., "Before Virus Outbreak."

x   **severe equipment shortages:** *Crimson Contagion 2019 Functional Exercise Draft After-Action Report*, 1–3.

x   **White House stood by its 2018 decision:** Deb Riechmann, "Trump Disbanded NSC Pandemic Unit That Experts Had Praised," AP, *AP News*, March 14, 2020, https://apnews.com/article/ce014d94b64e98b7203b873e56f80e9a.

x   **recommendations about school closures:** Sanger et al., "Before Virus Outbreak."

x   **pathogen passes harmful RNA:** Jonathan Corum and Carl Zimmer, "How Coronavirus Hijacks Your Cells," *The New York Times*, March 11, 2020, https://nytimes.com/interactive/2020/03/11/science/how-coronavirus-hijacks-your-cells.html.

xi   **the Huanan Seafood Wholesale Market:** Thomas J. Bollyky and Stewart M. Patrick, "Improving Pandemic Preparedness: Lessons from COVID-19," Council on Foreign Relations, Independent Task Force Report No. 78, October 2020, 36, https://cfr.org/report/pandemic-preparedness-lessons-COVID-19/.

xi   **released an "urgent notice":** Bollyky and Patrick, "Improving Pandemic Preparedness," 36.

xi   **for "spreading rumours":** Stephanie Hegarty, "The Chinese Doctor Who Tried to Warn Others about Coronavirus," *BBC News*, February 6, 2020, https://bbc.com/news/world-asia-china-51364382.

xi   **concerns to the World Health Organization:** Bollyky and Patrick, "Improving Pandemic Preparedness," 36.

xi   **springing up on the "US-based open-source":** Bollyky and Patrick, "Improving Pandemic Preparedness," 36.

xi   **twenty-seven cases in China's Hubei Province:** Louise Watt, "Taiwan Says It Tried to Warn the World about Coronavirus. Here's What It Really Knew and When," *Time*, May 19, 2020, https://time.com/5826025/taiwan-who-trump-coronavirus-covid19/; "News Scan for Dec 31, 2019," Center for Infectious Disease Research and Policy, accessed September 29, 2020, https://cidrap.umn.edu/news-perspective/2019/12/news-scan-dec-31-2019.

xi   **first COVID-19 death:** Derrick Bryson Taylor, "A Timeline of the Coronavirus Pandemic," *The New York Times*, August 6, 2020, https://nytimes.com/article/coronavirus-timeline.html.

xi   **no new cases since January 3:** Bollyky and Patrick, "Improving Pandemic Preparedness," 37.

xi   **virus sprang up in Thailand:** "Archived: WHO Timeline—COVID-19," World Health Organization, April 27, 2020, https://www.who.int/news/item/27-04-2020-who-timeline—covid-19.

xi   **spread to Japan and South Korea:** "Coronavirus Timeline: Tracking the Critical Moments of COVID-19," *NBC News*, accessed September 23, 2020, https://nbcnews.com/health/health-news/coronavirus-timeline-tracking-critical-moments-covid-19-n1154341.

xi   **reversed their January 11 announcement:** Bollyky and Patrick, "Improving Pandemic Preparedness," 37.

xi   **first American case was confirmed:** Bollyky and Patrick, "Improving Pandemic Preparedness," 40.

xi   **Chinese authorities suspended transportation:** Taylor, "Timeline of the Coronavirus Pandemic"; Bollyky and Patrick, "Improving Pandemic Preparedness," 40.

xi   **death toll had climbed to at least 360:** Taylor, "Timeline of the Coronavirus Pandemic."

xi   **moved cautiously, declaring:** Erin Schumaker, "Timeline: How Coronavirus Got Started," *ABC News,* September 22, 2020, https://abcnews.go.com/Health/timeline -coronavirus-started/story?id=69435165; Sui-Lee Wee, Donald G. McNeil Jr., and Javier C. Hernández, "W.H.O. Declares Global Emergency as Wuhan Coronavirus Spreads," *The New York Times,* April 16, 2020, https://nytimes.com/2020/01/30/health /coronavirus-world-health-organization.html.

xii   **an American with no travel history:** Schumaker, "How Coronavirus Got Started."

xii   **On March 11, the WHO:** Bill Chappell, "Coronavirus: COVID-19 Is Now Officially a Pandemic, WHO Says," National Public Radio, March 11, 2020, https://npr.org /sections/goatsandsoda/2020/03/11/814474930/coronavirus-covid-19-is-now-officially -a-pandemic-who-says.

xii   **reported global infections passed two hundred thousand:** Jeannette Jiang, Emily Peterson, and Robert Heimer, "COVID-19 Updated Data & Developments—March 18, 2020," Yale School of Medicine, March 18, 2020, https://medicine.yale.edu /news-article/23224/, citing https://coronavirus.jhu.edu/map.html.

xii   **borne witness to countless pandemics:** Bollyky and Patrick, "Improving Pandemic Preparedness," 22.

xiv   **warns of pneumonia of unknown cause:** Bollyky and Patrick, "Improving Pandemic Preparedness," 36.

xiv   **outbreak is posted to ProMED platform:** Bollyky and Patrick, "Improving Pandemic Preparedness," 36, 38.

xiv   **The WHO requests verification:** Bollyky and Patrick, "Improving Pandemic Preparedness," 36, 38.

xiv   **China announces its first virus death:** Taylor, "Timeline of the Coronavirus Pandemic."

xiv   **first case outside of China in Thailand:** "Archived: WHO Timeline—COVID-19," April 27, 2020.

xiv   **United States confirms its first case:** Taylor, "Timeline of the Coronavirus Pandemic."

xiv   **infected more than 570:** Taylor, "Timeline of the Coronavirus Pandemic."

xiv   **global death toll reaches at least 360:** Taylor, "Timeline of the Coronavirus Pandemic."

xiv   **outside of China in the Philippines:** "Novel Coronavirus (2019-nCoV) Situation Report—13," World Health Organization, February 2, 2020, https://who.int/docs /default-source/coronaviruse/situation-reports/20200202-sitrep-13-ncov-v3 .pdf?sfvrsn=195f4010_6.

xv   **no travel history to an outbreak area:** Schumaker, "How Coronavirus Got Started";
Erin Schumaker, Morgan Winsor, and Ivan Pereira, "Latest American Infected with
Coronavirus Has No Relevant Travel History: CDC," *ABC News*, February 26, 2020,
https://abcnews.go.com/International/us-military-coronavirus-patient-cases-surge-italy
-south/story?id=69225004.

xv   **reports its first COVID-19 death:** Taylor, "Timeline of the Coronavirus Pandemic."

xv   **died from it earlier:** Stephanie Soucheray, "Coroner: First US COVID-19 Death
Occurred in Early February," Center for Infectious Disease Research and Policy, April
22, 2020, https://cidrap.umn.edu/news-perspective/2020/04/coroner-first-us-covid-19
-death-occurred-early-february.

xv   **declares COVID-19 a "pandemic":** Chappell, "Coronavirus: COVID-19 Is Now
Officially a Pandemic, WHO Says."

xv   **Thirty-eight Americans have died:** "March 11 Coronavirus News," *CNN*, March 12,
2020, https://cnn.com/world/live-news/coronavirus-outbreak-03-11-20-intl-hnk/index.html.

xv   **Pfizer-BioNTech COVID-19 vaccine:** "FDA Takes Key Action in Fight against
COVID-19 by Issuing Emergency Use Authorization for First COVID-19 Vaccine,"
FDA News Release, December 11, 2020, https://fda.gov/news-events/press
-announcements/fda-takes-key-action-fight-against-covid-19-issuing-emergency-use
-authorization-first-covid-19.

xv   **Moderna COVID-19 vaccine:** "Moderna COVID-19 Vaccine," FDA News Release,
updated February 3, 2020, https://fda.gov/emergency-preparedness-and-response
/coronavirus-disease-2019-covid-19/moderna-covid-19-vaccine.

xv   **Johnson & Johnson vaccine:** "FDA Issues Emergency Use Authorization for Third
COVID-19 Vaccine," FDA News Release, February 27, 2021, https://fda.gov/news
-events/press-announcements/fda-issues-emergency-use-authorization-third-covid
-19-vaccine.

xv   **only 2.8 million have received:** Rebecca Robbins, Frances Robles, and Tim Arango,
"Here's Why Distribution of the Vaccine Is Taking Longer Than Expected," *The New
York Times*, December 31, 2020, https://nytimes.com/2020/12/31/health/vaccine-
distribution-delays.html.

xv   **Five hundred thousand Americans have died:** Pien Huang, "'A Loss to the Whole
Society': U.S. COVID-19 Death Tolll Reaches 500,000," NPR, February 22, 2021,
https://www.npr.org/sections/health-shots/2021/02/22/969494791/a-loss-to-the-whole
-society-u-s-covid-19-death-toll-reaches-500-000.

Chapter 1: What If?

5   **given command of the USS *Dobbin*:** Yeoman Second Class Kenneth Isaacs and Eliza
Isaacs, "USS *Dobbin*," in *Remembering Pearl Harbor*, eds. Robert S. La Forte and
Ronald E. Marcello (Wilmington, DE: Scholarly Resources, 1991), 197–98.

5   **forward positioned from the West Coast:** Roberta Wohlstetter, *Pearl Harbor: Warning
and Decision* (Stanford, CA: Stanford University Press, 1962), 80–81.

6   **quiet man and an avid hiker:** Isaacs and Isaacs, "USS *Dobbin*," 197.

6   **Once, he injured his arm while hiking:** Isaacs and Isaacs, "USS *Dobbin*," 197–98.

6   **Clad in a hat, a khaki uniform:** Isaacs and Isaacs, "USS *Dobbin*," 197.

7   **Just before 8:00 A.M.:** "The Path to Pearl Harbor," The National WWII Museum, New Orleans, accessed September 24, 2020, https://nationalww2museum.org/war/articles /path-pearl-harbor.

7   **launching 353 bomber:** Kenneth Hoffman, "Remembering Pearl Harbor: A Pearl Harbor Fact Sheet," The National WWII Museum, accessed October 6, 2020, https:// census.gov/history/pdf/pearl-harbor-fact-sheet-1.pdf.

7   **8 battleships severely damaged or destroyed:** Hoffman, "Remembering Pearl Harbor"; Tara Tyrrell, "American Ships Sunk at Pearl Harbor," pearlharbor.org, October 20, 2016, https://pearlharbor.org/sunk-not-forgotten-american-ships-sank-pearl-harbor-attack/.

7   **11 other vessels bombed and strafed:** These include four auxiliaries damaged, one auxiliary destroyed, three cruisers damaged, and three destroyers damaged. Hoffman, "Remembering Pearl Harbor."

8   **conducted regular war games:** Major Jeff Wong, "Interwar-Period Gaming Today for Conflicts Tomorrow: Press 'Start' to Play, Pt. 2," Center for International Maritime Security, May 8, 2017, http://cimsec.org/interwar-period-gaming-today-conflicts -tomorrow-press-start-play-pt-2/31712.

8   **aggressive expansion in Manchuria:** "The Path to Pearl Harbor," The National WWII Museum, New Orleans.

8   **embargoes on oil and scrap metal:** Wohlstetter, *Pearl Harbor*, 99, 131, 157, 163.

8   **more complex when Nazi Germany:** Wohlstetter, *Pearl Harbor*, 345–46.

8   **securing a political and economic order:** Wohlstetter, *Pearl Harbor*, 346–47.

8   **broken the Japanese code:** Wohlstetter, *Pearl Harbor*, 170.

8   **intercepted a coded message:** Wohlstetter, *Pearl Harbor*, 346–47.

8   **report on American military facilities:** Wohlstetter, *Pearl Harbor*, 211–12.

8   **Simultaneously, the US military, government sources:** Wohlstetter, *Pearl Harbor*, 37, 55, 124, 128, 158.

Chapter 2: Damocles and Me

15   **heavy sword hung from:** Marcus Tullius Cicero, *Cicero's Tusculan Disputations*, Project, https://gutenberg.org/files/14988/14988-h/14988-h.htm.

19   **in their book *Radical Uncertainty*:** John Kay and Mervyn King, *Radical Uncertainty: Decision-Making Beyond the Numbers* (New York: W.W. Norton & Company, 2020).

23   **gunfight in Somalia's smoldering capital:** Michael R. Gordon and Thomas L. Friedman, "Details of U.S. Raid in Somalia: Success So Near, a Loss So Deep," *The New York Times*, October 25, 1993, https://nytimes.com/1993/10/25/world/details-of-us -raid-in-somalia-success-so-near-a-loss-so-deep.html; Mark Bowden, "The Legacy of Black Hawk Down," *Smithsonian Magazine*, January/February 2019, https:// smithsonianmag.com/history/legacy-black-hawk-down-180971000.

23   **reluctantly deployed in 1995:** Steven Metz, "The American Army in the Balkans: Strategic Alternatives and Implications," Strategic Studies Institute, US Army War College, January 2001, 37–38.

25   **holding fifty-three American hostages:** Mark Bowden, "The Desert One Debacle," *The Atlantic*, May 1, 2006, https://theatlantic.com/magazine/archive/2006/05 /the-desert-one-debacle/304803/.

26   **On April 11, 1980:** Bowden, "Desert One Debacle."

26   **Air Force General David Jones:** Bowden, "Desert One Debacle."

26   **founder of America's nascent counterterrorist:** Bowden, "Desert One Debacle."

26   **intensive planning and rehearsals:** Bowden, "Desert One Debacle."

26   **85 percent probability of success:** Email exchange with Colonel (Retired) Keith Nightingale, one of the mission planners, March 2, 2020.

26   **secured by a truly active guard:** Email exchange with Colonel (Retired) Keith Nightingale, March 2, 2020.

26   **casualties among the operators:** Email exchange with Colonel (Retired) Keith Nightingale, March 2, 2020.

27   **Jones and Beckwith indicated:** Email exchange with Colonel (Retired) Keith Nightingale, March 2, 2020.

27   **Launching from an aircraft carrier:** Bowden, "Desert One Debacle."

27   **Infiltration involved flying:** Bowden, "Desert One Debacle"; Edward T. Russell, "Crisis in Iran: Operation EAGLE CLAW," in *Short of War: Major USAF Contingency Operations, 1947–1977*, ed. A. Timothy Warnock (Air Force History and Museums Program in association with Air University Press, 2000), 128–29.

27   **securing Tehran's soccer stadium:** Bowden, "Desert One Debacle"; Edward T. Russell, "Crisis in Iran: Operation EAGLE CLAW" in *Short of War: Major USAF Contingency Operations, 1947–1977*, ed. A. Timothy Warnock, (Air Force History and Museums Program in association with Air University Press, 2000), 130–131.

29   *fixed wing (F/W) and rotary*: Bowden, "Desert One Debacle"; Russell, "Crisis in Iran: Operation EAGLE CLAW," 128–29.

29   **they'd wait (undetected) during:** Russell, "Crisis in Iran: Operation EAGLE CLAW," 129.

29   **extract the hostages using:** Russell, "Crisis in Iran: Operation EAGLE CLAW," 129.

30   **five months of diplomatic impasse:** Elaine Kamarck, "The Iranian Hostage Crisis and Its Effect on American Politics," Brookings, November 4, 2019, https://brookings.edu /blog/order-from-chaos/2019/11/04/the-iranian-hostage-crisis-and-its-effect-on-american -politics/.

30   **been mitigated, as much as possible:** Email exchange with Colonel (Retired) Keith Nightingale, September 29, 2020.

30   **reduced periods of darkness would:** Email exchange with Colonel (Retired) Keith Nightingale, September 29, 2020.

31   **bring higher returns:** And sometimes, higher losses.

32   **an EC-130 and RH-53 collided:** Russell, "Crisis in Iran: Operation EAGLE CLAW," 133; Laura Lambert, "Operation Eagle Claw," *Encyclopedia Britannica*

Online, accessed October 26, 2020, https://britannica.com/event/Operation-Eagle
-Claw.

33   **poor eyesight:** Roberta Wohlstetter, *Pearl Harbor: Warning and Decision* (Stanford, CA: Stanford University Press, 1962), 337–38.

34   **batted .406 in 1941:** Bill Francis, "Ted's Pursuit of .400," National Baseball Hall of Fame, accessed October 26, 2020, https://baseballhall.org/discover-more/stories /baseball-history/teds-williams-pursuit-of-400.

Chapter 3: Communication

39   **lifting of an early morning fog:** Jim Bradshaw, "Battle of New Orleans," 64 Parishes—Louisiana Endowment for the Humanities, accessed March 21, 2021, https://64parishes.org/entry/battle-of-new-orleans-2.

39   **polyglot force:** "Battle of New Orleans," *History*, updated September 26, 2019, https://history.com/topics/war-of-1812/battle-of-new-orleans; "The Battle of New Orleans," White House Historical Association, accessed March 21, 2020, https://whitehousehistory.org/the-battle-of-new-orleans.

39   **earthworks reinforced:** "The Battle of New Orleans," White House Historical Association.

39   **whose casualties totaled:** This includes the dead, the wounded, the missing, and the captured. Bradshaw, "Battle of New Orleans"; "Battle of New Orleans," History; "New Orleans Chalmette Plantation," American Battlefield Trust, accessed March 21, 2021, https://battlefields.org/learn/war-1812/battles/new-orleans.

39   **thirteen Americans were killed:** Bradshaw, "Battle of New Orleans"; "New Orleans Chalmette Plantation," American Battlefield Trust.

40   **moving to withdraw guns:** "Battle of Balaklava," National Army Museum, accessed September 25, 2020, https://nam.ac.uk/explore/battle-balaklava; Tony Bunting, "Battle of Balaklava," *Encyclopedia Britannica Online*, last updated October 18, 2020, https:// britannica.com/event/Battle-of-Balaklava.

40   **order from Lord Raglan:** Bunting, "Battle of Balaklava."

40   **lost more than 110 men and 375 horses:** Bunting, "Battle of Balaklava."

41   **his famous hierarchy of needs:** Abraham Maslow offers a five-tier model of human needs. These begin with physiological needs (like food, water, etc.) progress to safety needs, ones for belonging and love, esteem, and finally, self-actualization.

45   **When nineteen hijackers passed unhindered:** National Commission on Terrorist Attacks upon the United States, *The 9/11 Commission Report: Executive Summary. Final Report of the National Commission on Terrorist Attacks upon the United States*, 2, 7, https://govinfo.library.unt.edu/911/report/911Report_Exec.pdf.

46   **"benefit and handicap of hindsight":** National Commission on Terrorist Attacks upon the United States, *The 9/11 Commission Report: Final Report of the National Commission on Terrorist Attacks upon the United States*, 339, https://govinfo.library.unt .edu/911/report/911Report.pdf.

46   **relevant information was not disseminated:** National Commission on Terrorist Attacks upon the United States, *9/11 Commission Report*, 254–77, 353.

46   **United States possessed sufficient information:** National Commission on Terrorist Attacks upon the United States, *9/11 Commission Report*, 344–48.

46   **CIA selected between six and eight:** National Commission on Terrorist Attacks upon the United States, *9/11 Commission Report*, 254.

46   **In the eight months prior:** National Commission on Terrorist Attacks upon the United States, *9/11 Commission Report*, 254.

46   **reporting "reached a crescendo":** On June 28, 2001, Richard Clarke, a counterterrorism policy official, is reported to have said that the pattern of al-Qaeda activity indicating attack planning over the past six weeks "had reached a crescendo." National Commission on Terrorist Attacks upon the United States, *9/11 Commission Report*, 257.

46   **with at least six separate intelligence reports:** National Commission on Terrorist Attacks upon the United States, *9/11 Commission Report*, 257.

46   **potential attacks in Yemen, Saudi Arabia:** National Commission on Terrorist Attacks upon the United States, *9/11 Commission Report*, 256–57.

46   **report on June 28 summed it up:** National Commission on Terrorist Attacks upon the United States, *9/11 Commission Report*, 257.

46   **President Bush explicitly requested:** National Commission on Terrorist Attacks upon the United States, *9/11 Commission Report*, 260.

47   **"[N]o one working on these":** National Commission on Terrorist Attacks upon the United States, *9/11 Commission Report*, 277.

47   **air traffic controller couldn't get ahold:** National Commission on Terrorist Attacks upon the United States, *9/11 Commission Report*, 18–19.

48   **"We have some planes":** National Commission on Terrorist Attacks upon the United States, *9/11 Commission Report*, 19.

48   **"Nobody move. Everything will be okay":** National Commission on Terrorist Attacks upon the United States, *9/11 Commission Report*, 19.

48   **Unable to fully discern the first:** National Commission on Terrorist Attacks upon the United States, *9/11 Commission Report*, 19.

48   **third and fourth words:** National Commission on Terrorist Attacks upon the United States, *9/11 Commission Report*, 23.

48   **The hijacker pilot evidently:** Another theory was that one of the crew members could have intentionally used the radio microphone to communicate with air traffic controllers. Matthew L. Wald and Kevin Sack, "'We Have Some Planes,' Hijacker Told Controller," *The New York Times*, October 16, 2001, https://nytimes.com/2001/10/16/national/we-have-some-planes-hijacker-told-controller.html.

48   **A simple communication error:** National Commission on Terrorist Attacks upon the United States, *9/11 Commission Report*, 23–25.

48   **"The most important failure":** National Commission on Terrorist Attacks upon the United States, *9/11 Commission Report: Executive Summary*, 9.

49   **"the system was blinking red":** National Commission on Terrorist Attacks upon the United States, *9/11 Commission Report*, 259.

50   **Part of a larger, aggressive influence:** "Joseph Goebbels," *American Experience*, PBS, accessed September 25, 2020, https://pbs.org/wgbh/americanexperience/features /goebbels-biography/; Helmut Heiber, "Joseph Goebbels," *Encyclopedia Britannica Online*, last updated October 25, 2020, https://britannica.com/biography/Joseph -Goebbels.

50   **"Effective propaganda must":** Adolf Hitler, *Mein Kampf*, trans. Ralph Manheim (Boston: Houghton Mifflin Company, 1943), chap. 6, Kindle.

50   **"the fact is real":** Hitler, *Mein Kampf*, chap. 6.

51   **linkage between smoking and lung cancer:** Allan M. Brandt, "Inventing Conflicts of Interest: A History of Tobacco Industry Tactics," *American Journal of Public Health* 102, no. 1 (January 2012): 63–71, https://doi.org/10.2105/AJPH.2011.300292.

51   **waged a more subtle effort:** Brandt, "Inventing Conflicts of Interest."

52   **"It is an obligation of the Tobacco":** Brandt, "Inventing Conflicts of Interest," 63–71, citing "Hill & Knowlton Inc Press release, re: Timothy V. Hartnett," Depositions and Trial Testimony Archive, Bates No. USX263293–USX263294, accessed October 20, 2011, http://legacy.library.ucsf.edu/tid/ppw36b00.

53   **Burgoyne's army of redcoats:** Kate Lohnes, "Battle of Saratoga," *US History: Pre-Columbian to the New Millennium*, accessed October 28, 2020, https://www.ushistory .org/US/11g.asp.

Chapter 4: Narrative

55   **roughly 180 defenders:** The estimate for the number of defenders ranges from 183 to 189 (and some historians suggest an even higher number). Jeff Wallenfeldt, "Texas Revolution: Santa Anna Responds: The Alamo and the Goliad Massacre," *Encyclopedia Britannica Online*, accessed December 20, 2020, https://britannica.com/topic /Texas-Revolution/Santa-Anna-responds-the-Alamo-and-the-Goliad-Massacre.

58   **"I wouldn't know, sir":** Martin Meredith, *The Fate of Africa: A History of the Continent since Independence* (New York: PublicAffairs, 2005), chap. 1, Kindle.

59   **Google's twenty-third employee:** Jessica Livingston, *Founders at Work: Stories of Startups' Early Days* (Apress, 2008), chap. 12, Kindle.

59   **He was sitting in a meeting:** Livingston, *Founders at Work*, chap. 12.

59   **temptations of some advertising agencies:** Livingston, *Founders at Work*, chap. 12.

60   **"'Don't be evil' is kind of funny":** Livingston, *Founders at Work*, chap. 12.

60   **"typical meaningless corporate statement":** Livingston, *Founders at Work*, chap. 12.

60   **Google's IPO registration incorporated:** See in particular the IPO registration's "Letters from the Founders" section, which addresses potential new stakeholders. Ken Hillis, Michael Petit, and Kylie Jarrett, *Google and the Culture of Search* (New York: Routledge, 2013), chap. 7.

60   **The company wrote:** Hillis, Petit, and Jarrett, *Google and the Culture of Search*, chap. 7.

60 **Revenue skyrocketed from:** Google, Form 10-K for the Fiscal Year Ended December 31, 2004, https://sec.gov/Archives/edgar/data/1288776/000119312505065298/d10k.htm; Google, Form 10-K for the Fiscal Year Ended December 31, 2006, https://sec.gov/Archives/edgar/data/1288776/000119312507044494/d10k.htm.

60 **Page, one of Google's founders:** Noam Scheiber and Kate Conger, "The Great Google Revolt," *The New York Times Magazine*, February 18, 2020, https://nytimes.com/interactive/2020/02/18/magazine/google-revolt.html; Google, Final Prospectus, April 18, 2004, https://sec.gov/Archives/edgar/data/1288776/000119312504143377/d424b4.htm.

60 **pairing their "staggering incomes":** Scheiber and Conger, "Great Google Revolt."

61 **Google would provide the DoD:** Scheiber and Conger, "Great Google Revolt."

61 **"AI arms race":** Cheryl Pellerin, "Project Maven to Deploy Computer Algorithms to War Zone by Year's End," US Department of Defense, July 21, 2017, https://defense.gov/Explore/News/Article/Article/1254719/project-maven-to-deploy-computer-algorithms-to-war-zone-by-years-end/.

61 **identifying as an AI company:** Pellerin, "Project Maven to Deploy Computer Algorithms to War Zone by Year's End."

61 **"customized AI surveillance engine":** Letter to Sundar Pinchai, https://static01.nyt.com/files/2018/technology/googleletter.pdf.

61 **both machine learning and deep learning:** Pellerin, "Project Maven to Deploy Computer Algorithms to War Zone by Year's End."

61 **track the movements:** Letter to Sundar Pinchai.

61 **software had greater success:** Scheiber and Conger, "Great Google Revolt."

62 **nineteenth-century minstrel shows:** Beatrice Dupuy, "No Evidence Former Slave Who Helped Launch Aunt Jemima Products Became a Millionaire," AP, June 19, 2020, https://apnews.com/afs:Content:9030960288.

62 **the "mammy" character:** Dupuy, "No Evidence Former Slave Who Helped Launch Aunt Jemima Products Became a Millionaire."

62 **Pearl Milling Company:** "Aunt Jemima Rebranded as Pearl Mining Company," PR Newswire, February 9, 2021, https://prnewswire.com/news-releases/aunt-jemima-rebrands-as-pearl-milling-company-301225441.html.

62 **Born into slavery:** Dupuy, "No Evidence Former Slave Who Helped Launch Aunt Jemima Products Became a Millionaire"; Sam Roberts, "Overlooked No More: Nancy Green, the Real Aunt Jemima," *The New York Times*, July 17, 2020, https://nytimes.com/2020/07/17/obituaries/nancy-green-aunt-jemima-overlooked.html.

62 **unmarked pauper's grave:** Sam Roberts, "Overlooked No More: Nancy Green, the Real Aunt Jemima."

62 **Encouraged to "act like owners":** Scheiber and Conger, "Great Google Revolt."

62 **Google employees put out feelers:** Scheiber and Conger, "Great Google Revolt."

62 **Liz Fong-Jones, then an engineer:** Scheiber and Conger, "Great Google Revolt."

63 **write an open letter:** Scheiber and Conger, "Great Google Revolt."

63 **they had two principal requests:** Letter to Sundar Pinchai.

63   "Google's stated values": Letter to Sundar Pinchai.

63   **employees worried that Google had stooped:** Letter to Sundar Pinchai.

63   **"irreparably damage Google's brand":** Letter to Sundar Pinchai.

63   **2004 prospectus:** Scheiber and Conger, "Great Google Revolt."

63   **dozen employees quit:** Kate Conger, "Google Employees Resign in Protest Against Pentagon Contract," Gizmodo, May 14, 2018, https://gizmodo.com/google-employees -resign-in-protest-against-pentagon-con-1825729300.

63   **renew the contract:** Scheiber and Conger, "Great Google Revolt."

63   **picked up by Palantir:** Tristan Greene, "Report: Palantir took over Project Maven, the military AI program too unethical for Google," The New Web, December 11, 2019, https://thenextweb.com/artificial-intelligence/2019/12/11/report-palantir-took-over -project-maven-the-military-ai-program-too-unethical-for-google/.

63   **Chinese government to censor search:** Scheiber and Conger, "Great Google Revolt."

63   *The Intercept* **exposed Google's dealings:** Scheiber and Conger, "Great Google Revolt."

63   **project was also scrutinized by Congress:** Issie Lapowsky, "Congress Challenges Google on China. Google Falls Short," *Wired*, September 26, 2018, https://wired.com /story/congress-google-project-dragonfly-questions/.

65   *I Want YOU for U.S. Army*: Kelly Knauer, "I Want You: The Story behind the Iconic Recruitment Poster," *Time Books*, April 6, 2017, https://time.com/4725856 /uncle-sam-poster-history/.

65   **cover of** *Leslie's Weekly* **magazine's:** Knauer, "I Want You."

65   **printing more than four million copies:** Knauer, "I Want You."

66   **As this 1959 advertisement captures:** *Recruiting Journal of the United States Army* (Washington, DC: The Service, 1959), 25.

66   *Today's Army Wants to Join You*: Beth Bailey, "The Army in the Marketplace: Recruiting an All-Volunteer Force," The Journal of American History 94, no. 1 (June 2007): 62.

66   *Be All You Can Be*: Matthew Cox, "Army Wants New Recruiting Slogan as Powerful as 'Be All You Can Be,'" *Military.com*, June 26, 2018, https://military.com/daily -news/2018/06/26/army-wants-new-recruiting-slogan-powerful-be-all-you-can-be.html.

67   *An Army of One*: The Army adopted this campaign in January 2001, eight months before 9/11. It lasted through 2006. Cox, "Army Wants New Recruiting Slogan."

67   **followed by** *Army Strong*: Cox, "Army Wants New Recruiting Slogan"; "'Army Strong' Replaces 'Army of One'" NBC News, October 9, 2006, https://nbcnews.com/id /wbna15197720.

67   **full of computer-generated images:** "What's Your Warrior? | Join Forces | GOARMY | Commercial," YouTube, uploaded by GoArmy, November 9, 2019, https://youtube .com/watch?v=7TprgnuYfyQ.

67   **Old French** *guerrier*: "Warrior," *Oxford Dictionary on Lexico.com*, accessed January 2, 2021, https://lexico.com/en/definition/warrior.

67   **"military anachronism":** Jim Gourley, "What's a Soldier? What's a Warrior? Well, Do You Want to Live in a State or in a Tribe?" Best Defense (blog by Thomas E. Ricks),

Foreign Policy, September 15, 2016, https://foreignpolicy.com/2016/09/15/whats-a
-soldier-whats-a-warrior-well-do-you-want-to-live-in-a-state-or-in-a-tribe/.

67   **"soldiers [have] replaced warriors"**: Gourley, "What's a Soldier? What's a Warrior?"

68   **describing them "as dedicated warriors"**: Dave Philipps, "Trump Clears Three
Service Members in War Crimes Cases," *The New York Times*, November 15, 2019,
https://nytimes.com/2019/11/15/us/trump-pardons.html.

68   **Described as "'warriors' and not traitors"**: Helene Cooper, Maggie Haberman, and
Thomas Gibbons-Neff, "Trump Says He Intervened in War Crimes Cases to Protect
'Warriors,'" *The New York Times*, November 25, 2019, https://nytimes.com/2019/11/25
/us/politics/mark-esper-seal-navy-secretary.html, citing President Trump.

69   **worldwide infection reached 118,000 people**: "WHO Director-General's Opening
Remarks at the Media Briefing on COVID-19," World Health Organization,
March 11, 2020, https://www.who.int/director-general/speeches/detail/who-director
-general-s-opening-remarks-at-the-media-briefing-on-covid-19---11-march-2020.

Chapter 5: Structure

71   **"Dutch, where's your division?"**: David Halberstam, *The Coldest Winter* (New York:
Hyperion, 2007), 269.

71   **Keiser's 2nd Infantry Division's**: Halberstam, *The Coldest Winter*, 268-269.

71   **called a "police action"**: "US Enters the Korean Conflict," National Archives, August
15, 2016, https://archives.gov/education/lessons/korean-conflict.

71   **Within days of hostilities**: Richard W. Stewart, ed., "The Korean War, 1950–1953,"
chap. 8 in *American Military History*, vol. 2, *The United States Army in a Global Era,
1917–2008* (Washington, DC: Center of American Military History, United States
Army, 2010), 223.

73   **forces stationed in Japan**: Stewart, "The Korean War, 1950–1953," 226.

75   **9/11 *Commission Report* uncovered**: National Commission on Terrorist Attacks upon
the United States, *The 9/11 Commission Report: Final Report of the National
Commission on Terrorist Attacks upon the United States*, 353, https://govinfo.library.unt
.edu/911/report/911Report.pdf.

78   **"cushy, high-end funeral parlor"**: Chase Untermeyer, "Location, Location, Location:
The West Wing of the White House," Lyndon B. Johnson Presidential Library, Austin,
Texas, June 9, 2015, http://untermeyer.com/location-location-location-the-west-wing-of
-the-white-house/.

78   **Tiny, sometimes windowless offices**: James F. Clarity and Warren Weaver Jr., "Briefing;
Buchanan's Window," *The New York Times*, December 24, 1985, https://nytimes
.com/1985/12/24/us/briefing-buchanan-s-window.html.

79   **"Proximity . . . is a source and sign"**: George Stephanopoulos, *All Too Human: A
Political Education* (New York: Little, Brown, 2008), chap. 7, Kindle.

79   **"more closely" with the president**: Stephanopoulos, *All Too Human*, chap. 7.

79   **"even if it were a matter of inches"**: Stephanopoulos, *All Too Human*, chap. 7.

79   **likening the Old Executive Office Building**: Stephanopoulos, *All Too Human*, chap. 7.

79   full, "protected" access to the president: Stephanopoulos, *All Too Human*, chap. 7.

80   Lehman Brothers had several formal mechanisms: Rosalind Z. Wiggins and Andrew Metrick, "The Lehman Brothers Bankruptcy B: Risk Limits and Stress Tests," *SSRN*, October 2014, 4, https://doi.org/10.2139/ssrn.2588547.

80   to enact new regulations: Kim Pernell, Jiwook Jung, and Frank Dobbin, "The Hazards of Expert Control: Chief Risk Officers and Risky Derivatives," *American Sociological Review* 82, no. 3 (May 31, 2017): 511–41, https://doi.org/10.1177/0003122417701115.

80   "Risk Assessment and Control Department": Bethany McLean and Peter Elkind, *The Smartest Guys in the Room: The Amazing Rise and Scandalous Fall of Enron* (New York: Portfolio /Penguin, 2013), 115.

80   mere administrative formality: McLean and Elkind, *Smartest Guys in the Room*, 116–17.

80   a "hurdle" to be overcome: McLean and Elkind, *Smartest Guys in the Room*, 116.

81   known as moral licensing: Pernell, Jung, and Dobbin, "Hazards of Expert Control."

81   like Joe Gregory at Lehman Brothers: Sorkin, *Too Big to Fail*, 124.

82   dedicated risk-management committee: Sorkin, *Too Big to Fail*, 370.

82   stopped inviting the CRO: Sorkin, *Too Big to Fail*, 124.

82   fully understand the complex derivative: Sorkin, *Too Big to Fail*, 204; Emilia Klepczarek, "The Importance of the Board of Directors. Lessons from Lehman's Failure," *Ekonomia I Prawo. Economics and Law* 16, no. 1 (March 2017): 63–64, https://doi.org/10.12775/EiP.2017.005.

82   "This is a day of disgrace!": Sorkin, *Too Big to Fail*, 371.

82   then "sidelined" her: "Not Too Big to Fail: Why Lehman Brothers Had to Go Bankrupt," *Knowledge @ Wharton*, September 28, 2018, https://knowledge.wharton .upenn.edu/article/the-good-reasons-why-lehman-failed/.

82   isolating the CRO: Sorkin, *Too Big to Fail*, 124; Wiggins and Metrick, "Lehman Brothers Bankruptcy B."

82   board was ill-equipped to understand: Grant Kirkpatrick, "The Corporate Governance Lessons from the Financial Crisis," *OECD Journal: Financial Market Trends*, no. 1 (September 2009): 61–87, https://doi.org/10.1787/fmt-v2009-art3-en.

82   made worse by increasing risk-appetite limits: Wiggins and Metrick, "Lehman Brothers Bankruptcy B: Risk Limits and Stress Tests", 4–10.

82   "core competencies of the firm": Wiggins and Metrick, "Lehman Brothers Bankruptcy B: Risk Limits and Stress Tests, 4.

Chapter 6: Technology

85   "We live in a society exquisitely": Carl Sagan, "Why We Need to Understand Science," *Skeptical Inquirer* 14, no. 3 (Spring 1990): 264, https://skepticalinquirer .org/1990/04/why-we-need-to-understand-science/.

86   September 26, 1983: Sewell Chan, "Stanislav Petrov, Soviet Officer Who Helped Avert Nuclear War, Is Dead at 77," *The New York Times*, September 18, 2017, https://nytimes .com/2017/09/18/world/europe/stanislav-petrov-nuclear-war-dead.html.

86   **no direct authority to initiate:** David Hoffman, "'I Had a Funny Feeling in My Gut,'" *The Washington Post Foreign Service*, February 10, 1999, p. A19, https://washingtonpost .com/wp-srv/inatl/longterm/coldwar/soviet10.htm; Chan, "Stanislav Petrov."

86   **single phone call of warning:** Chan, "Stanislav Petrov."

86   **five Minuteman intercontinental ballistic missiles:** Chan, "Stanislav Petrov."

86   **paused in shock:** Chan, "Stanislav Petrov."

86   **They understood well:** Chan, "Stanislav Petrov"; Hoffman, "'I Had a Funny Feeling in My Gut.'"

87   **Still, he knew the time:** Chan, "Stanislav Petrov."

87   **Petrov later explained:** Chan, "Stanislav Petrov"; Hoffman, "'I Had a Funny Feeling in My Gut.'"

87   **strange for the Americans to launch:** Chan, "Stanislav Petrov"; Hoffman, "'I Had a Funny Feeling in My Gut.'"

88   **"50-50" estimate of probability:** Chan, "Stanislav Petrov."

88   **early warning satellite constellation:** Chan, "Stanislav Petrov"; Hoffman, "'I Had a Funny Feeling in My Gut.'"

89   **he received a reprimand:** Chan, "Stanislav Petrov."

89   **faulted his improper note taking:** Hoffman, "'I Had a Funny Feeling in My Gut.'"

92   **O&I in detail in previous books:** Particularly in *Team of Teams: New Rules of Engagement for a Complex World* (New York: Portfolio/Penguin, 2015).

94   **possible that 95 percent of customer interactions:** Ed Lauder, "AI will power 95% of customer interactions by 2025," *AI Business*, March 10, 2017, https://aibusiness.com /document.asp?doc_id=760184.

94   **AI-enabled automated services have expanded:** Ryan W. Buell, "The Parts of Customer Service That Should Never Be Automated," *Harvard Business Review*, February 19, 2018, https://hbr.org/2018/02/the-parts-of-customer-service-that-should -never-be-automated.

97   **found that a normal nine-to-five workday:** Lindsay Tigar, "We're in the Midst of a Massive Work-from-Home Experiment. What If It Works?" *Fast Company*, March 26, 2020, https://.fastcompany.com/90481356/were-in-the-midst-of-a-massive-work-from -home-experiment-what-if-it-works.

Chapter 7: Diversity

99   **Edmund Pettus Bridge:** Anthony Cotton, "Marching with King: After 50 Years, a Coloradan Makes an Emotional Return to Selma," Colorado Public Radio, February 27, 2020, https://cpr.org/2020/02/27/marching-with-king-after-50-years-a-coloradan -makes-an-emotional-return-to-selma/.

99   **two hundred state police and deputized whites:** Matt Schudel, "Amelia Boynton Robinson, Activist Beaten on Selma Bridge, Dies at 104," *The Washington Post*, August 26, 2015, https://washingtonpost.com/national/amelia-boynton-robinson-activist-beaten -on-selma-bridge-dies-at-104/2015/08/26/9478d25e-4c11-11e5-bfb9-9736d04fc8e4 _story.html.

99   **led by Sheriff Jim Clark of Dallas County:** John Lewis, "Rep. John Lewis: An Oral History of Selma and the Struggle for the Voting Rights Act," *Time*, December 25, 2014, https://time.com/3647070/selma-john-lewis-voting-rights-act/.

99   **beating the marchers:** Christopher Klein, "How Selma's 'Bloody Sunday' Became a Turning Point in the Civil Rights Movement," *History*, March 6, 2015, https://history .com/news/selma-bloody-sunday-attack-civil-rights-movement.

99   **followed by two subsequent marches:** "Selma to Montgomery March," The Martin Luther King, Jr. Research and Education Institute, Stanford University, accessed September 21, 2020, https://kinginstitute.stanford.edu/encyclopedia/selma -montgomery-march.

103   **the CIA developed a series of plans:** "The Bay of Pigs," John F. Kennedy Presidential Library and Museum, accessed March 23, 2021, https://jfklibrary.org/learn/about-jfk /jfk-in-history/the-bay-of-pigs; Walter S. Poole, "The Joint Chiefs of Staff and National Policy, 1961–1964," Office of Joint History, Office of the Chairman of the Joint Chiefs of Staff, Washington, DC, 2011, 108, https://jcs.mil/Portals/36/Documents/History /Policy/Policy_V008.pdf.

103   **recommended to President-elect Kennedy:** Stephen Bates and Joshua L. Rosenbloom, "Kennedy and the Bay of Pigs," Kennedy School of Government Case Program, 1998, 3, https://sog.unc.edu/sites/www.sog.unc.edu/files/course_materials/Bay%20of %20Pigs%20case.pdf.

103   **quietly infiltrated onto the island:** Poole, "Joint Chiefs of Staff and National Policy," 108; Bates and Rosenbloom, "Kennedy and the Bay of Pigs," 2.

103   **conventionally organized invasion force:** Poole, "Joint Chiefs of Staff and National Policy," 114; "The Bay of Pigs," John F. Kennedy Presidential Library and Museum; "231. Memorandum No. 1 from the Cuba Study Group to President Kennedy," Office of the Historian, June 13, 1961, https://history.state.gov/historicaldocuments/frus1961 -63v10/d231.

103   **Escambray Mountains:** "The Bay of Pigs," John F. Kennedy Presidential Library and Museum.

103   **president met with his key advisers:** Robert Dallek, "JFK vs. the Military," *The Atlantic*, Fall 2003, https://theatlantic.com/magazine/archive/2013/08/jfk-vs-the-military/309496/; "The Bay of Pigs Invasion/Playa Girón: A Chronology of Events," National Security Archive, accessed October 12, 2020, https://nsarchive2.gwu.edu/bayofpigs/chron.html.

105   **prospects for the operation's success:** "Bay of Pigs Invasion/Playa Girón"; Poole, "Joint Chiefs of Staff and National Policy," 109.

105   **direct the Defense Department to more formally:** "Bay of Pigs Invasion/Playa Girón."

105   **the next two and a half months:** Poole, "Joint Chiefs of Staff and National Policy," 109–10.

106   **"just sat there nodding":** Jeffrey A. Friedman, *War and Chance: Assessing Uncertainty in International Politics* (New York: Oxford University Press, 2019), 146; Dallek, "JFK vs. the Military."

106   **equally mistrustful of Kennedy:** Dallek, "JFK vs. the Military."

106   **a series of noncommittal evaluations:** Friedman, *War and Chance*, 145–46; "Lyman Louis Lemnitzer," Joint Chiefs of Staff, accessed September 21, 2020, https://jcs.mil /About/The-Joint-Staff/Chairman/General-Lyman-Louis-Lemnitzer/; Poole, "Joint Chiefs of Staff and National Policy," 109-113.

106   **was a CIA operation:** Poole, "Joint Chiefs of Staff and National Policy," 116–117.

107   **members included Admiral Arleigh Burke:** Poole, "Joint Chiefs of Staff and National Policy," 2–4.

107   **highly publicized youthful dynamism:** Poole, "Joint Chiefs of Staff and National Policy," 2; Dallek, "JFK vs. the Military."

107   **significant doubts about the wisdom:** Irving L. Janis, "Groupthink," reprinted from *Psychology Today*, Ziff-Davis Publishing Company, 1971, 87, http://agcommtheory .pbworks.com/f/GroupThink.pdf.

107   **spent two years:** Janis, "Groupthink," 84.

107   **a group adopts a similar opinion:** Janis, "Groupthink," 84.

107   **groupthink silences deviant thoughts:** Janis, "Groupthink," 85.

107   **Janis defines eight "symptoms":** "Groupthink," 85.

108   **invulnerable to danger:** Janis, "Groupthink," 85.

108   **rationalizations to ignore:** Janis, "Groupthink," 86.

108   **They perpetuated stereotypes:** Janis, "Groupthink," 86.

108   **this phenomenon apply pressure:** Janis, "Groupthink," 87.

108   **likely participated in self-censorship:** Janis, "Groupthink," 85.

108   **were acting like mindguards:** Janis, "Groupthink," 88.

108   **appear to be unanimous:** Janis, "Groupthink," 87.

108   **On October 16, 1962:** Ernest R. May and Philip D. Zelikow, eds., *The Kennedy Tapes: Inside the White House During the Cuban Missile Crisis*, (New York: W. W. Norton & Company, 2002), 31–34; Robert F. Kennedy, *Thirteen Days: A Memoir of the Cuban Missile Crisis* (New York: W. W. Norton & Company, 1971), Section 1, "Address by President Kennedy: October 22, 1962," Kindle.

108   **USSR achieved a strategic advantage:** Kennedy, *Thirteen Days*, 149, "Address by President Kennedy."

108   **the missiles' flight distance:** Kennedy, *Thirteen Days*, Section 2.

109   **Surveillance imagery informs:** May and Zelikow, 32–33; Robert F. Kennedy, *Thirteen Days*, Section 1, "Address by President Kennedy: October 22, 1962."

109   **intermediate-range ballistic missile (IRBM) sites:** May and Zelikow, The Kennedy Tapes: Inside the White House During the Cuban Missile Crisis, 76.

109   **discuss and debate options:** May and Zelikow, The Kennedy Tapes: Inside the White House During the Cuban Missile Crisis, 109–137.

109   **settles on the "blockade-ultimatum":** May and Zelikow, The Kennedy Tapes: Inside the White House During the Cuban Missile Crisis, 136–138.

109   **formally convenes ExComm:** May and Zelikow, The Kennedy Tapes: Inside the White House During the Cuban Missile Crisis, 151.

109   **informs Congress of his decision:** May and Zelikow, The Kennedy Tapes: Inside the White House During the Cuban Missile Crisis, 163–183.

109   **addresses the American people:** May and Zelikow, The Kennedy Tapes: Inside the White House During the Cuban Missile Crisis, 183–189.

109   **letter to Chairman Khrushchev:** May and Zelikow, The Kennedy Tapes: Inside the White House During the Cuban Missile Crisis, 189–190.

109   **expressing grievance and frustration:** May and Zelikow, The Kennedy Tapes: Inside the White House During the Cuban Missile Crisis, 242–243.

109   **continue to ready their missile sites:** May and Zelikow, The Kennedy Tapes: Inside the White House During the Cuban Missile Crisis, 269.

109   **Soviet ships headed to Cuba:** May and Zelikow, The Kennedy Tapes: Inside the White House During the Cuban Missile Crisis, 297–99.

109   **seemingly contradictory letter:** May and Zelikow, The Kennedy Tapes: Inside the White House During the Cuban Missile Crisis, 311–14.

109   **American U-2 plane:** May and Zelikow, The Kennedy Tapes: Inside the White House During the Cuban Missile Crisis, 356–61.

109   **remove and dismantle their missiles:** May and Zelikow, The Kennedy Tapes: Inside the White House During the Cuban Missile Crisis, 402–404, 436–37.

110   **Executive Committee of the National Security Council:** Kennedy, Thirteen Days, Section 1; May and Zelikow, The Kennedy Tapes: Inside the White House During the Cuban Missile Crisis, 151.

110   **"the new chairman of the joint chiefs":** Josh Zeitz, "When Daily Intelligence Briefings Prevented a Nuclear War," Politico Magazine, December 12, 2016, https://politico.com/magazine/story/2016/12/trump-daily-intelligence-briefings-history-jfk-cuban-missile-crisis-214521.

110   **Edward Martin, as well as:** Kennedy, Thirteen Days, Section 1.

110   **significant changes to the JCS:** Poole, "Joint Chiefs of Staff and National Policy," 3.

110   **US forces conduct air strikes:** Dallek, "JFK vs. the Military"; May and Zelikow, The Kennedy Tapes: Inside the White House During the Cuban Missile Crisis 109–123.

110   **President Kennedy regarded air strikes:** Aleksandr Fursenko and Timothy Naftali, "One Hell of a Gamble": Khrushchev, Castro, and Kennedy, 1958-1964 (W. W. Norton & Company, 1998), chap. 12, Kindle; May and Zelikow, The Kennedy Tapes: Inside the White House During the Cuban Missile Crisis, 47–72.

110   **Dr. Strangelove:** In this film, a general fixed his sights on a massive nuclear war—other generals and politicians aim to stop his pursuits.

111   **coalesced into two major options:** Kennedy, Thirteen Days, Section 3; Poole, "Joint Chiefs of Staff and National Policy," 171; Fursenko and Naftali, One Hell of a Gamble, chap. 12.

111   **"the strongest case possible":** Fursenko and Naftali, One Hell of a Gamble, chap. 12.

111   **four members in particular:** Email exchange with Philip Zelikow, May 11, 2021; May and Zelikow, The Kennedy Tapes: Inside the White House During the Cuban Missile Crisis, 123–26, 136–37.

111   **"atypical:"** Email exchange with Philip Zelikow, May 11, 2021.

112   **"I think you're really making":** "'Why You've Got to Do It a Little Slower.' John F. Kennedy Consults Dwight D. Eisenhower during the Cuban Missile Crisis," UVA Miller Center, accessed October 14, 2020, https://millercenter.org/the-presidency /educational-resources/john-f-kennedy-and-dwight-eisenhower; May and Zelikow, *The Kennedy Tapes: Inside the White House During the Cuban Missile Crisis*, 144.

112   **communicated the blockade plan:** Kennedy, *Thirteen Days*, Section 4; May and Zelikow, *The Kennedy Tapes: Inside the White House During the Cuban Missile Crisis*, 183–89.

112   **another round of deliberations:** Kennedy, *Thirteen Days*, Section 9; May and Zelikow, *The Kennedy Tapes: Inside the White House During the Cuban Missile Crisis*, 311–388.

112   **Tensions rose as a U-2 was shot down:** May and Zelikow, The Kennedy Tapes: Inside the White House During the Cuban Missile Crisis, 356–61.

112   **"grave risk to the peace of the world":** May and Zelikow, The Kennedy Tapes: Inside the White House During the Cuban Missile Crisis, 388.

112   **shared this sentiment:** May and Zelikow, The Kennedy Tapes: Inside the White House During the Cuban Missile Crisis, 389–91. *Missile Crisis*, 388–91; Fursenko and Timothy, *"One Hell of a Gamble"* chap. 14.

112   **somewhat of an expert himself:** Zeitz, "When Daily Intelligence Briefings Prevented a Nuclear War."

113   **"From all this probing and examination":** Kennedy, *Thirteen Days*, Section 13.

113   **the most successful banks:** Chris Clearfield and András Tilcsik, *Meltdown: What Plane Crashes, Oil Spills, and Dumb Business Decisions Can Teach Us about How to Succeed at Work and at Home* (New York: Penguin Books, 2018), chap. 8, Kindle.

113   **three reasons for this:** Clearfield and Tilcsik, *Meltdown*, chap. 8.

114   **board's fundamental lack of diversity:** Clearfield and Tilcsik, *Meltdown*, chap. 8.

114   **But the Theranos board:** Clearfield and Tilcsik, *Meltdown*, chap. 8.

114   ***Wall Street Journal* article exposed:** Clearfield and Tilcsik, *Meltdown*, chap. 8.

114   **shut down in September 2018:** Reed Abelson, "Theranos is Shutting Down," *The New York Times*, September 5, 2018, https://nytimes.com/2018/09/05/health/theranos -shutting-down.html#:~:text=The%20Silicon%20Valley%20startup%20is,testing %20amid%20allegations%20of%20fraud.

114   **"makes the whole group more skeptical":** Clearfield and Tilcsik, *Meltdown*, chap. 8.

114   **Paraphrasing Sallie Krawcheck:** Clearfield and Tilcsik, *Meltdown*, chap. 8.

116   **fusion cells *fuse* intelligence:** Christopher Fussell, Trevor Hough, and Matthew Pedersen, "What Makes Fusion Cells Effective?" Naval Postgraduate School, 2009, https://apps.dtic.mil/dtic/tr/fulltext/u2/a514114.pdf.

116   **"operational focal point":** "Report on U.S. Hostage Policy," The White House, June 2015, 8, https://obamawhitehouse.archives.gov/sites/default/files/docs/report_on_us -_hostage_policy_final.pdf.

116   **The HRFC has five main hubs:** "A View from the CT Foxhole: Rob Saale, Former Director, U.S. Hostage Recovery Fusion Cell," Combating Terrorism Center at West

Point, January 23, 2020, https://ctc.usma.edu/view-ct-foxhole-rob-saale-former-director
-u-s-hostage-recovery-fusion-cell/

117 **investigating a plot to bomb:** "New York JTTF Celebrates 35 Years," Federal Bureau
of Investigation, December 8, 2015, https://fbi.gov/news/stories/new-york-jttf
-celebrates-35-years.

117 **the state of Missouri:** "State Leaders Tout Collaborative Response to Pandemic," *News
Tribune*, September 27, 2020, https://newstribune.com/news/local/story/2020/sep/27
/state-leaders-tout-collaborative-response-to-pandemic/843052.

Chapter 8: Bias

119 **"If slaves will make good soldiers":** James McPherson, Battle Cry of Freedom (New
York: Oxford University Press, 1988), 835.

119 **Patrick Byrne suspected:** Cade Metz and Julie Creswell, "Patrick Byrne, Overstock C.E.O.,
Resigns after Disclosing Romance with Russian Agent," *The New York Times*, August 22,
2019, https://nytimes.com/2019/08/22/business/overstock-ceo-patrick-byrne.html.

119 **working with the FBI:** Abha Bhattarai, "Overstock CEO Patrick Byrne resigns after
saying he aided in 'deep state' Russian Investigation," *The Washington Post*, August 22,
2019, https:// washingtonpost.com/business/2019/08/22/overstock-ceo-patrick-byrne
-resigns-after-saying-he-aided-deep-state-russia-investigation/; Abha Bhattari, "Inside
Overstock.com, Where a Firebrand CEO and 'Deep State' Intrigue Took Center Stage," *The
Washington Post*, September 27, 2019, https:// washingtonpost.com/business/2019/09/26
/inside-overstockcom-where-firebrand-ceo-deep-state-intrigue-took-center-stage/.

119 **working as a Russian agent:** Metz and Creswell, "Patrick Byrne, Overstock C.E.O.,
Resigns"; Bhattarai, "Overstock CEO Patrick Byrne Resigns"; Bhattarai, "Inside
Overstock.com."

119 **"Democrats and Republicans":** Patrick Byrne also endorsed election fraud conspiracy
theories about the corruption of the 2020 presidential election. Sheelah Kolhatkar, "A
Tycoon's Deep-State Conspiracy Dive," *The New Yorker*, December 7, 2020, https://
newyorker.com/magazine/2020/12/14/a-tycoons-deep-state-conspiracy-dive.

119 **"100 times bigger than Watergate":** Charles Gasparino and Lydia Moynihan, "Fmr.
Overstock CEO Patrick Byrne Wants to Explain Controversial Exit, Stock Sale and
Predicts More Deep State Revelations," *Fox Business*, October 7, 2019, https://fox
business.com/business-leaders/fmr-overstock-ceo-patrick-byrne-exit-stock-sale-deep-state.

119 **CEO of Overstock.com:** Metz and Creswell, "Patrick Byrne, Overstock C.E.O., Resigns."

120 **Dartmouth/Cambridge/Stanford pedigree:** Kolhatkar, "A Tycoon's Deep-State
Conspiracy Dive," *The New Yorker*.

120 **board was appropriately biased:** Tara Law, "Interim Overstock CEO Talks to TIME
about the Future after Scandal, and Patrick Byrne," *Time*, updated August 27, 2019,
https://time.com/5660763/overstock-patrick-byrne-jonathan-johnson/.

120 **stock price of Overstock crashed:** Abha Bhattarai, "Shares of Overstock Are
Plummeting after the CEO Says He Aided in 'Russian Investigation,'" *The Washington
Post*, August 14, 2019, https://washingtonpost.com/business/2019/08/14/shares
-overstock-are-plummeting-after-ceo-says-he-aided-russian-investigation/.

120   **underwriter of the firm's insurance:** Bhattarai, "Inside Overstock.com."

120   **regained 10 percent of its share value:** Jackie Wattles, "Overstock CEO Patrick Byrne Resigns," CNN *Business*, August 22, 2019, https://cnn.com/2019/08/22/business /overstock-ceo-patrick-byrne-resigns/index.html.

120   **Since 2009, Kalanick:** Kate Conger, "Uber Founder Travis Kalanick Leaves Board, Severing Last Tie," *The New York Times*, December 24, 2019, https://nytimes .com/2019/12/24/technology/uber-travis-kalanick.html.

120   **operated in more than seventy countries:** Mike Isaac, "Inside Uber's Aggressive, Unrestrained Workplace Culture," *The New York Times*, February 22, 2017, https:// nytimes.com/2017/02/22/technology/uber-workplace-culture.html.

121   **exchange the international coupons for American stamps:** Mary Darby, "In Ponzi We Trust," *Smithsonian Magazine*, December 1998, https://smithsonianmag.com/history /in-ponzi-we-trust-64016168/.

121   **investments would double:** Jeannette L. Nolen, "Ponzi Scheme," *Encyclopedia Britannica Online*, accessed September 22, 2020, https://britannica.com/topic /Ponzi-scheme; Darby, "In Ponzi We Trust."

121   **pay the phony returns:** "Ponzi Schemes," U.S. Securities and Exchange Commission, accessed October 6, 2020, https://sec.gov/fast-answers/answersponzihtm.html.

121   **defrauded $15 million:** Nolen, "Ponzi Scheme."

121   **fourteen company-wide cultural values:** Upon hearing complaints from employees about Uber's toxic work culture, the company hired a prestigious law firm to conduct an investigation on the workplace and offer recommendations. This quotes the report, and can be found in Meghann Farnsworth, "Read the Full Investigation into Uber's Troubled Culture and Management," *Vox*, June 13, 2017, https://vox.com/2017/6/13/15794412/read-entire-investigation-uber-culture -management-ethics-eric-holder.

121   **Workplace harassment reportedly:** Isaac, "Inside Uber's Aggressive, Unrestrained Workplace Culture."

121   **hands-off in reacting to allegations:** Isaac, "Inside Uber's Aggressive, Unrestrained Workplace Culture."

121   **hire a team of lawyers:** Farnsworth, "Read the Full Investigation into Uber's Troubled Culture and Management."

122   **The Securities and Exchange Commission (SEC) assumed that Madoff:** Stephanie Yang, "5 Years Ago Bernie Madoff Was Sentenced to 150 Years in Prison—Here's How His Scheme Worked," *Business Insider*, July 1, 2014, https://businessinsider.com /how-bernie-madoffs-ponzi-scheme-worked-2014-7.

122   **signs of money laundering:** "Bernie Madoff," *Encyclopedia Britannica Online*, accessed March 24, 2022, https://britannica.com/biography/Bernie-Madoff.

123   **ability to think in patterns:** Philip E. Tetlock and Dan Gardner, *Superforecasting: The Art and Science of Prediction* (New York: Broadway Books, 2015), 37.

123   **Common Information Sampling Bias:** James E. Hunton, "Mitigating the Common Information Sampling Bias Inherent in Small-Group Discussion," *Behavioral Research in Accounting* 13 (2001): 172.

123   **Confirmation Bias:** Shahram Heshmat, Ph.D, "What Is Confirmation Bias?" *Psychology Today*, accessed September 22, 2020, https://psychologytoday.com/blog /science-choice/201504/what-is-confirmation-bias.

123   **Halo Effect:** "Halo Effect: Definition and How It Affects Your Daily Life," *Healthline*, April 1, 2019, https://healthline.com/health/halo-effect.

123   **Status Quo Bias:** Kendra Cherry, "How the Status Quo Bias Affects Your Decisions," *Verywell Mind*, May 11, 2020, https://verywellmind.com/status-quo-bias-psychological -definition-4065385.

123   **Hindsight Bias:** Kendra Cherry, "How the Hindsight Bias Affects How We View the Past," *Verywell Mind*, May 6, 2020, https://verywellmind.com/what-is-a-hindsight -bias-2795236.

123   **Plan-Continuation Bias:** "Plan-Continuation Bias," APA *Dictionary of Psychology*, accessed September 22, 2020, https://dictionary.apa.org/plan-continuation-bias.

123   **Ingroup Bias:** "Ingroup Bias," APA *Dictionary of Psychology*, accessed September 22, 2020, https://dictionary.apa.org/ingroup-bias.

124   **"belief perseverance":** Tetlock and Gardner, *Superforecasting*, 160.

126   **first Africans were brought:** Some accounts say that enslaved Africans arrived earlier— some coming as early as 1565 with Spanish settlers in St. Augustine. Olivia B. Waxman, "The First Africans in Virginia Landed in 1619. It Was a Turning Point for Slavery in American History—But Not the Beginning," *Time*, August 20, 2019, https://time .com/5653369/august-1619-jamestown-history/.

126   **Mississippi was the wealthiest state:** William Cawthon, "Was the South Poor before the War?," Abbeville Institute, May 26, 2017, https://abbevilleinstitute.org/blog /was-the-south-poor-before-the-war/. Originally published as "The Affluent Section: The South on the Eve of the War between the States." under the direction of Emory Thomas at the University of Georgia, 1982.

127   **were wedded to "King Cotton":** "Confederate States of America," *Encyclopedia Britannica Online*, accessed October 16, 2020, https://britannica.com/topic /Confederate-States-of-America.

127   **more reticent to secede:** "Secession," *Encyclopedia Britannica Online*, accessed October 16, 2020, https://britannica.com/topic/secession.

127   **joined the Confederacy's rebellion:** "Voices of Secession," American Battlefield Trust, accessed October 16, 2020, https://battlefields.org/learn/articles/voices-secession.

127   **Samuel A. Cartwright:** Michael E. Ruane, "A Brief History of the Enduring Phony Science That Perpetuates White Supremacy," *The Washington Post*, April 30, 2019, https://washingtonpost.com/local/a-brief-history-of-the-enduring-phony-science-that -perpetuates-white-supremacy/2019/04/29/20e6aef0-5aeb-11e9-a00e-050dc7b82693 _story.html.

127   **majority of southern families were *not* slaveholders:** Ann Brown, "Fact Check: What Percentage of White Southerners Owned Slaves?" The Samuel Dubois Cook Center on Social Equity at Duke University, August 10, 2020, https://socialequity.duke.edu/news /fact-check-what-percentage-of-white-southerners-owned-slaves/.

128   **"It is impossible for us":** James W. Loewen, "Five Myths about Why the South Seceded," *The Washington Post*, February 26, 2011, https://washingtonpost.com /outlook/five-myths-about-why-the-south-seceded/2011/01/03/ABHr6jD_story.html.

128   **March 14, 2003:** Mike Rossiter, *Target Basra* (London: Bantam Press, 2008), chap. 6.

129   **The video showed neither:** Rossiter, *Target Basra*, chap. 6.

131   **Bush team diverged:** Senate Intelligence Committee Phase II Report, 152 Cong. Rec. S9243—S9246 (September 8, 2006), https://fas.org/irp/congress/2006_cr/s090806.html; Sharon Otterman, "IRAQ: America's Rationale for War," Council on Foreign Relations, March 19, 2007,. https://cfr.org/backgrounder/iraq-americas-rationale-war; "Terrorism Havens: Iraq," Council on Foreign Relations, December 1, 2005, https://cfr.org /backgrounder/terrorism-havens-iraq.

131   **expert assessment at the time:** Senate Intelligence Committee Phase II Report; "Terrorism Havens: Iraq"; Daniel Benjamin, "Saddam Hussein and Al Qaeda Are Not Allies," *The New York Times*, September 30, 2002, https://nytimes.com/2002/09/30 /opinion/saddam-hussein-and-al-qaeda-are-not-allies.html.

131   **al-Qaeda targeted regimes:** Benjamin, "Saddam Hussein and Al Qaeda are Not Allies"; Christopher M. Blanchard, "Al Qaeda: Statements and Evolving Ideology," *CRS Report for Congress*, updated July 9, 2007, https://fas.org/sgp/crs/terror/RL32759.pdf.

131   **agreeing that a Ba'ath and al-Qaeda partnership:** The CIA stated in a 2002 report that its "assessment of al-Qaida's ties to Iraq rests on a body of fragmented, conflicting reporting from sources of varying reliability," and that the "ties between Saddam and bin Laden appear much like those between rival intelligence services." In July of that year, the Defense Intelligence Agency assessed that "compelling evidence demonstrating direct cooperation between the government of Iraq and al-Qaida has not been established." Senate Intelligence Committee Phase II Report, 152 Cong. Rec. S9243—S9246 (September 8, 2006), https://fas.org/irp/congress/2006_cr/s090806.html.

131   **Iraq remained in possession of WMD:** Otterman, "IRAQ: America's Rationale for War; "Terrorism Havens: Iraq"; Senate Intelligence Committee Phase II Report.

132   **likely that the Hussein regime:** Kenneth M. Pollack, "Spies, Lies, and Weapons: What Went Wrong," *The Atlantic*, January/February 2004, https://theatlantic.com/magazine /archive/2004/01/spies-lies-and-weapons-what-went-wrong/302878/.

132   **developing more dangerous WMD:** Otterman, "IRAQ: America's Rationale for War."

132   **likely that the Iraqi dictator:** Senate Intelligence Committee Phase II Report.

133   **The National Security Council never even debated:** Michael J. Mazarr, *Leap of Faith: Hubris, Negligence, and America's Greatest Foreign Policy Tragedy* (New York: PublicAffairs, 2017), chap. 10, Kindle.

Chapter 9: Action

136   **"The United States did not act early":** Thomas J. Bollyky and Stewart M. Patrick, "Improving Pandemic Preparedness: Lessons from COVID-19," Council on Foreign Relations, Independent Task Force Report No. 78, October 2020, 52, https://cfr.org /report/pandemic-preparedness-lessons-COVID-19/.

136   **"A property of matter":** "Inertia," *Merriam-Webster Unabridged Online,* https://unabridged.merriam-webster.com/collegiate/inertia.

137   **al-Qaeda orchestrated the bombings:** "East African Embassy Bombings," Federal Bureau of Investigation, accessed September 22, 2020, https://fbi.gov/history/famous-cases/east-african-embassy-bombings.

137   **August 1998 missile strike:** Oriana Zill, "The Controversial U.S. Retaliatory Missile Strikes," Frontline, accessed March 24, 2021, https://pbs.org/wgbh/pages/frontline/shows/binladen/bombings/retaliation.html.

137   **armed unmanned aerial vehicle:** "Predator RQ-1/MQ-1/MQ-9 Reaper UAV," *Airforce Technology,* accessed October 26, 2020, https://airforce-technology.com/projects/predator-uav/.

139   **tie-dye and Hawaiian T-shirts:** Marc Randolph, *That Will Never Work: The Birth of Netflix and the Amazing Life of an Idea* (New York: Little, Brown, 2019), chap. 16, Kindle.

139   **behemoth Blockbuster for $50 million:** Randolph, *That Will Never Work,* chap. 16.

140   **Profiting off human forgetfulness:** Randolph, *That Will Never Work,* chap. 16.

140   **Netflix was David:** Randolph, *That Will Never Work,* chap. 15.

140   **revenue target of $5 million:** Randolph, *That Will Never Work,* chap. 15.

141   **If Blockbuster acquired Netflix:** Randolph, *That Will Never Work,* chap. 16.

141   **converting VHS into DVDs:** Gina Keating, *Netflixed: The Epic Battle for America's Eyeballs* (New York: Portfolio /Penguin, 2012), 66, Kindle; Randolph, *That Will Never Work,* chap. 16.

141   **buying out the competition:** Randolph, *That Will Never Work,* chap. 15.

141   **watching Antioco's face:** Randolph, *That Will Never Work,* chap. 16.

141   **Though his look lasted:** Randolph, *That Will Never Work,* chap. 16.

141   **Blockbuster claimed that e-commerce:** Randolph, *That Will Never Work,* chap. 16.

141   **Wasn't movie renting:** John Antioco, "How I Did It: Blockbuster's Former CEO on Sparring with an Activist Shareholder," *Harvard Business Review,* April 2011, https://hbr.org/2011/04/how-i-did-it-blockbusters-former-ceo-on-sparring-with-an-activist-shareholder.

141   **Blockbuster felt streaming:** Keating, *Netflixed,* chap. 4.

141   **conducted by Kagan Research:** Keating, *Netflixed,* chap. 4.

142   **current 100 million renters:** Keating, *Netflixed,* chap. 4.

142   **own in-store subscription model:** Keating, *Netflixed,* chap. 4.

142   **Blockbuster's assessment of digital rentals:** Keating, *Netflixed,* chap. 5.

142   **creating its own online platform:** Keating, *Netflixed,* chaps. 5, 6, 10.

142   **2007 analyst report highlighted:** "Forward Looking Statements: Blockbuster Inc. Presentation," Securities and Exchange Commission Archives, November 8, 2007, 23, https://sec.gov/Archives/edgar/data/1085734/000119312507239499/dex991.htm.

142   **"New Competitive Landscape":** "Forward Looking Statements: Blockbuster Inc. Presentation," 24.

144   **three million subscribers to Total Access:** Keating, *Netflixed,* chap. 12.

144 **gaining 70 percent of new subscribers:** Keating, *Netflixed*, chap. 10.

144 **"three years of gambles":** Keating, *Netflixed*, chap. 12.

144 **Hastings presented the final offer:** Keating, *Netflixed*, chap. 12.

144 **Blockbuster denied Netflix's proposition:** Keating, *Netflixed*, chap. 12.

144 **model was flawed:** Keating, *Netflixed*, chap. 12.

144 **"liquidity crisis":** Keating, *Netflixed,* chap. 12.

144 **While thrilled that Netflix admitted:** Keating, *Netflixed*, chap. 12.

145 **outside the Swedish Parliament:** Charlotte Alter, Suyin Haynes, and Justin Worland, "*Time* 2019 Person of the Year: Greta Thunberg," *Time*, accessed December 14, 2020, https://time.com/person-of-the-year-2019-greta-thunberg/.

145 **father picked her up:** Alter, Haynes, and Worland, "*Time* 2019 Person of the Year: Greta Thunberg."

145 **Fridays for Future movement:** Alter, Haynes, and Worland, "*Time* 2019 Person of the Year: Greta Thunberg."

145 **"We are in the beginning":** Alter, Haynes, and Worland, "*Time* 2019 Person of the Year: Greta Thunberg"; "Transcript: Greta Thunberg's Speech at the U.N. Climate Action Summit," National Public Radio, September 23, 2019, https://npr.org/2019 /09/23/763452863/transcript-greta-thunbergs-speech-at-the-u-n-climate-action-summit.

145 **Thunberg stresses that the clock:** "Transcript: Greta Thunberg's Speech at the U.N. Climate Action Summit."

145 **She implores leaders to:** "'I Want You to Panic': 16-Year-Old Issues Climate Warning at Davos," uploaded by *Guardian News*, January 25, 2019, https://youtube.com /watch?v=RjsLm5PCdVQ.

145 **A year later, she lamented:** Somini Sengupta, "Greta Thunberg's Message at Davos Forum: 'Our House Is Still on Fire,'" *The New York Times*, January 21, 2020, https:// nytimes.com/2020/01/21/climate/greta-thunberg-davos.html.

145 **The determined Thunberg has:** Alter, Haynes, and Worland, "*Time* 2019 Person of the Year: Greta Thunberg."

145 **defunded the Total Access program:** Keating, *Netflixed*, chap. 13.

145 **Meanwhile, Netflix "announced":** Ken Auletta, "Outside the Box: Netflix and the Future of Television," *The New Yorker*, January 27, 2014, https://newyorker.com /magazine/2014/02/03/outside-the-box-2.

146 **only one remaining Blockbuster:** Tiffany Hsu, "The World's Last Blockbuster Has No Plans to Close," *The New York Times*, March 6, 2019, https://nytimes.com/2019/03/06 /business/last-blockbuster-store.html.

146 **Shrewdly, in 2011:** Antioco, "How I Did It."

148 **Dr. King had been arrested:** "Letter from Birmingham Jail," *The Atlantic*, April 4, 2018, https://theatlantic.com/magazine/archive/2018/02/letter-from-a-birmingham -jail/552461/; General Stanley McChrystal, Jeff Eggers, and Jason Mangone, *Leaders: Myth and Reality* (New York: Portfolio/Penguin, 2018), 350.

148 **long letters to his critics:** Martin Luther King Jr., "Letter from Birmingham Jail," The Estate of Martin Luther King Jr., April 16, 1963, 1, https://swap.stanford.edu

/20141218230016/http://mlk-kpp01.stanford.edu/kingweb/popular%5Frequests
/frequentdocs/birmingham.pdf.

149   **"I have almost reached the regrettable"**: King, "Letter from Birmingham Jail," The Estate of Martin Luther King Jr., 4.

149   **"mouth pious irrelevancies"**: King, "Letter from Birmingham Jail," The Estate of Martin Luther King Jr., 7.

149   **Acknowledging the dangers of action**: King, "Letter from Birmingham Jail," The Estate of Martin Luther King Jr., 1–2.

150   **create "crisis" where negotiation**: King, "Letter from Birmingham Jail," The Estate of Martin Luther King Jr., 2.

151   **in 1963 as a mimeographed copy**: "Letter from Birmingham Jail," The Martin Luther King, Jr. Research and Education Institute at Stanford, May 17, 2017, https://kinginstitute.stanford.edu/encyclopedia/letter-birmingham-jail.

151   *Why We Can't Wait*: Dorothy Cotton, "Why We Can't Wait," The King Legacy Series, accessed April 9, 2020, http://thekinglegacy.org/books/why-we-cant-wait; "Letter from Birmingham Jail," The Martin Luther King, Jr. Research and Education Institute at Stanford.

153   **antithetical to the Afghan culture**: Azmat Khan, "Night Raids: Disrupting or Fueling the Afghan Insurgency?" *Frontline*, PBS, June 17, 2011, https://pbs.org/wgbh/frontline/article/night-raids-disrupting-or-fueli/.

153   **casualties among women or children**: Hamid Shalizi, "Karzai Wants Afghans to Take Control of Night Raids," *Reuters*, May 28, 2011, https://reuters.com/article/us-afghanistan-karzai-idUSTRE74R0YZ20110528.

153   **If our forces used dogs**: Khan, "Night Raids."

154   **Afghans also believed these**: Rod Nordland and Taimoor Shah, "Afghanistan Quietly Lifts Ban on Nighttime Raids," *The New York Times*, November 23, 2014, https://nytimes.com/2014/11/24/world/asia/afghanistan-quietly-lifts-ban-on-night-raids.html; Khan, "Night Raids."

154   **president of Afghanistan down to**: Joshua Partlow, "Karzai Wants U.S. to Reduce Military Operations in Afghanistan," *The Washington Post Foreign Service*, November 14, 2010, https://washingtonpost.com/wp-dyn/content/article/2010/11/13/AR2010111304001.html?sid=ST2010111305091.

154   **Velocity is defined as**: "Velocity," *Merriam-Webster Unabridged Online*, https://unabridged.merriam-webster.com/collegiate/velocity.

Chapter 10: Timing

157   **"can ask me for anything"**: The origins of this quote have been debated. While I cannot confirm an original source, this phrase was commonly accepted and quoted within the US military.

157   **The Public Warning System**: Chi-Mai Chen et al., "Containing COVID-19 among 627,386 Persons in Contact with the *Diamond Princess* Cruise Ship Passengers Who Disembarked in Taiwan: Big Data Analytics," *Journal of Medical Internet Research* 22, no. 5 (May 2020), https://doi.org/10.2196/19540; "CECC Advises Self-caution after

Diamond Princess Cruise Liner Visit," *Focus Taiwan—CNA English News*, February 7, 2020, https://focustaiwan.tw/society/202002070019.

157   **On February 5, 2020:** Eisuke Nakazawa, Hiroyasu Ino, and Akira Akabayashi, "Chronology of COVID-19 Cases on the *Diamond Princess* Cruise Ship and Ethical Considerations: A Report from Japan," *Disaster Medicine and Public Health Preparedness* 14 no. 4 (2020): 506–13, https://doi.org/10.1017/dmp.2020.50; Chi-Mai Chen et al., "Containing COVID-19 among 627,386 Persons."

157   **had disembarked onto Taiwanese soil:** Chen et al., "Containing COVID-19 among 627,386 Persons."

158   **officials instructed all 627,386 citizens:** Chen et al., "Containing COVID-19 among 627,386 Persons."

158   **painfully high density of cases:** Cheryl Lin et al., "Policy Decisions and Use of Information Technology to Fight COVID-19, Taiwan," *Emerging Infectious Diseases* 26, no. 7 (July 2020): 1506–12, https://doi.org/10.3201/eid2607.200574.

158   **seven as of May 2020:** Holly Williams, "How Taiwan Was Coronavirus-Ready While the U.S. Got Caught with Its 'Pants Down,'" *CBS News*, May 26, 2020, https://cbsnews.com/news/coronavirus-in-taiwan-how-taipei-was-ready-while-us-got-caught-with-pants-down-expert-says/.

158   **Taiwanese officials boarded planes:** Hilton Yip, "Taiwan Saw the Coronavirus Coming," *Foreign Policy*, March 16 2020, https://foreignpolicy.com/2020/03/16/taiwan-china-fear-coronavirus-success/; Lin et al., "Policy Decisions and Use of Information Technology to Fight COVID-19"; C. Jason Wang, Chung Y. Ng, and Robert H. Brook, "Response to COVID-19 in Taiwan: Big Data Analytics, New Technology, and Proactive Testing." *JAMA* 323, no. 14 (April 2020): 1341–42, https://doi.org/10.1001/jama.2020.3151.

158   **virus could spread human-to-human:** Thomas J. Bollyky and Stewart M. Patrick, "Improving Pandemic Preparedness: Lessons from COVID-19," Council on Foreign Relations, Independent Task Force Report No. 78, October 2020, 37, https://cfr.org/report/pandemic-preparedness-lessons-COVID-19/; Louise Watt, "Taiwan Says It Tried to Warn the World about Coronavirus. Here's What It Really Knew and When," *Time*, May 19, 2020, https://time.com/5826025/taiwan-who-trump-coronavirus-covid19/.

158   **Taiwanese government surveilled all citizens:** Watt, "Taiwan Says It Tried to Warn the World about Coronavirus"; C. Jason Wang, Chung Y. Ng, and Robert H. Brook, "Response to COVID-19 in Taiwan."

158   **Central Epidemic Command Center:** Cheryl Lin et al., "Policy Decisions and Use of Information Technology to Fight COVID-19"; C. Jason Wang, Chung Y. Ng, and Robert H. Brook, "Response to COVID-19 in Taiwan."

158   **124 action items:** C. Jason Wang, Chung Y. Ng, and Robert H. Brook, "Response to COVID-19 in Taiwan."

158   **decisions as early as January 17:** "Novel Coronavirus (2019-nCoV) Situation Report—3," World Health Organization, January 23, 2020, https://who.int/docs/default-source/coronaviruse/situation-reports/20200123-sitrep-3-2019-ncov.pdf.

158   **decided not to enforce domestic social distancing:** Erin Schumaker, "Timeline: How
       Coronavirus Got Started," *ABC News*, September 22, 2020, https://abcnews.go.com
       /Health/timeline-coronavirus-started/story?id=69435165.

159   **analysis conducted by Columbia University:** Bill Chappell, "U.S. Could Have Saved
       36,Lives If Social Distancing Started 1 Week Earlier: Study," National Public Radio,
       May 21, 2020, https://npr.org/sections/coronavirus-live-updates/2020/05/21/860077940
       /u-s-could-have-saved-36-000-lives-if-social-distancing-started-1-week-earlier-st; James
       Glanz and Campbell Robertson, "Lockdown Delays Cost at Least 36,000 Lives, Data
       Show," *The New York Times*, May 20, 2020, https://nytimes.com/2020/05/20/us
       /coronavirus-distancing-deaths.html.

159   **avoided 83 percent of deaths:** Glanz and Robertson, "Lockdown Delays Cost at Least
       36,000 Lives, Data Show."

161   **"the impossible but inevitable city":** Arjen Boin, Christer Brown, and James A.
       Richardson, *Managing Hurricane Katrina: Lessons from a Megacrisis* (Baton Rouge:
       Louisiana State University Press, 2019), 4. Original source was P. F. Lewis, *New
       Orleans: The Making of an Urban Landscape* (Cambridge, MA: Ballinger, 1976).

161   **It was inevitable because:** Boin, Brown, and Richardson, *Managing Hurricane Katrina*,
       4. Original source was Lewis, *New Orleans*.

161   **Category 5 storm:** "Hurricane Katrina," National Weather Service, National Oceanic
       and Atmospheric Administration, accessed September 24, 2020, https://weather.gov
       /jetstream/katrina.

161   **up to twelve thousand citizens:** This number does not include the citizens with special
       needs. Boin, Brown, and Richardson, *Managing Hurricane Katrina*, 43.

161   **small hole in the Superdome's:** "I Was There: Hurricane Katrina: Superdome
       Survivor," YouTube, uploaded by History, August 20, 2015, https://youtube.com
       /watch?v=Am-hb3ZCPUQ;

162   **makeshift shelter of "last resort":** Boin, Brown, and Richardson, *Managing Hurricane
       Katrina*, 9.

162   **twenty-five thousand Americans:** Boin, Brown, and Richardson, *Managing Hurricane
       Katrina*, 9.

162   **plumbing couldn't keep up:** "I Was There: Hurricane Katrina: Superdome Survivor."

162   **Elderly citizens who sought refuge:** "I Was There: Hurricane Katrina: Superdome
       Survivor."

162   **million people who had escaped:** Boin, Brown, and Richardson, *Managing Hurricane
       Katrina*, 15.

162   **between 1,200 and 1,800 deaths:** Boin, Brown, and Richardson, *Managing Hurricane
       Katrina*, 8.

162   **fourth most intense Atlantic hurricane:** "Meteorological History of Hurricane Katrina,"
       KLTV, August 16, 2006, https://kltv.com/story/5293566/meteorological-history-of
       -hurricane-katrina/; Talmon Joseph Smith, "Sunday Review: Remembering Katrina and
       Its Unlearned Lessons, 15 Years On," *The New York Times*, August 21, 2020, https://
       nytimes.com/2020/08/21/sunday-review/coronavirus-hurricane-katrina-anniversary.html.

162   **Dilatory pre-storm decision-making:** US House of Representatives, Select Bipartisan Committee to Investigate the Preparation for and Response to Hurricane Katrina, *A Failure of Initiative: Final Report of the Select Bipartisan Committee to Investigate the Preparation for and Response to Hurricane Katrina* (Washington, DC: US Government Printing Office, 2006), 1–5, 108–114, 133–36, https://nrc.gov/docs/ML1209 /ML12093A081.pdf.

163   **preceded by eleven other hurricanes:** Gaye S. Farris, "The Major Hurricanes of 2005: A Few Facts," in *Science and the Storms: The USGS Response to the Hurricanes of 2005,* accessed October 20, 2020, https://pubs.usgs.gov/circ/1306/pdf/c1306_ch2 _b.pdf.

163   **achieved hurricane status on the twenty-fifth:** Sarah Gibbens, "Hurricane Katrina, Explained," *National Geographic,* January 16, 2019, https://nationalgeographic.com /environment/natural-disasters/reference/hurricane-katrina/.

163   **mandatory evacuation only nineteen hours:** US House of Representatives, Select Bipartisan Committee to Investigate the Preparation for and Response to Hurricane Katrina, *Failure of Initiative,* 108–109.

163   **drivers the Regional Transit Authority:** Boin, Brown, and Richardson, *Managing Hurricane Katrina,* 42–43.

164   **city's other expected bus services:** Boin, Brown, and Richardson, *Managing Hurricane Katrina,* 43.

164   **formally request permission from FEMA:** Boin, Brown, and Richardson, *Managing Hurricane Katrina,* 91.

164   **"'logistics system in FEMA was broken'":** Boin, Brown, and Richardson, *Managing Hurricane Katrina,* 91.

164   **Governor Blanco personally redirected:** Boin, Brown, and Richardson, *Managing Hurricane Katrina,* 93.

164   **overrun with looters and murderers:** Boin, Brown, and Richardson, *Managing Hurricane Katrina,* 94.

164   **National Guard protect the buses:** Boin, Brown, and Richardson, *Managing Hurricane Katrina,* 94.

164   **the bus drivers got lost:** Boin, Brown, and Richardson, *Managing Hurricane Katrina,* 94.

165   **eight hundred buses evacuated:** Boin, Brown, and Richardson, *Managing Hurricane Katrina,* 94–95.

165   **last three hundred evacuees left:** Boin, Brown, and Richardson, *Managing Hurricane Katrina,* 94.

165   **nearby Convention Center:** Boin, Brown, and Richardson, *Managing Hurricane Katrina,* xvi, 145.

166   **For this 1998 Hungarian Grand Prix:** Mark Hughes, "Hungary 1998: How a Classic Schumacher/Brawn Gamble Snatched Victory from McLaren," *Formula 1®,* April 30, 2020, https://formula1.com/en/latest/article.hungary-1998-how-a-classic-schumacher -brawn-gamble-snatched-victory-from.6RIv63NqY0wBnDYlrdJCiC.html.

167   **the total prize payout:** Christian Sylt, "Ferrari's Sebastian Vettel Is F1's Top Prize Money Winner with $500 Million Haul," *Forbes*, April 20, 2019, https://forbes.com /sites/csylt/2019/04/20/ferraris-vettel-becomes-f1s-biggest-prize-money-winner-with-500 -million-haul/#343f27dd4804.

167   **fifty-two drivers have died:** "Deaths in Formula 1," *F1 Chronicle*, September 1, 2020, https://f1chronicle.com/deaths-in-formula-1/#Deaths-in-Formula-1.

167   **he recommended a nonconformist strategy:** Hughes, "Hungary 1998"; Ross Brawn and Adam Parr, *Total Competition: Lessons in Strategy from Formula One* (London: Simon & Schuster, 2016), Part 2, Section 13, Kindle.

167   **Pit stops are a crucial part:** Lawrence Barretto, "F1 Pit Stops Explained: Gone in 1.88s—Putting Together the Perfect F1 Pit Stop," *Formula 1®*, October 6, 2019, https:// formula1.com/en/latest/article.gone-in-1-88s-putting-together-the-perfect-f1-pit -stop.3lLKnEoPKdJgACsUn9IltC.html.

168   **the practice was banned:** Nate Saunders, "Why Drivers Support Return of Refueling in F1 Races," *ESPN*, June 25, 2019, https://espn.com/f1/story/_/id/27256436/why-drivers -support-return-refueling-f1-races.

168   **six and nine seconds:** "Refueling," *Technical F1-Dictionary*, accessed April 2, 2021, http://formula1-dictionary.net/refueling.html.

168   **0.365 seconds per lap:** Hughes, "Hungary 1998."

168   **drive 1.1 seconds faster:** Hughes, "Hungary 1998."

168   **"out of phase":** Brawn and Parr, *Total Competition: Lessons in Strategy from Formula One*, Part 2.

168   **Brawn recounts that three:** Ross Brawn and Adam Parr, *Total Competition: Lessons in Strategy from Formula One*, Part 2.

168   **made an astute tire choice:** Hughes, "Hungary 1998."

169   **refueling for only 6.8 seconds:** Hughes, "Hungary 1998."

169   **Apollo 13 accelerated as it approached:** Henry S. F. Cooper, *Thirteen: The Apollo Flight That Failed* (New York: Open Road, 1972), Section 4, Kindle.

169   **suffered a power shortage early:** Cooper, *Thirteen*, Section 1, 4.

169   **nail-biting two and a half hours:** Cooper, *Thirteen*, Section 4.

170   **did not make any adjustments to their strategy:** Hughes, "Hungary 1998."

170   **"19 qualifying laps":** Hughes, "Hungary 1998."

170   **took advantage of its lighter fuel load:** Hughes, "Hungary 1998."

170   **weren't able to grip the road:** Hughes, "Hungary 1998."

Chapter 11: Adaptability

173   **"Fosbury goes over the bar":** Bob Welsh and Dick Fosbury, *The Wizard of Foz: Dick Fosbury's One-Man High-Jump Revolution* (New York: Skyhorse Publishing, 2018), chap. 16, Kindle.

173   **blue shoe on one foot:** "How One Man Changed the High Jump Forever," *The Olympics on the Record*, YouTube, uploaded by Olympic Channel, April 1, 2018, https://youtube.com/watch?v=CZsH46Ek2ao.

173   **set at an intimidating 7' 4¼":** Joseph Durso, "Fearless Fosbury Flops to Glory," *The New York Times*, October 20, 1968, http://archive.nytimes.com/www.nytimes.com /packages/html/sports/year_in_sports/10.20.html?scp=7&sq=1968&st=cse.

173   **first two attempts:** "When High Jumper Dick Fosbury Changed the Game. Forever," Tokyo 2020, July 18, 2020, https://tokyo2020.org/en/news/when-high-jumper-dick -fosbury-changed-the-game-forever.

173   **victory was *itself* a surprise:** "When High Jumper Dick Fosbury Changed the Game. Forever," Tokyo 2020.

174   **center of gravity *below* the bar:** "How One Man Changed the High Jump Forever."

174   **hard landing grounds of the past:** Jacob Goldenberg et al., "How Do Revolutions Emerge?: Lessons from the Fosbury Flop," *International Studies of Management & Organization* 40, no. 2 (Summer 2010): 41, https://doi.org/10.2753/IMO0020 -8825400202; Welsh and Fosbury, *Wizard of Foz*, chap. 7.

174   **frantically read the rule books:** Goldenberg et al., "How Do Revolutions Emerge?," 40.

175   **twenty-eight out of forty jumpers:** "50 Years since the Day Dick Fosbury Revolutionised the High Jump," *World Athletics*, October 20, 2018, https:// worldathletics.org/news/feature/dick-fosbury-flop.

175   **adaptability in terms of survival:** "Definitions of Evolutionary Terms," Evolution Resources at the National Academies, The National Academies of Science, Engineering, and Medicine, accessed October 20, 2020, https://nationalacademies.org /evolution/definitions.

176   **"Marine-doubling-as-Metallica-fan":** Steve Knopper, *Appetite for Self-Destruction: The Spectacular Crash of the Record Industry in the Digital Age* (Steve Knopper, 2017), chap. 4, Kindle.

177   **Napster appeared publicly:** Stephen Dowling, "Napster Turns 20: How It Changed the Music Industry," *BBC*, May 31, 2019, https://bbc.com/culture/article/20190531-napster -turns-20-how-it-changed-the-music-industry.

177   **users could search for songs:** "Napster: Culture of Free," *The New York Times*, December 7, 2014, https://nytimes.com/video/technology/100000003275810/napster -culture-of-free.html; "How the Old Napster Worked," *HowStuffWorks*, accessed September 23, 2020, https://computer.howstuffworks.com/napster.htm; Dowling, "Napster Turns 20."

177   **designated their music directory:** Dowling, "Napster Turns 20."

177   **cost of purchasing CDs:** Knopper, *Appetite for Self-Destruction*, chap. 5; "Napster: Culture of Free," quoting Steve Knopper, contributing editor, *Rolling Stone*; Dowling, "Napster Turns 20."

177   **eventually brought Napster to court:** Knopper, *Appetite for Self-Destruction*, chap. 4.

177   **include filtering technologies:** Calvin K. M. Lam and Bernard C. Y. Tan, "The Internet Is Changing the Music Industry," *Communications of the ACM* 44, no. 8 (August 2001): 63, https://doi.org/10.1145/381641.381658.

177   **declined from 220 to 37:** Lam and Tan, "The Internet Is Changing the Music Industry."

177   **seventy million at the business's peak:** "Napster: Culture of Free."

177   **declared bankruptcy in 2002:** Knopper, *Appetite for Self-Destruction*, chap. 4; Dowling, "Napster Turns 20." Dowling, "Napster Turns 20."

177   **a new standard and expectation:** Dowling, "Napster Turns 20."

178   **Albhy Galuten, the senior vice president:** "Napster: Culture of Free."

178   **negotiating new record deals:** Knopper, *Appetite for Self-Destruction*, chap. 4.

178   **record labels had joined forces:** This calculation takes into account the introduction of a new subscription price, which could have cut Napster's users roughly in half. Knopper, *Appetite for Self-Destruction*, chap. 4.

178   **start-up's then 26.4 million users:** Knopper, *Appetite for Self-Destruction*, chap. 4.

178   **listeners were pirating music:** Knopper, *Appetite for Self-Destruction*, 196; Frank Rose, "The Civil War Inside Sony," *Wired*, February 1, 2003, https://wired.com/2003/02/sony-4/.

178   **"frozen by its fear of piracy":** Rose, "The Civil War Inside Sony."

179   **producing twenty-five million tons of steel:** William S. Dietrich II, "A Very Short History of Pittsburgh," *Pittsburgh Quarterly*, Fall 2008, accessed April 15, 2020, https://pittsburghquarterly.com/articles/a-very-brief-history-of-pittsburgh/.

179   **steel mills began to quiet:** Dietrich, "Very Short History of Pittsburgh"; Chris Isidore, "When American steel was king," CNN Business, March 18, 2019, https://money.cnn.com/2018/03/09/news/companies/american-steel-history/index.html.

179   **"eds and meds":** "Eds & Meds Thrive in Former Steel City," University of Pittsburgh, accessed March 25, 2021, https://225.pitt.edu/story/eds-meds-thrive-former-steel-city.

179   **an epicenter for start-ups:** "The Transformation of Pittsburgh," Metroguide, accessed March 25, 2021, https://pittsburghmetroguide.com/the-transformation-of-pittsburgh/.

179   **Flint did not have Pittsburgh's resources:** Andrew R. Highsmith, *Demolition Means Progress: Flint, Michigan, and the Fate of the American Metropolis* (Chicago: University of Chicago Press, 2015), Introduction.

180   **niche market that would rise:** Knopper, *Appetite for Self-Destruction*, chap. 5.

180   **prevent the piracy:** Knopper, *Appetite for Self-Destruction*, chap. 5; "Napster: Culture of Free."

180   **record labels had two choices:** "Napster: Culture of Free."

180   **Taylor Swift famously criticized:** Knopper, *Appetite for Self-Destruction*, chap. 7.

180   **time on the road touring:** "Napster: Culture of Free."

181   **Nokia Corporation, a multinational:** James Surowiecki, "Where Nokia Went Wrong," *The New Yorker*, September 3, 2013, https://newyorker.com/business/currency/where-nokia-went-wrong; "Our History," Nokia, accessed September 23, 2013, https://nokia.com/about-us/our-history/.

181   **paper mill in 1865:** "Our History," Nokia.

181   **top manufacturer of mobile phones:** BBC, "The Rise and Fall of Nokia," YouTube, uploaded by Educate Learning, August 31, 2018, https://youtube.com/watch?v=RDYedU7COEQ.

182   **50 percent of the market share:** Michael Krisgman, "Nokia Reinvented: Decline, Resurrection, and How CEOs Get Trapped," *ZDNet*, November 26, 2018, https://zdnet.com/article/nokia-reinvented-decline-resurrection-and-how-ceos-get-trapped/.

182 **"iPhone Killer"**: Risto Siilasmaa and Catherine Fredman, *Transforming NOKIA: The Power of Paranoid Optimism to Lead through Colossal Change* (New York: McGraw-Hill Education, 2019), chap. 3, Kindle.

182 **software company Symbian**: Siilasmaa and Fredman, *Transforming NOKIA*, chap. 1.

182 **source of Finnish national pride**: Krisgman, "Nokia Reinvented."

182 **Apple made a splash**: BBC, "The Rise and Fall of Nokia"; Siilasmaa and Fredman, *Transforming NOKIA*, chap. 2.

182 **shipping 115 million devices**: Siilasmaa and Fredman, *Transforming NOKIA*, chap. 2.

182 **15 percent share of the market**: Nokia, in comparison, had 40 percent of the market. Siilasmaa and Fredman, *Transforming NOKIA*, chap. 2.

182 **Android, Microsoft, and Apple**: Siilasmaa and Fredman, *Transforming NOKIA*, chap. 1.

182 **the purchasing psyche**: BBC, "The Rise and Fall of Nokia," quoting Ducan Lamb, Creative Director of Nokia, 2008–11.

182 **hemorrhaged 70 percent of its market value**: Siilasmaa and Fredman, *Transforming NOKIA*, chap. 3.

182 **By April 2012**: Siilasmaa and Fredman, *Transforming NOKIA*, chap. 9.

183 **fell 40 percent that year**: Siilasmaa and Fredman, *Transforming NOKIA*, chap. 9.

183 **forced to do the unthinkable**: Siilasmaa and Fredman, *Transforming NOKIA*, chap. 12, chap. 17.

183 **"Anytime anybody in the world"**: "Nokia Chairman Risto Siilasmaa: Lessons in Innovation," YouTube, uploaded by CXOTALK, October 29, 2018, https://youtube.com/watch?v=REn46ZEnXn4&feature=emb_title. Retrieved from Krisgman, "Nokia Reinvented."

183 **"distant cousin"**: Siilasmaa and Fredman, *Transforming NOKIA*, chap. 14.

183 **"corporate orphan"**: Siilasmaa and Fredman, *Transforming NOKIA*, chap. 11.

183 **NSN was an independent**: Siilasmaa and Fredman, *Transforming NOKIA*, chap. 2, 11.

183 **"money-losing sinkhole"**: Siilasmaa and Fredman, *Transforming NOKIA*, chap. 8.

183 **dominated by Chinese companies**: Siilasmaa and Fredman, *Transforming NOKIA*, chap. 4, 14.

183 **investment in mobile**: Siilasmaa and Fredman, *Transforming NOKIA*, 199–200.

183 **Nokia Solutions and Networks**: Martha DeGrasse, "NSN Becomes Nokia Solutions and Networks," *RCR Wireless News*, August 7, 2013, https://rcrwireless.com/20130807/network-infrastructure/nsn-becomes-nokia-solutions-and-networks.

183 **flailing devices and services unit afloat**: Siilasmaa and Fredman, *Transforming NOKIA*, chap. 14.

183 **As Siilasmaa recalls**: Siilasmaa and Fredman, *Transforming NOKIA*, chap. 14.

184 **Less than 1 percent**: Krisgman, "Nokia Reinvented."

184 **Nokia has also made a series**: Siilasmaa and Fredman, *Transforming NOKIA*, chap. 14, 16, 18.

184 **only end-to-end 5G network**: "Our History," Nokia.

Chapter 12: Leadership

186 **"I pledge you"**: Franklin D. Roosevelt, "Address Accepting the Presidential Nomination at the Democratic National Convention in Chicago," July 9, 1932, American Presidency Project, https://presidency.ucsb.edu/documents/address -accepting-the-presidential-nomination-the-democratic-national-convention-chicago-1.

186 **pedestal of stones**: "Braddock Cannon," Alexandria Times, February 5. 2009, https:// alexandriava.gov/uploadedFiles/historic/info/attic/2009 /Attic20090205BraddockCannon.pdf

186 **spring of 1755**: David L. Preston, Braddock's Defeat: The Battle of the Monongahela and the Road to Revolution (New York: Oxford University Press, 2015): chap. 3, Kindle.

186 **French regulars and Canadian militia**: Colonel (Ret.) (AUS) John P. Sinnott, "Major General Braddock's March on Fort Duquesne," Warfare History Network, accessed September 23, 2020, https://warfarehistorynetwork.com/2015/07/27/major-general -braddocks-march-on-fort-duquesne/.

186 **supported by Native American warriors**: Preston, Braddock's Defeat, chap. 4.

187 **force of 2,100 soldiers**: This included 1,400 British regulars and 700 provincials. "Edward Braddock," Encyclopedia Britannica Online, accessed March 26, 2021, https:// britannica.com/biography/Edward-Braddock.

187 **professional infantry regiments of British soldiers**: Preston, Braddock's Defeat, 55; Sinnott, "Major General Braddock's March on Fort Duquesne."

187 **militia from several**: Sinnott, "Major General Braddock's March on Fort Duquesne."

187 **120 miles of difficult**: Preston, Braddock's Defeat, chap. 5.

187 **ensure a trafficable supply**: Thomas E. Crocker, Braddock's March: How the Man Sent to Seize a Continent Changed American History (Yardley, PA: Westholme Publishing, 2009), chap. 12; Preston, Braddock's Defeat, chap. 5.

187 **inadequate supply of pack**: Sinnott, "Major General Braddock's March on Fort Duquesne."

187 **Militia leaders**: Preston, Braddock's Defeat, chap. 3.

187 **Duke of Cumberland**: Sinnott, "Major General Braddock's March on Fort Duquesne."

189 **sallied out to engage**: Sinnott, "Major General Braddock's March on Fort Duquesne."

189 **Although hoping to ambush**: Sinnott, "Major General Braddock's March on Fort Duquesne."

189 **collapsed into panicked retreat**: Crocker, Braddock's March, chap. 18.

189 **located and desecrated**: Crocker, Braddock's March, chap. 19.

189 **"These savages may, indeed"**: Crocker, Braddock's March, chap. 19.

189 **spring a clever ambush**: Sinnott, "Major General Braddock's March on Fort Duquesne."

189 **44th and 48th Regiments**: Preston, Braddock's Defeat, chap. 2.

190 **besiege Fort Duquesne**: Sinnott, "Major General Braddock's March on Fort Duquesne."

191   **"Braddock, of course, was"**: Douglas Southall Freeman, *George Washington*, vol. 2, *Young Washington* (New York: Scribner, 1949), 96.

193   **left partially paralyzed**: Amy Berish, "FDR and Polio," Franklin D. Roosevelt Presidential Library and Museum, accessed September 23, 2020, https://fdrlibrary.org/polio.

193   **America's gross domestic product**: Christina D. Romer and Richard H. Pells, "Great Depression," *Encyclopedia Britannica Online*, accessed March 26, 2021, https:// britannica.com/event/Great-Depression.

193   **ten thousand banks had failed**: Kim Phillips-Fein, "The Bitter Origins of the Fight over Big Government," *The Atlantic*, January 31, 2019, https://theatlantic.com /magazine/archive/2019/03/fdr-herbert-hoover-big-government/580456/.

193   **more than 24 percent of workers**: Steve H. Hanke, "A Great Depression?" Cato Institute, November 21, 2008, https://cato.org/publications/commentary/great-depression-1.

194   **"great experiment"**: This phrase is from a letter George Washington wrote to Catharine Sawbridge Macaulay Graham, on January 9, 1790. "From George Washington to Catharine Sawbridge Macaulay Graham," University of Virginia Press, accessed September 23, 2020, http://founders.archives.gov/documents /Washington/05-04-02-0363.

194   **plans for a "new deal"**: Roosevelt, "Address Accepting the Presidential Nomination."

194   **Beyond his memorable declaration**: Conrad Black, *Franklin Delano Roosevelt: Champion of Freedom* (New York: PublicAffairs, 2003), 270.

194   **On Sunday, March 5, 1933**: William L. Silber, "Why Did FDR's Bank Holiday Succeed?," *Federal Reserve Bank of New York Economic Policy Review* 15, no. 1 (July 2009): 19, https://newyorkfed.org/medialibrary/media/research/epr/09v15n1 /0907silb.pdf.

194   **extended the bank closure**: Silber, "Why Did FDR's Bank Holiday Succeed?," 19.

195   **"My friends, I want"**: "Franklin Delano Roosevelt First Fireside Chat: The Banking Crisis," YouTube, uploaded by Speeches, January 7, 2015, https://youtube.com /watch?v=r6nYKRLOFWg.

196   **"sufficiently solvent"**: William E. Leuchtenburg, "Franklin D. Roosevelt: Domestic Affairs," UVA Miller Center, accessed October 6, 2020, https://millercenter.org /president/fdroosevelt/domestic-affairs.

196   **During those fifteen minutes**: Silber, "Why Did FDR's Bank Holiday Succeed?," 19.

196   **"it is safer to keep"**: Franklin Delano Roosevelt First Fireside Chat," YouTube.

196   **more than half of the funds**: Silber, "Why Did FDR's Bank Holiday Succeed?," 19.

196   **largest percentage price increase**: Silber, "Why Did FDR's Bank Holiday Succeed?," 20.

196   **Banking Act of 1933**: Leuchtenburg, "Franklin D. Roosevelt: Domestic Affairs." "Banking Act of 1933 (Glass-Steagall)," Federal Reserve History, November 22, 2013, https:// www.federalreservehistory.org/essays/glass-steagall-act.

196   **"Brain Trust"**: Leuchtenburg, "Franklin D. Roosevelt: Domestic Affairs"; "Brain Trust," *Encyclopedia Britannica Online*, accessed March 26, 2021, https://britannica .com/topic/Brain-Trust.

196   **increasing the size of the court:** William Leuchtenburg, "When Franklin Roosevelt Clashed With the Supreme Court—and Lost," *Smithsonian Magazine*, May 2005, https://smithsonianmag.com/history/when-franklin-roosevelt-clashed-with-the-supreme -court-and-lost-78497994/.

198   **Prime Minister Jacinda Ardern:** Uri Friedman, "New Zealand's Prime Minister May Be the Most Effective Leader on the Planet," *The Atlantic*, April 19, 2020, https:// theatlantic.com/politics/archive/2020/04/jacinda-ardern-new-zealand-leadership -coronavirus/610237/.

198   **Taiwan, under Tsai Ing-wen:** Wang, Ng, and Brook, "Response to COVID-19 in Taiwan," 1341–42.

198   **Governor Gavin Newsom:** Ivan Pereira, "How California Lost Control over COVID-19 despite Early Successes," *ABC News*, August 1, 2020, https://abcnews.go.com/Health /california-lost-control-covid-19-early-successes/story?id=72008022.

Chapter 13: Game Time

205   **161 lane miles of roadways:** "The Big Dig: Project Background," Mass.gov, accessed December 16, 2020, https://mass.gov/info-details/the-big-dig-project-background#the -challenges-; National Academy of Engineering, National Research Council, and Transportation Research Board, "Executive Summary," in *Completing the 'Big Dig': Managing the Final Stages of Boston's Central Artery / Tunnel Project* (Washington, DC: The National Academies Press, 2003), https://doi.org/10.17226/10629.

205   **connect key roadways:** "The Big Dig: Project Background," Mass.gov, accessed December 16, 2020, https://mass.gov/info-details/the-big-dig-project-background; "The Big Dig: tunnels and bridges, Mass.gov, https://mass.gov/info-details/the-big-dig-tunnels -and-bridges.

205   **541,000 truckloads:** "The Big Dig: Facts and Figures," Mass.gov, accessed December 16, 2020, https://mass.gov/info-details/the-big-dig-facts-and-figures.

205   **3.8 million cubic yards:** "The Big Dig: Facts and Figures."

206   **sixteen years after construction:** Construction began in September 1991, and the majority of efforts were completed by 2006. "The Big Dig: Project Background."

206   **eight years behind plan:** "Executive Summary," in *Completing the "Big Dig"*; Anthony Flint, "10 Years Later, Did the Big Dig Deliver?," *The Boston Globe*, December 29, 2015, https://bostonglobe.com/magazine/2015/12/29/years-later-did-big-dig-deliver /tSb8PIMS4QJUETsMpA7SpI/story.html.

206   **original cost, estimated at $2.6 billion:** Virginia Greiman, "The Big Dig: Learning from a Mega Project," NASA Appel Knowledge Services, July 15, 2010, https://appel .nasa.gov/2010/07/15/the-big-dig-learning-from-a-mega-project/; Associated Press, "$14.8 Billion Later, Big Dig Finally Complete," *NBC News*, December 25, 2017, https:// nbcnews.com/id/wbna22394932.

206   **killed a motorist:** Flint, "10 Years Later, Did the Big Dig Deliver?"

206   **Corruption—some charged:** "Company Sentenced in Big Dig Fraud and False Statements Scheme," U.S Attorney's Office, September 14, 2009, retrieved from https:// archives.fbi.gov/archives/boston/press-releases/2009/bs091409a.htm.

206   **haphazard planning:** Greiman, "The Big Dig."

206   **"The political controversy"**: Andrew Natsios, *The NewsHour with Jim Lehrer*, American Archive of Public Broadcasting, August 8, 2008, https://americanarchive.org /catalog/cpb-aacip_507-4f1mg7gb7s.

207   **twenty-nine college institutions:** "Boston by the Numbers: 2020," Boston Planning & Development Agency Research Division, July 2020, 17, http://bostonplans.org /getattachment/51f1c894-4e5f-45e4-aca2-0ec3d0be80d6, citing "City of Boston Student Housing Trends: 2018–2019 Academic Year," Department of Neighborhood Development, excluding MIT. Boston also has two community colleges.

208   **175 executives of the biotechnology firm:** Philip Marcelo and Matt O'Brien, "After Spreading Coronavirus, Boston Biogen Meeting Serves as Stark Warning," *NBC Boston*, March 11, 2020, https://nbcboston.com/news/coronavirus/boston-biogen -meeting-coronavirus-warning/2089438/.

208   **"super-spreading event:"** Jonathan Saltzman, "Biogen Conference Likely Led to 20,000 COVID-19 Cases in Boston Area, Researchers Say," *The Boston Globe*, last updated August 25, 2020, https://bostonglobe.com/2020/08/25/business/biogen -conference-likely-led-20000-covid-19-cases-boston-area-researchers-say/.

208   **infection of twenty thousand:** Saltzman, "Biogen Conference Likely Led to 20,000 COVID-19 Cases in Boston Area," *The Boston Globe*.

208   **city recorded nine:** "COVID-19 Timeline," Boston Public Health Commission, accessed March 27, 2021, https://bphc.org/whatwedo/infectious-diseases/Infectious -Diseases-A-to-Z/covid-19/Pages/COVID-19-Timeline.aspx.

208   **declared a state of emergency:** "COVID-19 Timeline."

208   **On March 17:** "All Boston Public Schools to Close Starting Tuesday, March 17," City of Boston, March 13, 2020, https://boston.gov/news/all-boston-public-schools-close -students-starting-tuesday-march-17.

208   **On March 20:** "Mass. Health Officials Announce State's First Coronavirus-Related Death," *News 7 Boston*, March 20, 2020, https://whdh.com/news/mass-health-officials -announce-states-first-coronavirus-related-death/.

209   **city of roughly 695,000:** "Boston by the Numbers: 2020," 9, citing U.S. Census Bureau, 2018 1-year American Community Survey, BPDA Research Division Analysis.

209   **greater metropolitan population:** "Boston Region Population Now at Nearly 4.9 Million," *Curbed Boston*, April 23, 2019, https://boston.curbed.com/2019/4/23 /18511826/boston-region-population-2019, citing US Census Bureau, "New Census Bureau Estimates Show Counties in South and West Lead Nation in Population Growth," April 18, 2019, https://census.gov/newsroom/press-releases/2019/estimates -county-metro.html.

209   **more than nine feet of snow:** Angela Fritz, "Boston Clinches Snowiest Season on Record amid Winter of Superlatives," *The Washington Post*, March 15, 2019, https:// washingtonpost.com/news/capital-weather-gang/wp/2015/03/15/boston-clinches -snowiest-season-on-record-amid-winter-of-superlatives/.

209   **just over two feet:** Fritz, "Boston Clinches Snowiest Season on Record amid Winter of Superlatives," *Washington Post*.

210 **"snow farms":** Lucy Perkins, "The Last Boston 'Snow Farm' Finally Melts," National Public Radio, July 14, 2015, https://npr.org/sections/thetwo-way/2015/07/14/422939198 /the-last-boston-snow-farm-finally-melts.

211 **The student was isolated:** Interview with Mayor Marty Walsh, September 12, 2020.

211 **Rosengren devoted thirty-five minutes:** Interview with Mayor Marty Walsh, September 12, 2020.

212 **Not long after, Brian Golden:** Interview with Mayor Marty Walsh, September 12, 2020.

216 **Walsh rejected the idea:** Interview with Mayor Marty Walsh, September 12, 2020.

216 **"I was just doing my part":** Interview with Mayor Marty Walsh, September 12, 2020.

Chapter 14: Building the Capacity

219 **"All things are ready":** William Shakespeare, *Henry V*, Folger Shakespeare Library (New York: Simon & Schuster, 1995), 4.3.73, https://shakespeare.folger.edu/downloads /pdf/henry-v_PDF_FolgerShakespeare.pdf.

219 **5:12 A.M. on a Wednesday:** "The Great San Francisco Earthquake," USGS, accessed March 27, 2021, https://earthquake.usgs.gov/earthquakes/events/1906calif/18april/; "San Francisco Earthquake of 1906," *Encyclopedia Britannica Online*, accessed October 30, 2020, https://britannica.com/event/San-Francisco-earthquake-of-1906.

219 **the equivalent of 7.9:** "San Francisco Earthquake of 1906," *Encyclopedia Britannica Online*.

219 **But the fires:** "1906 Earthquake: Firefighting," National Park Service, accessed October 29, 2020, https://nps.gov/prsf/learn/historyculture/1906-earthquake-fire-fighting.htm.

219 **Exacerbated by the use of dynamite:** "1906 Earthquake: Firefighting."

219 **Adding to this challenge:** "Death of Fire Chief Engineer Dennis T. Sullivan," The Museum of the City of San Francisco, accessed February 12, 2021, http://sfmuseum .org/hist10/dtsullivan.html.

219 **80 percent of the city was destroyed:** "From the Archives: 112 Years Ago: Images from San Francisco's Devastating 1906 Earthquake," *Los Angeles Times*, April 18, 2016, https://latimes.com/local/lanow/la-me-110th-anniversary-san-francisco-earthquake -pictures-20160413-htmlstory.html.

219 **three thousand lives:** "From the Archives: 112 Years Ago"; "San Francisco Earthquake of 1906," *Encyclopedia Britannica Online*; "San Francisco Earthquake, 1906," The Center for Legislative Archives, accessed September 26, 2020, https://archives.gov /legislative/features/sf.

219 **population was left homeless:** "San Francisco Earthquake, 1906."

220 **In 1906, the risk of earthquakes:** "1906 Marked the Dawn of the Scientific Revolution," USGS, accessed October 29, 2020, https://earthquake.usgs.gov /earthquakes/events/1906calif/18april/revolution.php.

220 **Advancements in geophysics:** "1906 Marked the Dawn of the Scientific Revolution."

220   **earthquake *caused* faults to form:** "1906 Earthquake Centennial," National Park Service Park News, 2, accessed December 12, 2020, https://nps.gov/pore/learn/upload /resourcenewsletter_1906earthquakecentennial.pdf.

220   **the State Earthquake Investigation Commission:** "1906 Marked the Dawn of the Scientific Revolution"; "1906 Earthquake Centennial."

221   **"integrated government-commissioned scientific investigation":** "1906 Marked the Dawn of the Scientific Revolution."

221   **hiked the full distance:** "1906 Marked the Dawn of the Scientific Revolution"; "1906 Earthquake Centennial."

221   **examining the local soil:** "1906 Marked the Dawn of the Scientific Revolution."

221   **conducted triangulation surveys:** "1906 Marked the Dawn of the Scientific Revolution."

221   **"theory of elastic rebound":** "1906 Earthquake Centennial"; "1906 Marked the Dawn of the Scientific Revolution."

221   **"undistorted state":** "1906 Marked the Dawn of the Scientific Revolution."

221   **Lawson report:** "1906 Marked the Dawn of the Scientific Revolution"; "1906 Earthquake Centennial."

221   **research has helped forecast:** "1906 Marked the Dawn of the Scientific Revolution."

Chapter 15: Assessing the System

228   **roughly 180 defenders:** Wallenfeldt, "Texas Revolution: Santa Anna Responds: The Alamo and the Goliad Massacre," *Encyclopedia Britannica Online.* https://www .britannica.com/topic/Texas-Revolution/Santa-Anna-responds-the-Alamo-and-the -Goliad-Massacre

228   **prevent 4,000 Mexican soldiers:** "Remember the Alamo," *American Experience*, PBS, aired February 2, 2004, https://pbs.org/wgbh/americanexperience/films/alamo/.

229   **German Wehrmacht fresh:** "The German Invasion of Western Europe, 1940," Democracy at War: Canadian Newspapers and the Second World War, Canadian War Museum, accessed December 20, 2020, https://warmuseum.ca/cwm/exhibitions /newspapers/operations/westerneurope_e.html/.

230   **historically and quantitatively, France's military:** John Graham Royde-Smith, "World War II: The Invasion of Low Countries and France," *Encyclopedia Britannica Online*, accessed December 20, 2020, https://britannica.com/event/World-War-II; John Graham Royde-Smith, "World War II: Forces and Resources of the European Combatants, 1939," *Encyclopedia Britannica Online*, accessed December 20, 2020, https:// britannica.com/event/World-War-II/Forces-and-resources-of-the-European -combatants-1939.

230   **Germany's campaign lasted:** Dr. Gary Shefield, "The Fall of France," *BBC*, last updated March 30, 2011, http://bbc.co.uk/history/worldwars/wwtwo/fall_france_01.shtml.

230   **boasted more powerful guns:** Royde-Smith, "Forces and Resources of the European Combatants"; Royde-Smith, "The Invasion of Low Countries and France."

234   **newly installed automated control system:** Michael Laris, "Changes to Flawed Boeing 737 Max Were Kept from Pilots, DeFazio Says," *The Washington Post*, June 19, 2019,

https://washingtonpost.com/local/trafficandcommuting/changes-to-flawed-boeing-737
-max-were-kept-from-pilots-defazio-says/2019/06/19/553522f0-92bc-11e9-aadb
-74e6b2b46f6a_story.html.

234   **pilots *could* have responded:** Jack Nicas, James Glanz, and David Gelles, "In Test of
Boeing Jet, Pilots Had 40 Seconds to Fix Error," *The New York Times*, March 25, 2019,
https://nytimes.com/2019/03/25/business/boeing-simulation-error.html.

234   **But the updated control system:** Laris, "Changes to Flawed Boeing 737 Max Were
Kept from Pilots."

Chapter 17: Solutions

251   **most volatile expense:** United, Form 10-K for the Fiscal Year Ended December 31,
2017, 14, https://ir.united.com/static-files/9ac6c8bb-ec7a-4f84-b64c-c0502de0cc86.

251   **fuel hedging:** United, Form 10-K for the Fiscal Year Ended December 31, 2017, 14;
Southwest, Form 10-K for the Fiscal Year ended December 31, 2016, 20, http://otp
.investis.com/clients/us/southwest/SEC/sec-show.aspx?Type=html&FilingId=11
830166&Cik=0000092380.

251   **International and political circumstances:** United, Form 10-K for the Fiscal Year
Ended December 31, 2017, 20; Southwest, Form 10-K for the Fiscal Year Ended
December 31, 2016, 20–21.

253   **the morning of July 2, 1863:** Richard A. Sauers, *Gettysburg: The Meade-Sickles
Controversy* (Washington, DC: Potomac Books, 2003), chap. 3, Kindle; Campbell,
"Death of the III Corps."

253   **repositioning his III Corps:** "Daniel Edgar Sickles," American Battlefield Trust,
accessed December 16, 2020, https://battlefields.org/learn/biographies/daniel-e-sickles;
Eric A. Campbell, "Death of the III Corps," *HistoryNet*, accessed December 16, 2020,
https://historynet.com/death-iii-corps.htm.

256   **airline's expenses are fixed:** United, Form 10-K for the Fiscal Year Ended
December 31, 2017.

260   **seven infantry and one cavalry:** "Civil War Series: The Battle of Gettysburg," National
Park Service, accessed December 16, 2020, https://nps.gov/parkhistory/online_books
/civil_war_series/16/sec2.htm.

262   **evacuated at 8:57 A.M.:** National Commission on Terrorist Attacks upon the United
States, *The 9/11 Commission Report. Final Report of the National Commission on
Terrorist Attacks upon the United States*, 318, https://govinfo.library.unt.edu/911
/report/911Report.pdf.

266   **response to the influenza pandemic:** *Crimson Contagion 2019 Functional Exercise
Draft After-Action Report*, Coordinating Draft, U.S. Department of Health and Human
Services, Office of the Assistant Secretary for Preparedness and Response, October
2019, 4, https://int.nyt.com/data/documenthelper/6824-2019-10-key-findings-and
-after/05bd797500ea55be0724/optimized/full.pdf#page=.

266   **presented two tabletop exercises:** Specifically, where DHS and FEMA were not
the lead agencies. *Crimson Contagion 2019 Functional Exercise Draft After-Action
Report*, 4.

266   **series used a stair-step approach:** The first Tabletop was an internal HHS exercise, while the second was for Chicago and Illinois specifically, including participants from the city and state, as well as interagency partners.

266   **The Seminar in May 2019:** *Crimson Contagion 2019 Functional Exercise Draft After-Action Report,* 5.

266   **war game, a four-day functional:** *Crimson Contagion 2019 Functional Exercise Draft After-Action Report,* 5.

266   **"whole-of-community" response:** *Crimson Contagion 2019 Functional Exercise Draft After-Action Report,* 5.

271   **action, reaction, and counteraction:** Brigadier General (Ret.) Tom Maffey, discussion about war games, June 17, 2020.

274   **Millennium Challenge 2002:** Blake Stilwell, "That Time a Marine General Led a Fictional Iran against the US Military—and Won," *We Are the Mighty,* June 17, 2020, https://wearethemighty.com/articles/that-time-a-marine-general-led-a-fictional-iran -against-the-us-military-and-won.

274   **Van Riper's team beat:** Malcolm Gladwell, *Blink* (New York: Little, Brown, 2005), chap. 4, Kindle.

274   **Van Riper was criticized:** Gladwell, *Blink,* chap. 4.

274   **Dick Fosbury's famous:** "How One Man Changed the High Jump Forever," *The Olympics on the Record,* YouTube, uploaded by Olympic Channel, April 1, 2018, https://youtube.com/watch?v=CZsH46Ek2ao.

275   **"collision between two centers of gravity":** Joseph L. Strange and Richard Iron, "Center of Gravity: What Clausewitz Really Meant," *Joint Force Quarterly,* no. 35 (Quantico, VA: Marine Corps War College, 2004), 21, https://apps.dtic.mil/dtic/tr /fulltext/u2/a520980.pdf.

Epilogue: The Myth of Helplessness

285   **"The more we value things":** Epictetus, *Discourses and Selected Writings,* Book IV, 23, Kindle.

285   **King Canute the Great:** Dorothy Whitelock, "Canute (I)," *Encyclopedia Britannica Online,* last updated November 8, 2020, https://britannica.com/biography/Canute-I.

286   **twentieth-century fashion icon:** General Stanley McChrystal, Jeff Eggers, and Jason Mangone, *Leaders: Myth and Reality* (New York: Portfolio/Penguin, 2018), 70–90.

Image Credits

Page xiii: Library of Congress (LC-DIG-ds-01290)

Page 6: via Wikimedia Commons

Page 7 (left): Copyrighted 1941. AP. 2184324:0221PF. Used by permission of Wright's Media

Page 50: via Wikimedia Commons

Page 61: Flickr, Tangi Bertin, via CC BY 2.0 (creativecommons.org/licenses/by/2.0/legalcode)

Page 65: Library of Congress (LC-DIG-ppmsc-03521)

Page 73: Photo by Sgt. 1st Class Raymond Piper, via DVIDS

Page 78: by Sarfa, via Wikimedia Commons

Page 126: photo by Cville dog, Wikmedia Commons, via CC BY-SA 3.0 (creativecommons.org/licenses/by-sa/3.0/legalcode)

Page 130: Department of Defense photo by Helene C. Stikkel

Page 138: U.S. Air Force photo/Tech. Sgt. Sabrina Johnson

Page 146: Photo by Anders Hellberg. Wikimedia Commons via CC BY-SA 4.0 (creativecommons.org/licenses/by-sa/4.0/legalcode)

Page 153: U.S. Marine Corps photo by Lance Corporal Shawn M. Statz/Released

Page 181: Photo by Oldmobil, Wikimedia Commons via CC BY-SA 3.0 (creativecommons.org/licenses/by-sa/3.0/legalcode)

Page 207: by MrJARichard, Wikimedia Commons via CC BY-SA 4.0 (https://creativecommons.org/licenses/by/4.0/legalcode), remixed

Page 220: Courtesy US Army Center of Military History

Page 224: Photo by Capt. Veronica Aguila, courtesy of Ranger Recruiting Liaison office, Fort Benning, via DVIDS.

Page 254: National Archives, 111-B-258

Page 271: Photo by Javier Chagoya, Naval Postgraduate School, via DVIDS

Page 281: Photo by Staff Sgt. Matt Scotten, via DVIDS

Index

Page numbers in italics refer to illustrations.